# AMC V-8 Engines 1966–1991

## HOW TO REBUILD & MODIFY

Tony Pontillo

CarTech®

**CarTech®**

CarTech®, Inc.
6118 Main Street
North Branch, MN 55056
Phone: 651-277-1200 or 800-551-4754
Fax: 651-277-1203
www.cartechbooks.com



Edit by Wes Eisenschenk
Layout by Connie DeFlorin

ISBN 978-1-61325-599-5
Item No. SA504

Library of Congress Cataloging-in-Publication Data Available

Written, edited, and designed in the U.S.A.
Printed in China
10 9 8 7 6 5 4 3 2 1



DISTRIBUTION BY:

***Europe***
PGUK
63 Hatton Garden
London EC1N 8LE, England
Phone: 020 7061 1980 • Fax: 020 7242 3725
www.pguk.co.uk

***Australia***
Renniks Publications Ltd.
3/37-39 Green Street
Banksmeadow, NSW 2109, Australia
Phone: 2 9695 7055 • Fax: 2 9695 7355
www.renniks.com

***Canada***
Login Canada
300 Saulteaux Crescent
Winnipeg, MB, R3J 3T2 Canada
Phone: 800 665 1148 • Fax: 800 665 0103
www.lb.ca

# CONTENTS

# Acknowledgments

After many years of rebuilding American Motors Company (AMC) engines, it has become normal for me to receive about a dozen phone calls a month (even from other machine shops) with rebuilding questions. I am one of the lucky ones who honestly can say I cannot wait to get to my job. Any time I can pass this information onto someone who is rebuilding an AMC or even another machine shop, it makes me feel great.

Don's Auto Parts & Machine Shop was first opened in 1957 under the name Kenosha Crankshaft. In the first years of business, Kenosha Crankshaft did business grinding crankshafts in-house and laying underneath a tractor out in the fields. That's right, they used to go out and grind only one rod journal in a tractor engine just by laying underneath it.

In 1961, Kenosha Crankshaft moved to a new building and changed its name to Don's Auto Parts & Machine Shop. At that time, it became a full-service machine shop. The town was thriving as AMC supplied good-paying jobs to a large percentage of local families who became very loyal to the AMC brand.

I was an employee at Don's Auto Parts & Machine Shop for Don Jones and his son Jim Jones for many years. Later in life, I purchased the business from the family and greatly enjoy it. I am often asked why I didn't change the name. Well, when a business has been around since 1961 with the same name, I believed I owed it to the family to keep the name. My name is Tony, but more people call me Don!

I am very thankful that CarTech has provided an opportunity to share my knowledge with anyone who wants to rebuild an AMC engine. My company rebuilds about 30 to 50 AMC engines a year, so I knew I could handle writing this book.

Thank you to all of my employees for putting up with me having them stop what they're doing so that I could take photos of each step. They would see me coming out of the office with a camera and would say, "Oh boy, more pictures and documentation." Every one of them pitched in to help write this book.

Thank you to Jimmy Jones for the camera and for teaching me how to take good photos. Luckily for me, years ago he took up photography as a hobby. Thank you to the rest of our employees; each of you provided some type of help during this process.

Most importantly thank you to my wife, Karla, and our children, Kaitlyn, Megan, Tyler, and Tanner, for missing me at all those family dinners because I would stay late at the shop to work on the book. There were many weekends when I headed back to the shop to put in some hours writing.

In addition, some customers contributed—even though their engines might have taken a little longer during this process, and I apologize for that. They were extremely patient with me and excited to be involved. Most AMC enthusiasts are very dedicated and knowledgeable about the history behind their car.

Ken Kinnucan is the owner of the dual-quad engine that is shown throughout the book. Ken has a few nostalgia Super Stock cars in his collection. He is a customer who brought his AMC engine all the way from California to Wisconsin to have it built. We can't thank him enough for all his help and patience.

Tom Roughalo is another customer who had his engine built while the book was being written. While we were building his engine, his car was painted at a local body shop.

I would like to thank Dave Furlin, another customer, for his research and information. He supplied me with a boatload of history from the engine plant. If you ever get a chance to visit him, Dave probably has one of the largest libraries of AMC photos that exists. It is common to see his AMC-only car photos posted every day on Facebook. Most of the car enthusiasts in Kenosha feel a bit of loyalty to the AMC cars and Jeeps.

All of this wouldn't be possible without all the little vendors that remake AMC parts. AMC engine building lives on due to these companies. Thank you. They are listed in the source guide. Please patronize them.

Lastly, thank you to the Automotive Engine Rebuilders Association (AERA), which provided the engine specifications. The association is where your local machine shops find crankshaft sizes, bore sizes, engine bulletins, and engine diagrams. If you work for a local machine shop that is not a member of the association, check it out; it offers a great value.

# Introduction

*There's no better feeling than dropping your refreshed and rebuilt 360 engine back between the fenders of your restored 1973 AMC Javelin. (Photo Courtesy Mary Bongaard)*

Taking on a project such as rebuilding an AMC engine can be overwhelming. The best advice that I can provide is to reach out for help when questions arise. Going into this project, recognize your level of ability and ask your machine shop to help with the rest.

If this is your first engine build, let your machine shop know that you are relatively new to this. When a customer mentions that it is his or her first engine rebuild, we go out of our way to ensure that the customer understands everything. We even put instruction tags on items to help. The success of your engine rebuild is just as important (or more important) to your machine shop.

Even though we tried to keep this book aimed toward the beginner, we have included many of the specialty oil modifications. These modifications are often unknown to machine shops that do not rebuild many AMC engines.

We receive phone calls from many shops that ask how we do some of these modifications. I compiled this information in a book for you and your engine builder to use. Keep in mind that every engine builder will have thoughts as to what is correct. Over the years, many of these modifications have changed and/or developed for the better due to input from many people.

When restoring a classic car, just remember that if an engine rebuild goes wrong, it will leave you stranded and cost you thousands of dollars. When corners are cut on some bodywork, you may be the only one who can notice it. However, there are some items in an engine build that you should not omit.

Always listen to the machine shop's recommendations. If you are looking for a qualified machine shop to rebuild your engine in your area, start by looking on the AERA website for members. If a machine shop is a member, that is a great sign that it takes its business seriously. You can also call the AERA, as it deals with machine shops from around the world and will steer you in the right direction to find a quality machine shop.

### Engines

In 1966–1967, the 290-ci engine was developed for the Rambler Rogue. By 1967, the 343-ci V-8 had been released. This was the beginning of the very popular V-8 engine lineup. In 1968, the first design of the 390-ci engine was released. Although the engine blocks are considered the

***Most AMC engine rebuilds begin right here. Underneath all of that dust and grime is a 390, which is the heart of this 1969 SC/Rambler. Nothing short of a full engine rebuild will suffice for this car. (Photo Courtesy Wes Eisenschenk)***

same in design, the 390-ci engine was labeled as being a new design. The 290-ci engine block later developed into the popular 304-ci engine. The 343-ci engine grew up to become the 360-ci engine.

In 1970, the second design of the 390 was released. This block had the same displacement as the 1968–1969 engine but had major design changes. This engine is the rarest due to the fact it was only produced for one year.

All 1968–1970 390 engines had the chrome dress-up kit with the popular chrome valve covers. This was part of the "AMX Package" for all models of the Ambassador, AMX, Javelin, Rebel, and Hurst SC/Rambler.

All of the AMC V-8 engines have their displacement (in cubic inches) cast in the block on both sides just above the oil-pan rails. The bore and stroke stayed the same, but the cylinder deck height was taller, the connecting rod was longer, and the 7/16-inch head bolts were changed out for 1/2-inch head bolts.

In 1971, the SC/360 Hornet was released, and it was designed to be a performance vehicle that was a little more economical. It was also designed to be more friendly to the insurance companies. The Hornets were not looked at as a muscle car back in 1970. AMC only built 784 SC/360s from August 1970 through February 1971, which makes the SC/360 rarer than the SC/Rambler, the Rebel Machine, and even the total number of AMXs painted in the Big Bad colors in the prior two years.

In 1971, the release of the 401 became the last design change of the legendary V-8 engine lineup. Every once in a while, a customer will bring in an AMC 401 painted all red. This is how we can identify the International 401s. They were used in 1974–1975 when International had a shortage of its 392 engines. The AMC engine was used in the Scouts and mini school buses between 1972 and 1980.

### Group 19

AMC's history wouldn't be complete without talking about the Group 19 performance parts. These parts have become known to AMC owners as "Group 19" parts. This term is used simply because of the way that AMC organized its parts books. Group 1 was engine parts, Group 2 was cooling, Group 3 was electrical, etc. Group 19 was the section devoted to high-performance equipment.

Carl Chakmakian, AMC's performance director, contributed to the Group 19 parts design. Group 19 was not limited to engine performance parts and included rear adjustable spoiler wings, a front fiberglass spoiler, etc.

According to AMC dealers, the Group 19 parts were available up until about 1974. Group 19 performance parts were considered to be expensive back then, but it was nothing compared to what these items cost today.

# DESIGN YOUR BUILD

One of the first things to think about when designing your engine build is to determine how the vehicle will be used. A popular choice is a numbers-matching restoration using as close to stock parts as possible. Another option is a mild performance build for the street. Other choices that we have seen customers select range from a full drag-race engine to a road-race engine with boosted applications (nitrous oxide, supercharging, turbocharging). Recently, a popular request is an engine that would be good for the Hot Rod Power Tours.

## Build Options

If you are like most gearheads, you have been thinking about this for a few years and want to get started. Let's talk about a stock restoration first.

### Mild Build

Even when doing a numbers-matching restoration, we have been asked if we can improve the engine's performance. Most of the time, a larger camshaft can be installed and internal modifications can be made to increase horsepower. These small modifications are internal and are blind to the judges.

Even with a mild build, we recommend some oil modifications. This is discussed in the later chapters. If you plan a mild build, you will reuse the cylinder heads, engine block, valve covers, etc. Some people go to the extreme of sending items, such as the water pump, out to be rebuilt so that they can keep the original numbers on the engine. The nice aspect regarding this type of build is that the cost is lower because all of the performance parts aren't necessary to purchase.

### A Step Above Mild

Another option is to build a mild performance engine for the street or maybe some days at the local dragstrip. This kind of build can get out of hand very quickly with really no limits except your bank account. This is my favorite kind of build because you can spend hours looking at different intake manifolds, aftermarket cylinder heads, camshaft options, pistons, carburetors, and now many different fuel-injection units.

Here are some things to consider when designing your engine. It is kind of like the trickle-down effect: the more horsepower you make, the more it affects the complete drivetrain. Most of the drivetrain components are good for about 400 to 450 hp and less without any major updating. As the horsepower increases, internal items must be upgraded as well. Keep in mind the octane level of fuel that will be used. If you are looking to run pump gas (90 to 93 octane), this is important for the correct compression ratio.

One of the first updates should be to replace the connecting-rod bolts with ARP bolts. The connecting rods and crankshaft on AMC engines are probably some of the strongest stock items that AMC ever built. Other replacements include using aftermarket bolts or studs in the main caps or even aftermarket main caps with four bolts.

The engine builder will have two main questions: 1) What is your target horsepower? and 2) What's your budget?

### High-Performance Build

Most race car engine builds fall into the same category no matter the type of racing. For building an all-out drag-racing engine, options include using an aluminum engine block or the stock cast-iron block. Cylinder heads have options from highly modified cast-iron cylinder heads (such as that of a National Hot Rod Association [NHRA] stock application) to the aluminum heads offered by Edelbrock and Indy Cylinder Head. Road-racing and boosted applications have all of the same performance parts from which to choose. Most importantly, you will need to select the right combination of these parts for your application.

## Build Budgeting

Classify your build based on the aforementioned build types. Let's say that your build of choice is a restoration with a step-up camshaft. Start with a notebook to list all of the items that are needed. We have done many AMC rebuilds, so I can get a customer real close on the engine build.

You can call your local machine shop and get a rough quote for machine work. However, most machine shops say that it is hard to quote machine work over the phone without physically seeing the block. Without seeing the engine in person, a machine shop cannot assess whether the crankshaft needs to be ground or just polished, and there is a pretty big price difference between the two.

During disassembly, pay attention to how everything looks. This can help determine how much machine work will be needed. For example, crankshaft bearings can indicate a lot about an engine. If any bearings are spun or welded to the crankshaft, the cost of the machine work will increase.

Hopefully your engine was running but was just tired and in need of a rebuild. On the other hand, if it just sat around and digested water in the cylinders for years, your machine shop costs will increase.

## Parts Purchasing

After getting the quote back from the machine shop, enter this information into your notebook. Now you can start looking up parts for the engine build. I believe in supporting your machine shop when purchasing parts. Most machine shops have become competitive with mail-order companies. However, even if you are paying a little more for the parts, remember that you are paying for the machine shop's knowledge. Also, when you need help with your project, the machine shop is there for you.

With the machine shop's quote and the parts list, you are close to knowing the approximate cost. Keep in mind that rebuilding an AMC is not like a small-block Chevy. Many parts are not off-the-shelf items. If you want something other than a stock cast piston, most pistons are custom made.

As you complete your price sheet, don't forget the external items, such as a distributor, water pump, carburetor, spark plugs, break-in oil, belts, and hoses. We always tell customers that the little items to finish an engine can easily add up to more than $1,000.

### Machine Shop Help

After disassembly, let those working at the machine shop know what kind of build you want and bring the following items to the machine shop:

- Engine block with main caps
- Crankshaft
- Connecting rods
- Cylinder heads

Make sure that the machine shop does the following:

- Hot tank the engine block
- Magnaflux the block and check the bores
- Clean and check the crankshaft
- Clean and check the connecting rods
- Disassemble the cylinder heads and magnaflux and estimate

*This is the donor engine. It has been sitting around for a long time. The first step is to make sure that it has a rebuildable core.*

### Cutting Corners

What if your quote is a few thousand dollars over your budget? There are always places to save some money, but you should not cut corners on some items. For example, if you decide not to bore your block, you will not need to spend money on new pistons. However, is it worth going through all of this work to have an engine that smokes a little?

Maybe a friend has a glass-bead machine, and you can take some of the tinwork to the car wash, degrease it, and glass bead it yourself. This is a better option than cutting corners on machine work. For example, we just finished a complete stock AMC 390 build from intake to oil pan, including running the engine with camshaft break-in for $7,400.

This process is similar for other types of engine builds. Aftermarket parts will change and add to the overall budget. Many various performance options are available. The more horsepower that is made, the more it will affect your overall budget. It is important for the machine shop to know and understand your project so that it can recommend the correct parts.

### When to Splurge

An item that is very high on the list that affects the overall budget is upgrading to a hydraulic-roller camshaft. I recommend this option even if a customer has to wait a few extra weeks to pay for it. Another expensive item on which to splurge is aluminum cylinder heads.

These two items can add $4,000 to a build once all the options are added together.

## Identifying Your AMC V-8 Engine

***Notice the displacement (in cubic inches) markings in the casting? Our donor block is easily recognized as 401 engine with these markings on the side of the block.***

The V-8 engines began with the 290 2V code H and the 290 4V code N. The engine code is the seventh digit of the vehicle identification number (VIN). This only applies if the engine is original to the vehicle. On most AMC vehicles, the VIN is located on the driver-side front door panel, or on the upper-left corner of the dash.

On all V-8 engine blocks, the displacement (in cubic inches) is cast into both sides of the engine block just above the oil pan. These numbers are raised and big and bold. There are only a few cases where the numbers are not on the side of the blocks; these unnumbered blocks were most often used in NASCAR, some crate engines, and drag-racing packages.

When a customer had a major engine failure and the dealership deemed that a new engine was needed, the dealerships had what we now call "crate engines" sitting on the shelf. Since the engines were so much alike but had different displacement, the crate engines did not have numbers on them. The replacement engine could have been a 343, 360, 390, or 401.

Engines that were exported were reported to not have any numbers on them. There also was a number of blocks produced without casting numbers in 1970–1971. Some call them the Traco, Machine, or Donohue blocks, and they are usually set up for a four-bolt main. So, that's where the rumor came from that the racing organizations could not determine the engine's displacement from the outside.

| Engine Displacement | Year Range | Code |
|---|---|---|
| 290 2V | 1966–1969 | H |
| 290 4V | 1966–1969 | N |
| 304 2V | 1970–1981 | H |
| 343 2V | 1967–1969 | S |
| 343 4V | 1967–1969 | Z |
| 360 2V | 1970–1991 | N |
| 360 4V | 1970–1991 | P |
| 390 4V | 1968–1970 | W 68-69 |
| 390 4V | 1968–1970 | X 70 |
| 390 4V | 1969 | Y SS/AMX |
| 390 4V | 1970 | Machine |
| 401 4V | 1971–1978 | Z |

## Valve Cover Tag

On nearly all AMC V-8s through the 1970s, there was a small, thin, metal tag attached with a Phillips screw on the passenger-side valve cover facing toward the front of the engine. The engine code and build date are listed there. These numbers do not reference which body was used. This makes it impossible to prove that the engine was originally installed in a particular vehicle.

The first digit on the tag represents the year that the engine was built. (Note that if the car was a January or February build, it was possible for the engine tag to be one year prior.) The second and third digits represent the month in which the engine was built, and the fourth digit represents the engine code. The final digits represent the day of the month in which the engine was built.

Tags are often moved from engine to engine, and it is common practice for these tags to move around and even be restamped. The date listed should precede the car's original build date by about a month.

Over the years, we have also seen various letters on the tag that signify various oversizes. We once had a tag with an *L* on it. We asked numerous people if they knew what that meant, but no one knew.

***The tag on this valve cover reads as follows: The first digit (1) represents the year 1968, the second and third digits (10) represent the month of October, the fourth digit (Z) corresponds with having a 343-ci engine, and the last two digits (12) are the day of the month. So, this 343-ci engine was built on October 12, 1968.***

### Tag Breakdown

| Digit | Representation |
|---|---|
| First Digit | The year that the engine was built |
| Second and Third Digits | The month that the engine was built |
| Fourth Digit | Should match the seventh digit of the VIN, which is always the engine size |
| Fifth and Sixth Digits | The day of the month that the engine was built |

The first digit on the valve cover tag corresponds to the following build dates:

| First Digit | Year |
|---|---|
| 1 | 1959 |
| 2 | 1960 |
| 3 | 1961 |
| 4 | 1962 |
| 5 | 1963 |
| 6 | 1964 |
| 7 | 1965 |
| 8 | 1966 |
| 9 | 1967 |
| 1 | 1968 |
| 2 | 1969 |
| 3 | 1970 |
| 4 | 1971 |
| 5 | 1972 |
| 6 | 1973 |
| 7 | 1974 |
| 8 | 1975 |
| 9 | 1976 |
| 1 | 1977 |
| 2 | 1978 |
| 3 | 1979 |
| 0 | 1980 |
| 1 | 1981 VIN Code B |
| 2 | 1982 VIN Code C |
| 3 | 1983 VIN Code D |
| 4 | 1984 VIN Code E |
| 5 | 1985 VIN Code F |
| 6 | 1986 VIN Code G |
| 7 | 1987 VIN Code H |
| 8 | 1988 VIN Code J |

The second and third digits represent the following:

| Second and Third Digits | Month |
|---|---|
| 01 | January |
| 02 | February |
| 03 | March |
| 04 | April |
| 05 | May |
| 06 | June |
| 07 | July |
| 08 | August |
| 09 | September |
| 10 | October |
| 11 | November |
| 12 | December |

The fourth digit matches the seventh digit of the VIN code.

| Fourth Digit | Engine Specification |
|---|---|
| W | 390-ci 4-barrel engine |
| X | 390-ci other engines |
| Z | 343 V-8 Typhoon 4-barrel |

During the rebuild, we found one lifter hole that was 0.010-inch oversize and next to the lifter bore was an *OS* stamped on it. We could only assume that the lifter bore was cut oversize on the assembly line and repaired by just oversizing one lifter bore. To save the block, we measured the old lifters to find the 0.010-inch lifter. We disassembled the lifter and sent it to a company that regrinds lifters.

One year, we saw about a dozen of the *C* tags, and this was one of the toughest to deal with. For some of them, we took camshaft bearings and turned down the outside diameter; for others, we used to bore the camshaft tunnel out to the correct size. Here is a list of documented letters that were common to see stamped on the tags:

| Letter | Representation |
|---|---|
| B | Cylinder bore 0.010-inch oversize |
| M | Main bearings 0.010-inch undersize |
| P | Connecting rod bearings 0.010-inch undersize |
| C | Camshaft bore 0.010-inch undersize |
| PM | Mains and rods 0.010-inch undersize |

Planethoustonamx.com offers valve cover and carburetor tag restamps that are very similar to the OEM tags. The website has a huge listing of the history of the AMC brand.

| Engine Casting Numbers | | | |
|---|---|---|---|
| Engine Casting Numbers | Displacement (cubic inches) | Year | Comments |
| 3144932 | 327 | 1957–1961 | |
| 3147230 | 327 | 1957–1962 | |
| 3153044 | 327 | 1957–1962 | |
| 3153055 | 327 | 1957–1962 | |
| 3153077 | 250 | 1956–1961 | |
| 3153677 | 327 | 1957–1961 | |
| 3166463 | 327 | 1963–1967 | |
| 3169824 | 287 | 1963–1966 | |
| 3179062 | 290 | 1966–1969 | |
| 3179063 | 343 | 1967–1969 | |
| 3190079 | 401 | 1971 | |
| 3190806 | 390 | 1968–1969 | 7/16-inch head bolt |
| 3190808 | 232, 390 | 1964–1971 | |
| 3195292 | 304 | 1970–1971 | |
| 3195527 | 304 | 1970–1982 | |
| 3195528 | 360 | 1970–1984 | |
| 3195528 | 390, 401 | 1970–1980 | |
| 3195529 | 390 | 1969–1970 | 1/2-inch head bolt |
| 3195529 | 401 | 1972–1976 | |
| 3198951 | 401 | 1971–1978 | |
| 3414725 | 401 | 1972–1974 | |
| 3220411 | 401 | 1975–1978 | |
| 4160275 | 327 | 1963–1966 | |
| 440275 | 327 | 1958–1962 | |
| 446527 | 320 | 1955 | |
| 4486279 | 390 | 1968–1970 | |
| 4487211 | 304 | 1970–1976 | |
| 4488874 | 401 | 1971–1976 | |

(Table Courtesy Todd Jesme and planethoustonamx.com)

## AMC Engines

The following table shows the AMC engines that were produced from 1966 to 1991. It provides all of the different bore and stroke combinations that were manufactured. Although six engines with various displacements (in cubic inches) were produced, they were similar in design. The overall design of the engine block and cylinder heads stayed the same. The only variances were the size of bores, valves, and main bearing housing bores. They all used hydraulic flat-tappet camshafts, and the 4-barrel carburetors were all Carter designs.

| V-8 Specifications | | | | | | | | |
|---|---|---|---|---|---|---|---|---|
| Engine | Type | Bore and Stroke | Displacement | Compression Ratio (:1) | Carburetor | Horsepower | Torque | Valve Lifters |
| 290-ci V-8 | OHV V-8 | 3.75x3.28 | 290 ci | 9.0 | A.M. 2-barrel | 200 (at 4,600 rpm) | 285 (at 2,800 rpm) | Hydraulic |
| 290-ci V-8 | OHV V-8 | 3.75x3.28 | 290 ci | 10.0 | Carter 4-barrel | 225 (at 4,700 rpm) | 300 (at 3,200 rpm) | Hydraulic |
| 343-ci V-8 | OHV V-8 | 4.08x3.28 | 343 ci | 9.0 | A.M. 2-barrel | 235 (at 4,400 rpm) | 345 (at 2,600 rpm) | Hydraulic |
| 343-ci V-8 | OHV V-8 | 4.08x3.28 | 343 ci | 10.2 | Carter 4-barrel | 280 (at 4,800 rpm) | 365 (at 3,000 rpm) | Hydraulic |
| 390-ci V-8 | OHV V-8 | 4.165x3.574 | 390 ci | 10.2 | Carter 4-barrel | 315 (at 4,600 rpm) | 425 (at 3,200 rpm) | Hydraulic |
| 401-ci V-8 | OHV V-8 | 4.165x3.68 | 401 ci | 10.2 | Carter 4-barrel | 330 (at 5,000 rpm) | 430 (at 3,400 rpm) | Hydraulic |

## Build Types

By now, you have researched your engine and know which size of AMC engine you are rebuilding. For the most part, you have decided on the type of engine build. Most engine-build customers modify this as the build progresses.

### *Stock Rebuild*

A stock rebuild, also known as a numbers-matching rebuild, is the easiest option. It is common for customers who own rare AMC cars to restore them to their factory-stock appearance. It might be a factory race car that is being restored right down to the decals from years ago. This type of restoration requires every nut and bolt to be reused. The factory bolts have a distinctive look and must be retained for that reason.

The external parts that will be reused (or sourced) are the intake manifold, carburetor, exhaust manifolds, distributor, and all other stock items on the exterior of the engine. If an original exhaust manifold is damaged, search swap meets and the internet to find a numbers-matching manifold. For some car enthusiasts, the challenge of coming up with all the numbers-matching parts is what drives them to restore a car.

To this day, all of the mechanical items needed to rebuild an engine can still be purchased. Pistons, valves, camshafts, lifters, and pushrods can be bought new in the aftermarket world. The engine can appear stock, but internal items can be changed or upgraded to modern items. The distributor can appear stock, but the old points can be removed and a PerTronix module can be installed to upgrade the distributor.

Even when building a stock-appearing engine, the camshaft can be upgraded by installing a hydraulic-roller camshaft. Other options include upgrading the rocker arms and valvetrain. A stock rebuild uses the original valve covers, so stay with stock replacements for rocker arms. All these items will keep the engine appearing stock but will provide the reliability of a modern engine. As long as the camshaft is updated to a roller, performance will be improved.

***Except for the intake manifold and carburetor, this is a completely stock restored AMC with original valve covers and the manufacturing tag on the passenger-side valve cover. It was painted with Seymour EN-66 Blue engine paint.***

### *Street-Performance Build*

Street-performance builds are very popular because the car may not have the original engine or the original engine may have been modified already. This type of engine build should be reliable and street friendly.

When selecting a camshaft for this type of build, larger is not always better. A camshaft can only work as well as the heads and intake can support. With a good hydraulic-roller camshaft, camshaft lift can be increased significantly from stock. Most of our designs are in the 0.525- to 0.600-inch lift range.

Duration is very important to the build. This is an important question: Does the vehicle have power brakes or will they be installed in the future? If power brakes are in the equation, we recommend that the duration stay below 0.234 degrees duration at 0.050 lift. Options are available to create extra vacuum with a tank or an electric vacuum pump that work well. The Bullet Racing camshaft is a popular camshaft that we use with manual brakes. If using power brakes, an electric vacuum pump is needed. This is about the largest street-driven camshaft that we like to use.

For this camshaft to work, the engine needs good-flowing cylinder heads, a convertor stall or manual transmission, and a good intake and carburetor combination. This is a really aggressive street camshaft for a hydraulic roller. A good hydraulic-roller lifter is needed for this camshaft. We recommend purchasing the Bullet Cams H/D lifter. This camshaft has the same valve lift across the board and seems to work well, but we have also used a split lift that at times has worked better.

| Bullet Racing Cams SNS84780 | | |
|---|---|---|
| | Intake | Exhaust |
| Duration at 0.050 | 0.250 | 0.256 |
| Gross lift | 0.626 | 0.626 |
| Intake lobe: We used this camshaft with a 104 and a 106 intake centerline. | | |

Aftermarket cylinder heads from Edelbrock are popular for this type of build. One reason is the price. Rebuilding the stock cast-iron cylinder heads and updating them with a larger hydraulic-roller camshaft can approach $1,200 with parts. Currently, a set of Edelbrock cylinder heads can be purchased for about $2,100 a set.

Edelbrock has a variety of aftermarket cylinder heads available. Both the Edelbrock performer and RPM performer offer great performance options.

There are advantages to running aluminum cylinder heads. You can run a little more compression in the engine due to the fact that they dissipate heat in the combustion chamber better than a cast-iron head. They also remove weight from the front end of the vehicle. If you are interested in using aftermarket aluminum cylinder heads but would rather keep a stock look and paint the complete engine, we machine the logo off the ends of the cylinder heads and glass bead the heads so that the paint will stick to it.

The intake manifold and carburetor are important to this build also. The street dual-plane intake creates more low-end torque and horsepower. A single-plane intake is designed to build top-end power at a higher RPM. Other items from which to choose include custom valve covers, water pumps, pulley systems, and ignition systems (potentially a custom MSD ignition system).

### Race-Engine Build

When building a race engine, there are many similarities among drag-race, road-race, and boosted engines. Combining parts is where these engines differ. The machining on the engine block is the most important for this build. There are four major oil-system modifications, lifter bore bushings, extra cylinder head bolts, and blueprinting that are required to provide a reliable engine block.

## Aftermarket Parts Options

Many aftermarket parts are available: a crankshaft (for serious horsepower), forged pistons, solid-roller lifters and camshafts, and an aluminum intake manifold and cylinder heads. If you thought that an AMC engine wouldn't have many options, you'd be wrong.

### Block and Crankshafts

Indy Cylinder Head has a full-race-style AMC block that has removable cylinder liners and is engineered for all-out race engines.

There are not as many options for crankshafts. The stock forged crankshaft is a decent piece and can hold up to quite a beating, but for an all-out race engine you will have to step up to an aftermarket crankshaft. Aftermarket crankshafts are available from Molnar and K1.

### Forged Pistons

Forged pistons are easier to purchase because all of the major piston manufacturers offer custom-made pistons. Some of the most popular piston companies that offer an AMC 401 forged piston are Diamond Pistons, RaceTec, Wiseco, and Federal-Mogul.

The Federal-Mogul piston is heavy compared to the other aftermarket companies. This piston was a

This is a replacement piston that is manufactured by Diamond Pistons. It provides a little more compression and features a performance ring pack.

good entry-level performance piston that was available in the early years. The new-design lightweight forged pistons proved to be just as strong but would increase RPM faster.

When balancing the lighter-weight pistons, it makes the engine balancing a lot easier and more economical. Most of the time, weight is removed from the crankshaft counterweights rather than adding expensive heavy metal.

***Cometic offers multilayer steel (MLS) cylinder head gaskets in many different thicknesses. Usually, gaskets are available in 0.010-inch increments to adjust the compression ratio as needed.***

### *Camshafts, Connecting Rods, and Rod Journals*

Camshafts are available through most major camshaft companies, although not all camshaft companies have cores for grinding hydraulic-roller camshafts. One of the leading camshaft companies for AMC camshafts is Bullet Cams.

For aftermarket connecting rods, the K1 rods allow you to keep the AMC factory connecting-rod journal sizes. If you stay with the AMC rod journal size, the best option is K1.

All aftermarket crankshafts have the rod journals turned down to the size of small-block-Chevy journals. On race engines where the stock crankshaft is used, we grind the journals to the small-block Chevy connecting-rod size of 2.100 inch. When doing this, it gives the engine builder a vast assortment of connecting rods from which to choose.

### *Head Gaskets*

Fel-Pro offers the stock-replacement cylinder head gasket with steel on the block side of the gasket and a composite material on the side against the cylinder head. For engines with higher compression and for all race car applications, we use Cometic multilayer steel (MLS) head gaskets. For cylinder head-gasket stock replacement and for some mild performance, we use Fel-Pro head gaskets. For all-out race applications, we use Cometic MLS head gaskets.

### *Rocker Arms*

There are many options for rocker arms. Most of the big rocker-arm suppliers list having AMC rocker arms available, but the part number will often be the same as a small-block Ford. Harland Sharp offers various part numbers, and one of them is a shaft rocker-arm option. In addition, T&D Machine Products and Jesel offer high-end shaft rocker-arm kits. These kits can be made with any rocker-arm ratio that is needed.

***Harland Sharp offers rocker arms that were designed to replace AMC rocker arms. Unlike many other companies that just repackaged Ford 1.6 rocker arms as AMC, Harland Sharp designed a rocker specifically for AMC owners.***

# Teardown

Once the engine is removed from the car, it's time to prepare for the teardown. Find a good location to do this. The average garage will work well. It is helpful to use a rolling cart to organize all the parts during disassembly. This prevents parts from being scattered throughout the entire garage. The engine rebuild may take a few months, so keep the parts organized to make reassembly easier.

## Engine Stands

When looking to purchase an engine stand, the cheapest option is not always the best option. A four-leg engine stand works the best and can provide many years of use. A three-leg engine stand can be unstable, especially if the concrete garage floor is not flat.

When installing the engine on the stand, attach the engine as centered as possible. This makes rotating the engine a one-person job. If the engine is top-heavy, it will roll over very easily. However, getting it right-side up will take considerable effort.

Remove the flexplate or flywheel before installing the engine onto the engine stand. These bolts are almost impossible to remove after the engine is on the stand. Once the engine is on the stand, drain the engine oil (if it hasn't been done already). It can be a big mess if you forget to drain the oil.

## Exhaust Manifold Removal

Our 401 donor engine is replacing a 304 engine in a Javelin. This engine was purchased from a junkyard in California that removed as few accessories as possible. Begin removing the old accessories, starting with the exhaust manifolds. If this is not done correctly, you will have to drill out several broken exhaust bolts.

Air tubes were only required on vehicles being shipped to California. We started by spraying PB B'laster on the exhaust-manifold bolt threads a few days before removing the. Then, a torch was used to heat up the cylinder head. It is important to only heat the

***The first step to the engine teardown is to remove all of the accessories. Since we purchased this core with all the accessories attached, we will box these up, label them, and hang on to them in case a part is missing or damaged.***

*When removing exhaust-manifold bolts, using impact wrench will most likely break them off, which will leave you with hours of drilling them out or a large bill from the machine shop. Use a torch to add heat to the threaded part of the bolt. Once the bolt is heated, break it loose very slowly and add more heat if it is not turning.*

*Now start removing all the accessories from the front of the engine. Take photos to document the process. It can be helpful during reassembly.*

boss that the manifold bolt threads into. As soon as the bolt boss gets slightly red in color, carefully use a 9/16-inch socket and give it a turn. If it does not turn at all, go back to heating. It's okay to spray WD-40 right after heating to the exposed threads.

About 95 percent of the exhaust-manifold bolts will come out with this process. Sometimes after the bolt begins to move, you can go in short movements back and forth while spraying with WD-40.

## Front Accessory Removal

Next, remove all of the pulleys, belts, and the water pump from the front of the engine. Most of these items usually unbolt with very few issues. Most of the water pump and front-cover bolts will use a 9/16-inch socket to remove.

As bolts are removed, put them into small Ziplock bags with a description of what they were used for. Since this engine will not have air-conditioning, we will separate out those items.

Some of the water-pump bolts go all the way through the front cover and into the block. Make sure that you hang on to these bolts for the reinstallation. We do so many AMC rebuilds that we had stainless bolts made to replace the stock ones.

## Carburetor Removal

Remove the old carburetor from the intake manifold. Take photos during disassembly. We are not using the stock carburetor or intake manifold for this build, so we didn't take photos of those items. Remove all of the lines, the EGR valve, and the heater control valve on the rear of the intake.

*Remove the carburetor and set it aside. We will not be using it for this build, but if we were going to use it, we would send it to a carburetor restoration company. Remove all throttle-linkage brackets and accessory brackets from the intake. These items will more than likely bolt right up to the new intake manifold.*

Even though we are putting an aftermarket Edelbrock intake manifold on this engine, we need to remove the tray on the bottom on the stock intake because Edelbrock does not supply this item. So, do not sell the intake manifold quite yet. Notice the valley-pan intake gasket from the factory. This is mentioned this in future chapters.

## Distributor Removal

The distributor is mounted in the front of the engine, unlike a Chevy. Begin by removing the mounting bracket bolt with a 9/16-inch wrench. Put the distributor hold-down bracket in a safe place; this is another one of those hard-to-replace items that you should keep.

After removing the bracket, wiggle the distributor while pulling it up and out of the block. Because this engine has been sitting for years, the distributor will most likely take a little bit of prying to remove. Use a screwdriver with light pressure to pry the distributor evenly. When removing the distributor, take a quick look at the distributor gear for abnormal wear. The distributor gear is an important item in the rebuild.

## Rocker-Arm and Pushrod Removal

After removing the valve covers, note that this engine has the bridge rocker arms, which indicates that this is the newer engine design. The older versions had a rocker-arm stud with a shoulder on it. Most of the time, we convert these rockers over to a stud style. However, if you reuse them, we keep the rockers together with the bridges because they have developed a wear pattern on the rocker arm. Even if we had a stud-mounted rocker arm, keep these items together and numbered.

If reusing the pushrods, put them into a bag and label them "intake pushrod" and "exhaust pushrod" with the adjacent cylinder. A lot of times, the length of the pushrod changes depending on camshaft selection. So, on complete restorations or rebuilds, the consumable items (such as rockers and pushrods) are almost always replaced. This will save time because cleaning, numbering, and bagging these items for reassembly is not necessary.

## Intake Manifold Removal

Begin by removing all of the intake manifold bolts. For bolt removal, a regular 9/16-inch socket and wrench work well. However, for easier removal, use a 9/16-inch short swivel socket. For a stock rebuild, the factory bolts had a distinctive look to them. Since aftermarket bolts would look different, keep and clean the original bolts.

Once all of the manifold bolts are removed, take a flat-blade screwdriver and slide it between the intake and the engine block. A flat, wide blade should be used so that no damage is done to the intake or the block. Gently pry up on the intake,

*With the accessories out of the way, the bracket that holds the distributor in place is visible. Remove this bracket. Then, lightly pry the distributor out of the front cover. Usually it will come right out, but since this engine has been sitting for years it required the use of light pressure.*

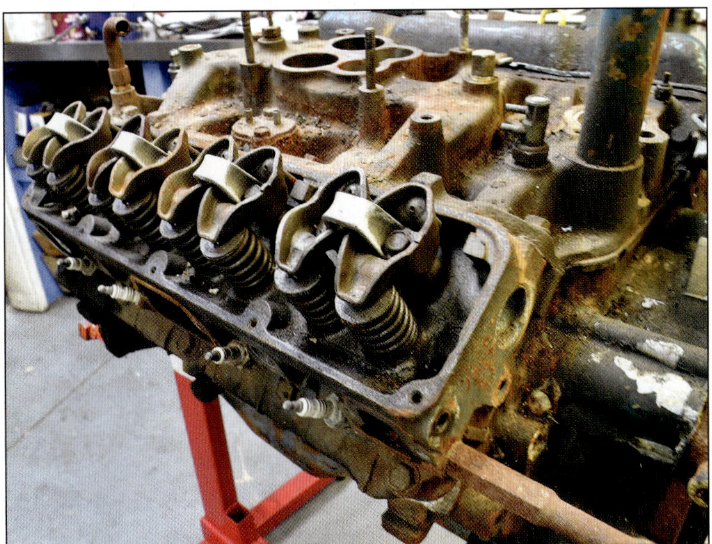

*With the valve covers removed, it is easier to see that the rocker arms are held down with bridges. This indicates that the valvetrain is nonadjustable and that it is a late-1970s-and-up engine.*

Now that the intake is removed, the factory intake valley pan is visible. Take a close look at this because they can be very tricky to seal during reassembly.

Judging by the looks of this oil pan, we will have to magnaflux this engine block to make sure that it is not cracked. You can see some water in it due to sitting around for several years.

and move from the front to the back a little at a time.

If the manifold does not seem to be moving, check to make sure that all bolts were removed from the intake. Once you have verified this, continue to work your flat-blade screwdriver from side to side. After it pops, lift the intake manifold off the block.

The factory manifold gasket is a steel valley-pan gasket. These are a little harder to get sealed up than a normal paper intake gasket. Normally, the type of intake gasket will indicate whether a manifold has ever been removed.

The oil pickup tube is threaded into the bottom of the engine block. To remove it, simply grab the tube and turn counterclockwise. They usually thread out rather easily.

## Oil Pan Removal

The factory oil pan bolts are 7/16 inch. To make removing these bolts easier, use a 3/8-inch ratchet extension to get above the oil pan. Remove the oil-pan bolts, put them in a bag, and label them.

To remove the pan, use a small, thin putty knife to help separate the pan from the block. Work the pan on both sides a little bit at a time. The more that the oil pan is deformed, the greater the chance will be for oil leaks during installation. If the oil pan is rusted, get a new pan for the reassembly. These pans are being reproduced for the Jeeps.

The oil pan will have a radiused notch in the front for a steering-arm linkage to clear. This is the only difference between the car pan and the Jeep pan. To our knowledge, no aftermarket suppliers reproduce the car-only pan.

Notice that the oil pickup tube threads into the engine block. To remove it, just turn it in a counterclockwise rotation. Sometimes you can clean and reuse the pickup screen. However, in this case, we are installing a new Melling oil pickup tube.

## Front Cover Removal

Before removing the front cover, remove the harmonic balancer. It is important to use a harmonic-balancer-removal tool. First, remove the harmonic-balancer bolts with a 3/4-inch socket. When removing the front cover assembly, be careful not to damage it. Sometimes it is easier to first remove the stud that goes all the way into the block. The through bolts that thread through the front cover and into the block can corrode and seize in the cover.

After the timing cover is removed, most stock engines have an oil slinger on the snout of the crankshaft. On AMC race engines, the slinger is not reinstalled unless doing a complete stock rebuild. We have seen these oil slingers crack and cause trouble in the front cover.

The timing chain is bolted on with a camshaft gear bolt, a fuel pump eccentric, and the gear that drives the distributor. Sometimes these items stick on the end of the camshaft. Use a small prybar with very light pressure to aid in removing these items. For now, remove them to remove the chain.

***From the factory, there was an oil slinger behind the front cover. The slinger has a keyway slot and slides over the snout of the crankshaft. This was designed to keep oil from slinging out of the front-cover seal. On race applications, we do not reuse these because we have seen them get torn up in a high-RPM engine.***

***Using a harmonic-balancer puller, thread the 3/8-16-inch bolts into the front of the crankshaft. Using a 7/8-inch socket, thread the mandrel into the remover, and the harmonic balancer will start to press off the snout of the crankshaft.***

## Cylinder Head Removal

It is now time to remove the cylinder heads. Start by removing all 14 cylinder head bolts with a 5/8-inch six-point deep-well socket. To remove the bolts, loosen them

***The timing chain is held on by the camshaft bolt, camshaft distributor gear, and fuel pump eccentric. Reproductions of the eccentric and camshaft bolt kit are available from EngineQuest. If the front camshaft gear and fuel pump eccentric are stuck on the snout of the camshaft, use a flat-blade screwdriver or a small pry bar to gently free up the gear and the eccentric. Once they are free, remove both items for future inspection.***

*With this kind of rust in the cylinder, soak the cylinders with a penetration oil overnight. The hope is that will free up the piston enough so that it can be removed.*

*Use a drill and a wire brush attachment to remove as much of the large deposits of rust as possible.*

starting at the center and going outward. There are two cylinder head dowel pins that register in the block to align the cylinder head.

If the cylinder head is stuck on the dowel pins and a little stubborn, take a dead-blow hammer and tap each side of the cylinder head. AMC cylinder heads can be bolted to either side of the engine, so there is not necessarily a left and a right cylinder head. However, as common practice, we still stamp the heads as "left" and "right."

This engine was left outside, and water entered the cylinder head. With the cylinder heads off, spray all of the cylinders down with a penetrating oil and let the engine soak for a few days. Hopefully, the pistons can be loosened just enough to remove them. If they do not move, break them out. Before trying to remove them, use a drill with a wire brush to remove as much of the scale rust as possible.

### Dipstick Tube Removal

When removing the dipstick tube, you will notice the factory bracket that is used to locate and hold down the tube. Although this bracket is missing on many engines, some companies remake it. Most of the time, this bracket can be reused, so hang on to it.

*Take off the bracket that holds down the oil-dipstick tube before removing the dipstick tube itself.*

## Piston and Rod Removal

It is now time to remove the piston and rod assemblies. Now the engine has been turned over after soaking, we can remove the pistons.

The first step is to stamp your connecting rods and main bearing caps. The connecting rods are numbered 1–8 from front to back. Your main bearing caps are also numbered 1–5 from front to back. On the connecting rods, always stamp the outside of the connecting rod, which is the side facing the pan rail. You are now ready to remove the first piston-and-rod assembly.

The stock connecting-rod nuts will take a 9/16-inch 12-point socket. Aftermarket rod bolts can vary in socket size, but most are have a 6-point nut. Remove the bearing-cap nuts and set them aside. To remove the rod cap, it may be necessary to tap on the rod to get it to move down into the bore. If you have to resort to hitting the rod bolts, use a piece of brass to tap them. Once the cap is loose, remove it from the connecting rod.

The next step is to install connecting-rod boots on the bolts.

We have seen rod bolts nick crankshafts bad enough that grinding the crankshaft 0.010 inch does not clean them up. You don't want to have to grind your crank any more than you have to. Use a rubber mallet to begin to tap the piston assembly out of the bore. Keep your hand on the cylinder side to catch the piston so that it does not fall on the floor.

When removing the piston-and-rod assembly, support the connecting rod so that it does not damage the cylinder bore. Repeat this procedure to remove the other seven pistons. Even though the connecting rods have been numbered, get into the habit of reinstalling the rod caps back onto the rods. Remember that all AMC engines have the bearing notches on the same side.

*Before removing the connecting rods, make sure that they are numbered 1–8 from front to rear. The rods should be numbered on the pan rail side of the rod and should be stamped both on the rod cap and the rod itself.*

**1**

*After removing the bearing cap, install the connecting-rod boots so that when you remove the rod assembly, you do not nick the crankshaft.*

**2**

*To remove a connecting rod bearing cap that is not removable by hand, use a brass punch and lightly tap the rod bolt squarely on the surface just enough to pop the cap free. We will install new ARP rod bolts in these rods, but if you plan to reuse the rod bolts, just lightly tap the bolt with a dead-blow hammer so that the bolt isn't damaged.*

**3**

*Once the rod cap is free, remove it from the connecting rod.*

4

To remove the piston-and-rod assembly, tap it with a dead-blow piston hammer that is designed for this purpose.

5

Once the piston is out of the cylinder bore, use two hands to guide the connecting rod out of the cylinder. Do not scratch the cylinder bore, even if you are planning on boring the engine.

## Bearing Bolt Removal

When the pistons are all removed, unbolt the main-bearing bolts. Removal of the stock factory bolts requires a 13/16-inch socket. From the factory, the AMC main bearing caps have arrows pointing to the front, and they have the numbers 1–5 forged in the main cap.

There is a stamped number 2 on our cap. This is a number stamped from a previous build and is not correct. Use a dead-blow hammer to lightly tap the main cap from side to side. Once loose, remove the cap.

The main thrust bearing is located on the number-3 cap. AMC used a thrust on both the upper and lower bearing. When removing the rear cap, check the condition of the rear-main seal.

Once all of the main bearing caps are removed, lift the crankshaft out of the block. Lift the crankshaft straight up and out of the block, being careful not to nick the journals. Keep all of the old bearings until the project is done.

Look at the back of the bearings to see if the engine has had the crankshaft ground or not. All undersize bearings are stamped on the back side of the bearings (for example, 0.010, 0.020, or 0.030). The rule of thumb is that if the bearing does not have any stamping on it, it is standard.

1

AMC had arrows and numbers forged right into the castings. They are numbered from front to back. Notice the stamped number 2 on our number-1 cap. This was stamped wrong from the last engine rebuild. At least it was on in the correct position.

2

Using a 13/16-inch socket with an electric impact gun, remove the main-bearing-cap bolts.

3

*Using a dead-blow hammer, lightly tap the main cap after the bolts are loose to break it free.*

4

*The thrust bearing on all AMC V-8 engines is located on the number-3 main cap. AMC used a thrust on the upper and lower bearing.*

5

*The rear-main cap houses the rear-main seal. Inspect the seal during disassembly.*

6

*Grab the crankshaft from both the front and rear and start to break it loose. Lift straight up and try not to hit the journals.*

7

*When the crankshaft is clear of the engine block, set it down on the rear flange. It should stand up on its own.*

## Camshaft Removal

Once the crankshaft is removed, remove the camshaft. We wait until the crankshaft is out of the way just in case we have to use a large pry bar to help the camshaft slide through the bearings.

On an engine that has been sitting for a while, it is common for the camshaft to need a little persuasion. Using a long, flat-blade screwdriver or a pry bar, lightly pry forward on the camshaft. If not reusing the camshaft, do not worry about damaging the cam. However, if you plan to reuse the camshaft, do not pry on the lobes. Once the camshaft is loose, begin to walk it out of the bores.

The camshaft lifters should just fall out or just need a slight tap to remove them. Always remove the lifters prior to removing the camshaft so that the lobes do not get stuck on the lifters. This comes out quick.

After removing the camshaft, we noticed some notches in cylinders number-1 and number-2. The other cylinders do not have this notch at the bottom, which is what gives it away. After looking more closely at the cylinder bores, we noticed that the engine had two connecting-rod failures. Cylinders number-1 and number-2 had sleeves installed prior to our rebuild. There is no way to know what kind of sleeve job was done. Will water leak from behind the sleeves? You can put a lot of money into the block and not really know what you have.

1

*After many years of storage, it is common for the camshaft to be stuck in the bore. Use a small pry bar or a large screwdriver to free the camshaft. Most of the time, a new camshaft will be installed. However, in keeping with good disassembly practices, do not pry on the camshaft lobes.*

2

*Once the camshaft is free, support the rear of the camshaft and walk it out of the engine block.*

3

*Notice the different notches in the front two cylinders. This is a sign that at one time this engine broke two connecting rods. The cylinders were damaged enough that they had to install two cylinder sleeves to repair. This is a questionable engine block to use because we do not know the severity of the repair because the cylinder sleeve is hiding it. If you put a lot of money into this engine block and it decides to leak water into the engine oil down the road, that would be devastating.*

## Freeze Plug Removal

Now that the block is stripped, remove the freeze plugs. Most customers leave this step for the machine shop. If you want to give it a shot, use a medium punch to hit them on one side or the other side of the plug. The idea is to tip it and not punch it all the way into the block. If it happens to fall into the block, fish it out by grabbing it with locking pliers.

*To remove the freeze plugs, use a medium-length punch and tap them on one side to tip them. Use a pair of locking pliers to remove them. Be careful, and if they fall into the block, retrieve them.*

## Camshaft Bearing Removal

Unless you have a removal tool, leave camshaft bearing removal for the machine shop. The camshaft bearing tool is an expanding mandrel that fits the inside diameter of the camshaft bearing. Once it is expanded, the driver has a centering cone that helps keep the tool straight.

Document where the oil holes are aligned before you remove the bearings. If you are not careful, you could remove material from the inside diameter of the camshaft housing. While holding the centering cone, hit the mandrel with a large hammer to remove the bearing.

*Unless you have a removal tool, leave the camshaft bearing removal for the machine shop. The tool is an expandible driver that expands to fit the inside diameter of the camshaft bearing. Then, hit the driver with a hammer to remove the bearing.*

## Valve-Spring Removal

To remove the valve springs, a valve-spring-removal tool is required. The machine shop has air versions to speed up the process. Manual valve-spring-removal tools are available that will work for one set of heads. The tool centers on the back of the valve while compressing the valve spring and the retainer.

Once the spring is compressed, remove the valve locks from the valve and release the spring compressor. Remove the spring and retainer. Once it is removed, take the valve out. On these cylinder heads, we used a small punch to tap the valves out of the rusted valve guides. We already know these heads will be getting new valves, but if you want to reuse the valves, be careful not to damage them.

*If you want to remove the valve springs from the cylinder head, some basic manual tools are available. This model is air driven, but the manually driven tool is the same concept. It's just a little slower.*

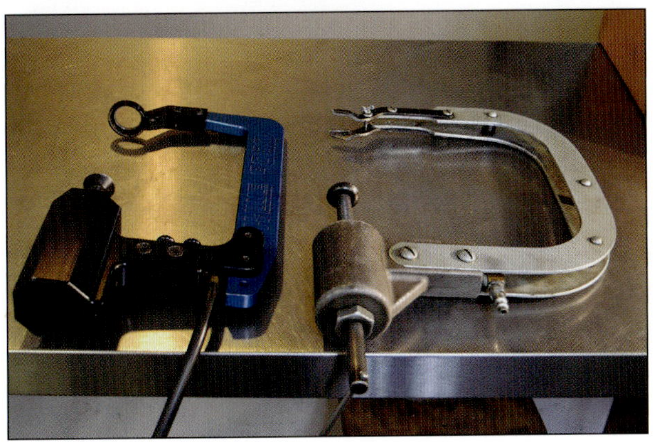

*The valve compressor on the left is for high valve spring pressure, such as in a solid-roller engine. The valve-spring compressor on the right is a typical compressor that is used on stock and mild performance springs.*

# ENGINE BLOCK INSPECTION AND MACHINING

After the block has been completely stripped, it is ready for the cleaning operation. First, conduct a visual inspection before sending it through the cleaning process.

This particular block was very greasy and rusted, which made it somewhat difficult to visually inspect. By removing the crankshaft, we know that this engine does not have any spun main bearings. However, we will inspect the main housing bore one last time.

Another area to check is the lifter valley (both sides) because this is where the block will crack if it has ever been frozen. Use a flashlight to inspect the lifter-valley area. When a block freezes, it will usually crack between the lifter area and the cylinder deck. These cracks will almost always crack from front to rear on the block. When water freezes, it expands and will push the block out. These cracks are sometimes visible, and the bulge can be felt. Sometimes a water trail is visible from the crack down into the valley. These small hints can save you the expense of having a machine shop check for you and charge you.

*The engine block has been stripped of freeze plugs, oil gallery plugs, and camshaft bearings. It is now ready for the hot-tank operation.*

The other area to visually inspect is the outside of the block (both sides) by the freeze plugs. Look for the same effect's cracks and/or water leaks. Keep in mind that this check is only for the obvious cracks and defects. Have your local machine shop magnaflux the block after the cleaning process.

## Hot Tanking and Magnafluxing

After hot tanking, the engine block is ready for magnafluxing. Some blocks should soak in the bottom of the tank over the weekend to loosen up the grease. Once the jet washing is complete, the block goes into a rinse booth, where it is rinsed with hot water. Then, the block is blow dried. Next, it is magnafluxed. If you're building an AMC engine, it is possible that the engine may be 30 to 50 years old.

With the Midwest's freezing temperatures, owners are concerned about engines being winterized cor-

*After the first run in the spray washer, the engine block is completely degreased. This is a caustic hot tank that is heated to 180°F.*

*This handheld magnafluxing machine is from Goodson Shop Supplies. It uses a yellow powder, and when the magnetic field is applied, the magnetic powder will find its way directly to the crack.*

rectly. Freeze cracks are very common in the lifter valley, freeze plug area, and cylinder bores. These areas are surrounded by water that could have frozen in its lifetime.

Another reason that a block could crack is from heat or a spun rod. It could also crack because the main bearing creates a lot of heat in the main housing bore. If there are discolored or burnt areas, pay extra attention to them. The AMC V-8 engines were known for having some main-bearing oil problems, especially at high RPM.

## Align Hone, Bore, and Cylinder Deck Inspection

After we know that we have a solid block on which to begin our build, the next items to check are the align hone, cylinder deck, and bores. To check the align hone, torque the main caps onto the block in the correct number locations. It is especially important to make sure that the mating surface of the main caps is clean of any dirt, grease, burrs, and high spots.

Run a file board or a surface stone over the block. The main caps should have the same thing done to the mating surface. After a complete cleaning, wipe the surfaces with some brake or parts cleaner and blow them dry with compressed air.

Use a Sunnen dial bore gauge to check all five main bores. This specification will have a high and low limit; most machine shops set up the gauge to the middle of the specification. If you are doing a complete engine build and are interested in blueprinting your engine, do the align hone even if the bore is good. Performance applications will usually have ARP main studs installed and aligned honed.

Cylinder bores are checked the same way as the align bore. The cylinder bores can be a little more difficult to check, depending on the condition of the block. Sometimes we have to rough bore the cylinder block to determine the oversize piston that is needed.

Final honing should always be done after the machine shop has the pistons. The proper way is to measure the pistons per the manufacturer's recommendations and measure the clearance accordingly. Our project block ingested water and damaged two cylinders enough to require that sleeves were installed. The cylinder deck will be resurfaced in most rebuilds. From the factory, the piston sits below the deck.

AMC blocks actually are pretty close to a zero deck from the factory, unlike the Chevy engines, where it was common to have the piston in the hole 0.020 inch. AMC engines will only have about 0.005 to 0.012 inch to remove from the deck to get to a zero deck.

When inspecting the deck, pay attention to low or water-damaged areas. If the machine shop concludes that the deck needs more than 0.005 to 0.012 inch removed, it can order the pistons with the compression height (CH) moved. Sinking the piston into the block a little more will provide more room for the block to clean up.

When a zero deck is discussed, most machine shops put the piston

*With the main caps torqued in the proper locations, the align bore is checked with a Sunnen dial bore gauge.*

*Using a Sunnen dial bore gauge, check the cylinder bores to get a close idea of their condition. Often, the block has to be rough bored to determine the oversize piston that is needed.*

in the hole at 0.005 inch. This will allow room for the connecting rod and piston to grow when they are at full temperature. When increasing the compression ratio of an engine block, resurfacing the block is very important for the head-gasket sealing. The cylinder deck can be resurfaced, or it can be square decked.

## Resurfacing versus Square Decking

When disassembling the engine, check the piston height in the four outer cylinders. You may find that number-1 piston in the hole is 0.005 inch, and at the other end of the block, it is 0.009 inch. This indicates that the block is out of square.

AMC is by far the closest out of the factory machined engine blocks made. When blueprinting, you want the cylinder deck to be square to the main bearing housing bore. For a perfect machined engine square, decking is the only way to go.

This completes the engine inspection. With all of this information, your machine shop will be able to explain the machining that is needed on the engine block and provide the piston bore size that is needed. Depending on the application for your build, they will give you different options for machining and parts.

## Oven Cleaning and Blasting

Now that the engine block has been completely checked over, the cleaning process can be completed. The production order for checking an engine block is planned out. If we went ahead and cleaned a block fully before magnafluxing and then found a crack, we would have spent a lot of time (and money) cleaning an engine block that was no good.

Years ago, to clean an engine block so that it looked brand new involved different chemicals and different acid baths. Some shops may still clean blocks that way, but the cost of disposing of these chemicals has changed the cleaning industry.

The popular, new way to clean engine blocks is to place the engine block into an oven system. The oven

*This is the new Van Norman oven cleaning machine, which is the most efficient and EPA-friendly way of cleaning an engine block.*

Here is a completed engine block after oven cleaning, shot blasting, and tumbling in a Van Norman cabinet.

Here's the engine block in a stainless-steel shot blast cabinet. The two cylinders that were rusted are on the right. You still can see the damaged area, but a lot of it was surface damage only.

heats up the block to 400°F to bake all of the grease and oils off the block. After this process is complete, the engine block is moved into a shop blast cabinet while it's still hot.

Stainless-steel shot or steel shot are the popular choices. These types of machines have impellor blades in the bottom that spray the steel shot onto the engine block while it is spinning. This process is done while the block is hot so that no moisture left in it. In addition, while the block is hot, the least amount of shot will stick in the block.

After the block comes out of the blast cabinet, it goes into a tumbler machine. This machine shakes it to remove as much steel shot as possible. If we were just freshening an engine or honing it, we would not do this process. The steel shot does rough up the machined surfaces a little. That is okay as long as the bores and the cylinder deck surface will be machined.

## Block Machining and Blueprinting

There is a certain order in which block machining is completed. This order is necessary because each machining step is blueprinted off the first step. First is the align bore and align hone. The next step is to chamfer and stone all surfaces on the bottom of the engine block. Then, check the housing bore with a dial bore gauge to determine if any caps need to be recut. After the align hone, we like to etch the main bearing bolt or stud torque on the oil-pan rail.

### Align Bore and Align Hone

As mentioned before, there are different options depending on your build application and horsepower. There are some companies that offer a billet main bearing cap kit. Bulltear offers a nice kit that is recommended for extreme high-horsepower builds and boosted applications. For a stock or very mild build, reusing the stock main bolts is okay. Milodon main bolt stud kit (part number 81187) is used when building a high-performance or race engine.

The purpose of cutting the main caps is to make the main housing bore smaller. It is important to get this bore as close as possible when cutting the caps. Once this is done, the align hone mandrel is used to hone the bore back to the factory dimension.

The Bulltear four-bolt billet main bearing cap kit is used for extreme horsepower. (Photo Courtesy Bulltear)

*Using an ARP thread chaser, clean all the main bearing cap holes. After chasing the threads, use a bristle brush to clean the holes.*

*The Milodon main cap stud kit has been around forever. Milodon was one of the first to produce the main stud kit for an AMC engine.*

Removing as little as possible is important. Removing more material moves the crankshaft centerline closer to the crankshaft. This will naturally create some play in the timing chain. There are some timing chain manufacturers that offer a 0.005- and 0.010-inch undersize timing chain set for this reason.

The first step in the align hone is to chase all the threads in the main bearing cap holes. If any threads don't feel right or show any signs of pulling out, repair them. ARP makes thread-chasing taps that are designed to clean the threads but not remove any material.

Since torquing bolts is all based on friction, it is very important to have the threads cleaned thoroughly and blown out. It is easier to stone and debur the main cap surfaces before installing the studs. To clean the bolt holes, run a small bristle brush with brake cleaner in the hole. After the threads are completely cleaned, install the Milodon studs. Before threading them in, put a dab of oil on the studs and follow the instruction from either Milodon or ARP.

*With a stone block and some mineral spirits, remove all sharp edges on the oil-pan rails and the main cap pads.*

### *Chamfer and Stone the Block*

All sharp edges are removed from the block. If the main bearing caps are not numbered very clearly, stamp the appropriate number into the cap so it is clear to read. The main caps are always numbered from front to back.

Every once in a while, someone will bring in an engine block that does not have the correct main caps with it. Not having the correct main caps makes the job very difficult. Sometimes the caps will fit close enough for us to align bore and then align hone the block. Always be cautious about buying a block without the correct main caps.

The concept of an align hone is to make the housing bore smaller than the original dimension. The key to making this step go well is trying to keep the housing bore consistent all the way through. It is important that the bores do not vary in size much. The mandrel used to align hone will hone all five main caps at the same time. This machine uses a diamond wheel to cut the caps. Be careful to cut the same amount off each cap.

*The main caps lock into the Sunnen cap grinder for grinding. The object is to remove the least amount and the same amount from each main cap.*

*The align hone mandrel is stroked through the housing bore evenly with slight over-stroking to keep the stones wearing evenly.*

*After the main caps are installed and torqued, run the dial bore gauge through the housing bore to see how close the dimensions are. It is common to have to remove a cap or two and grind them a little more.*

Most shops have a Sunnen align hone machine. Although there are a few different machines out there, the Sunnen is the most popular. While honing the housing bore, keep in mind that the more material that is honed out, the closer the crankshaft moves to the timing chain. Some of the newer machines will actually bore each housing bore separately. In this case, having all five main caps close to the same size is not as important. The newest machines to enter this market are CNC controlled.

### Checking with the Dial Bore Gauge

After caps are all cut, they are reinstalled onto the engine and torqued using the Milodon torque instructions. Then, check the housing bore with a dial bore gauge to determine if any caps need to be recut. The closer the align bore is, the easier it will be for the hone to provide a perfect result.

When setting up the dial bore gauge, most engine specifications will provide a housing bore range. Engine builders usually hone the housing bore to the middle of the specification, which provides the most flexibility when setting up the bearing clearances. Even though a large specification is provided on the housing bore, keep it in the middle of the specification to keep the main bearing crush correct. If the main bearing does not have the correct crush, it is easy for the bearing to spin in the housing.

When engine builders talk about bearing crush, it is a totally different topic than bearing clearance. When the main bearing cap is torqued, the two edges of the main bearings make contact before the cap is torqued. The point where the upper and lower bearing make contact is the bearing crush.

The correct amount of bearing crush provided by most engine bearing manufacturers is 0.0005 to 0.0012 inch. If bearing crush is too much, it will buckle the edges of the bearing and cause a tight spot. If more bearing clearance is needed, it is better to machine the crankshaft diameters rather than open the housing bore.

#### Final Sizing the Main Housing Bore

Using the align hone mandrel, the housing bore is honed back out to the factory dimension. Sometimes the engine block needs to be rotated around to achieve perfect results. The key for the machine shop is to keep the hone mandrel stones the same size, and the proper use of overstroking helps with this.

Some caps will become close to the final housing bore size first, so loosen up the cap as to not remove as much material. After loosening the main caps that are close to size, the mandrel is run through a couple more times and then rechecked with the dial bore gauge. This might take a few times to get perfect.

#### Main Bearing Bolt Torque Etching

After the align hone, etch the main bearing bolt or stud torque on the oil pan rail. This is especially nice if you are performing the assembly at home because it makes it very clear how much torque to use on the mains. Also, if anyone else ever has to disassemble the engine, that person will know the torque value to use during the rebuild.

## Boring and Honing

Since our project engine had major rust damage, we will demonstrate the machining that is needed to install sleeves. Rough boring is done in a Rottler F5. The cutters on the Rottler are set up with a precision micrometer. Remember that when boring an engine 0.020 over, it is only removing 0.010 inch from each side of the cylinder bore. This is why it sometimes takes more than you would think to clean up a cylinder.

#### Cylinder Sleeve

Most cylinder sleeves come in two different thicknesses: 0.063 and 0.125. Depending on our final bore size, pick the correct thickness sleeve. When complete, the sleeve should not be thin, which would increase the probability of cracking. To keep the cylinder sleeve from moving in the bore, machine a step at the bottom of the bore. When the cylinder sleeve is pressed all the way in, it will sit on the step in the bottom of the bore.

When boring for a cylinder sleeve, we leave a 0.0015-inch press fit. Before installation, put the cylinder sleeve in the freezer for a few hours. This will shrink the sleeve for easier installation.

The cylinder sleeve is installed with a homemade driver just larger than the outside diameter (OD) of the sleeve. Use a large sledgehammer to drive in the sleeve. Even with only a 0.0015-inch press fit and shrinking the sleeve in the freezer, it still pounds in rather hard. When the sleeve hits the step on the bottom, the tone will change when pounding in the sleeve. At that time, give it one more tap just to make sure that it is bottomed and you are done.

*After align honing is complete, etch on the main bearing torque to make it easier for the engine assembler. Also, years down the road, the next rebuild will be easier without having to determine the torque values.*

## Sleeving the Engine

**1**

*The Rottler F5 is used for boring the cylinders. The boring bar locates and bores the cylinders off the main housing bore. This ensures that the bores are perfectly straight with the centerline of the mains.*

**2**

*The cutters are set up with a precision micrometer before cutting. This machine can cut as much as 0.050 inch in one cut.*

**3**

*When boring for a cylinder sleeve, a step is left at the bottom of the bore. This makes it impossible for the sleeve to fall down.*

**4**

*Before sleeve installation, the sleeve is put in the freezer to shrink it for easier installation. With only a 0.0015-inch press fit, it will drive in harder than you would think.*

**5**

*The sleeve is pressed into the bore with a homemade driver that is just larger than the OD of the sleeve and a large sledgehammer.*

*The leftover sleeve is topped cut to within 0.005 inch of the deck. The rest will be milled off during the square decking.*

*The sleeve is rough bored to the same dimension as the other cylinders.*

The cylinder sleeve is just a bit long, so top it off to about 0.005 inch above the deck. The rest will be removed during the square decking. The sleeved cylinder is rough bored to the same bore size of the other cylinders, preparing it for final honing. Older machines consisted of a boring bar that would bolt to the deck of the cylinder block.

In this application, square deck the cylinder block before boring. When blueprinting a block, the bores need to be bored off the centerline of the main bearing housing bore (crankshaft centerline). That way, we know that the bores are straight to the crankshaft.

From the factory, it is common to see the bores so far off that they do not clean up when boring off the crank centerline. If the cylinder has a heavy ridge, it is common for this ridge to be much heavier on one side than the other. When this happens, the block may need to be bored larger than was first anticipated. This is why you should never order pistons before the machine shop determines what size to order.

Try to purchase parts from the machine shop that is doing the work, even if the parts cost a little more. Remember that this shop is doing the machining, and you want the best possible job done.

Most pistons are special order or custom made for the AMC family, which makes the pistons nonreturnable if you guess wrong. Sometimes we even have to rough bore the block to be able to tell the customer what size piston is needed.

### *Square Deck the Cylinder Block*

After installing the cylinder sleeve and rough boring, the next step is to square deck the cylinder block. To do this, install a BHJ fixture in the main housing bore.

This fixture has a 2-inch bar that sits in the main bearing housing bore. Rings are installed that are the correct size for the AMC housing bore. The end plate is located on the 2-inch bar and with a rod through the camshaft tunnel. The plate is used to indicate in the deck. It is common for blocks to be out of square as much as 0.010 to 0.015 inch.

If an engine block is out of square, it changes the piston-to-deck clearance. There may be one piston at a zero deck on one side and on the other side one that is at -0.010 inch. This changes the compression ratio in each cylinder. This is one of the major items to check when blueprinting an engine block.

Once the BHJ fixture is installed, measure from the cylinder deck down to the 2-inch bar with a depth mic. This will yield the cylinder deck height. From the factory, you might

*The BHJ square decking fixture is installed on the engine block.*

Both sides are indicated in before decking begins. The BHJ fixture ensures that the deck heights will be square from side to side.

Honing an engine with a torque plate simulates the cylinder head being torqued on. This provides the best overall piston ring seal.

*It is important to find the cylinder deck that is the worst and start with that side. Otherwise, you will have to go back and recut the first side if the deck heights do not match.*

The ARP cylinder head bolt kit is specifically for Edelbrock cylinder heads. Depending on the choice of cylinder head, ARP offers a head bolt or stud for your application.

find that this measurement differs from side to side and even from end to end. After machining many different makes and models of engines, we found that the AMC engines were machined pretty accurately from the factory.

### Deck Height

Before decking, another item to calculate is where the deck height should be. In determining this, your desired compression ratio is needed. An engine makes the most power when the piston is at a zero deck or what we call a -0.005-inch deck to allow for growth.

To figure out the deck height needed, the crankshaft stroke, connecting-rod length, and piston compression height (CH) are needed. Once the desired deck height is determined, you are ready to begin machining. After the decking is complete, chamfer all of the bolt holes. The surfacing will leave large burs on the bolt holes; a light chamfer using a drill with a countersink tool installed is all that it takes to debur.

### Torque Plate

Whenever possible, ask to have the block final honed with a torque plate. Not many shops will have a torque plate for an AMC. Just using any torque plate does not ensure that the job is being done correctly. The machine shop should use the same head gasket that will be installed during assembly.

If you are using ARP studs or new head bolts, these are also needed when torque plate honing. As long as you are going through the motion of installing a torque plate, it does not take much more effort to do it correctly. When using ARP studs, the torque value changes. So, it is very important that the torque plate is torqued on with the same torque.

### *Final Honing*

The engine block is now ready for the final honing process. Install the torque plate on the block with the cylinder head gasket and the cylinder head bolts or studs that will be used. When mounting the engine block into the Sunnen hone, secure the block with the bar that goes through the center of the main bearing caps. All caps are torqued on the engine block for honing.

With the torque plate installed on the outside of the cylinders, the smaller 5/16-inch bolts are threaded into the engine block. These are extra cylinder head bolts that are covered in more detail in the upcoming chapters. This is for higher-compression engines or engines with boost. The engine block is installed into a CV/10 Sunnen diamond hone to finish honing.

The Sunnen diamond hone is an automated machine that does not generate as much heat as the older process using stones. The machine keeps track of where the cylinder wall is tighter and automatically repairs the cylinders by stopping in the tight spots repeatedly.

Using diamonds has many advantages. It keeps the cylinder walls cooler during the honing process. This keeps the cylinder walls from expanding or getting an hourglass effect during honing. When using stones, it was common to have to let the engine block cool down for a couple hours and then come back

*It is important that the main bearing caps are installed and torqued on the engine block before final honing begins. It may be overkill, but the idea is to keep as many items torqued on the engine to keep the cylinders as straight as possible for final honing. All V-8 engine blocks are mounted in the machine with a bar that travels through the main housing bore.*

*The torque plate is installed on the outside of the cylinders, and smaller 5/16-inch bolts are threaded into the engine block. These are the extra cylinder head bolts for higher-compression engines or engines with boost.*

*The newest Sunnen honing machines are diamond hones. The diamonds don't create as much cylinder heat as the old stone method. This is one of many benefits to the new diamond hone machines.*

*This is an example of a perfect crosshatch for good oil control and long piston-ring life.*

and finish after the cylinder walls shrank back down.

The different crosshatch patterns available in the new diamond hone is unlimited. We use various crosshatch angles for different applications. For street driving, you want good long-term oil control and ring seal. For drag racing, you are willing to give up a little life for less drag and more horsepower.

Once the final honing is complete, install brushes on the hone and take about three strokes through to give it a perfect finish. Before taking the engine out of the hone using a lifter broach tool, the lifter bores are broached to remove any burrs from the cleaning process. It is especially important when running a hydraulic flat-tappet camshaft that the lifters spin freely in the bores.

### Pistons

For our project engine, we chose Diamond Pistons. Diamond always includes measuring instructions in the box. Notice that the desired clearances recommended will change for particular applications. My teacher years ago used to always say no one will ever know if your piston is a little too loose, but everyone will know if you're too tight. These instructions also show where to measure your pistons.

Keep in mind that the material and process to make pistons has changed over the last 10 years. Over the years, the piston-to-wall clearance needed has become less and less. This means that the newly designed pistons do no grow as much as the old-school forged pistons. Remember to always follow the piston manufacturer on piston-to-wall clearance. After that, you can add your own personal experience to that equation.

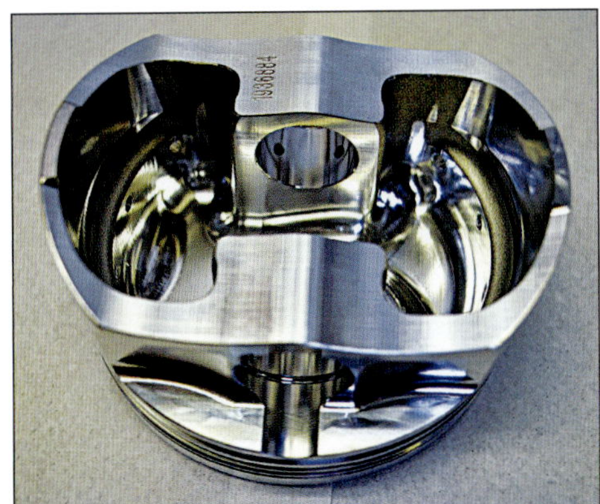

*For this project, we chose Diamond pistons. To measure the pistons, make sure that they are at room temperature. Then, follow the instructions that the piston manufacturer supplied in the box. The manufacturer will also provide direction regarding where to measure the pistons. Always follow the manufacturer's guidelines.*

*A small piston ring package is designed for less ring drag and uses the new single piston clips instead of the spiro locks.*

*This Diamond piston was built with a slight dome. The compression ratio of this engine will be 13.5:1.*

### Cylinder Wall Chamfering

After the torque plate is removed, chamfer the cylinder walls. Chamfering the cylinders needs to be uniform and not too big. The idea is to just break the edge to help the piston rings slide into the bore without any trouble. This makes installing the pistons with rings a lot easier.

The piston ring seal is one of the most important items. If the rings do not seal up on the break-in, sometimes they never will. This is why the first few minutes of an engine are so important. If the piston rings get washed with fuel, it is very hard to get them to come back around. Normally, the only choice is to disassemble the engine and hone it. As previously mentioned, using a good break-in oil is also important.

This is the last step of the normal machining process. The engine can be removed and final washed for assembly. Of course, many different performance upgrades can be done.

## Performance Options for Machining

Let's cover some performance machining options. Each one of these steps has its own purpose. As

*With the lifter bushing installed in one side but not the other, you can see how the oil flow is controlled much better in a high-RPM engine.*

the horsepower level keeps going up, each of these machining steps have a role in making an AMC engine live at a high RPM. Keep in mind that some of these machining steps have different purposes depending on the application: drag racing, road racing, and/or boosted applications.

### *Lifter Bushings*

The first option that we will cover is installing lifter bushings. For most applications, the stock lifter bores are satisfactory. If you are building a high-RPM, solid-roller engine, whether it is used for drag racing or road racing, the benefits of the oil control gained by installing lifter bushings helps keep the crankshaft bearings oiled.

In this application, we are installing lifter bushings to install solid-roller small-block Chevy lifters. The argument could be made to install a larger-diameter lifter instead of a small-block Chevy lifter. The lifters were ordered from Bullet racing with an AMC-spaced link bar installed.

The lifter bushings were supplied by Trend. Yes, we did order a few extra custom lifter bushings. We used one for our setup just in case we ruined one. To control oil and restrict oil to the top of the engine for the solid roller, we drilled a 0.187-inch hole in the lifter bushings before installing them.

This oil hole will considerably restrict oil to the top of the engine. We are running full roller rocker arms, and these do not need nearly as much oil. AMC engines struggle to get enough oil to the main bearings, so making all these oil changes will help the bottom end stay properly lubricated.

Once the BHJ lifter truing fixture is bolted to the block, it is installed on a floating table in our Peterson machine. This machine allows us to float and level the block in every direction. Although there are CNC machines that can do this job in a more automated setup, our manual Peterson provides the same results without the large price tag. When talking about blueprinting with the lifter bores, this setup is making sure that the lifters are both at the proper angle and locations in reference to the camshaft.

The BHJ fixture can be used on multiple different engine blocks, but for each type of engine, there is a different locater plate. These fixtures are pretty expensive, so your machine shop may not have the AMC lifter plate.

Some of the larger Rottler automated machining centers that are CNC controlled do not need all of the different fixtures. They simply can be programed to machine the lifter bores. This makes the job a whole lot easier, but the machine payment is quite a bit. With the lifter locating plate installed, the final reaming for the busing is completed.

### *Drilled Bushings for Better Oil Flow*

All 16 lifter bushings are drilled to 0.187 inch. Carefully measure the hole location. The oil hole location in the lifter bore is very important for the oil travel. We always wait to have our new lifters in our hands before determining the location of the oil hole.

*Using a BHJ lifter truing fixture, the block is mounted in our Peterson machine. If there is any lifter bore misalignment, it will get blueprinted back to the correct location with the BHJ fixture.*

*With the lifter locating plate installed, the final reaming for the busing is completed in the Peterson machine.*

For the location of the oil hole, we installed the front and rear camshaft bearing and the camshaft. While putting a lifter in the hole, watch the lifter travel closely to determine the best location for the oil hole. With large-lift AMC cams, watch to make sure that the oil band on the lifter does not come out of the bore both on top and bottom.

Years ago, there were a few brands of lifters that would bleed off oil pressure only when running very large camshaft lobes because the oil band would travel out of the lifter bore. In recent times, it seems that most lifter companies have caught on to this and have relocated the oil band. This is something that you or your engine builder should pay attention to.

With a bushing installation tool that we made with the lathe, we aligned the lifter hole and pressed in the bushings, being careful not to press the lifter bushing in too far. Before pressing in the bushing, deburr the oil holes both on the inside diameter (ID) and the outside diameter (OD). This is much easier before installation.

Using a Sunnen adjustable hand, hone the lifter bores carefully to the correct size. Be very careful not to hone them too much, as this will bleed off oil pressure, and the only way to repair it is to remove the bushing and install a new one. Using a lifter, check the clearance. The lifter should slide up and down freely with no resistance.

Carefully check the lifter bore clearance with a dial bore gauge, making sure to not hone too much out. A lifter clearance of 0.0012 to 0.0015 inch works fine for most applications. With all the lifters installed, the oil holes all lined up, and the lifter bores honed to size, we are ready to move on to the next step.

## Drilling and Installing the Bushings

**1**

*The new, smaller oil holes are drilled in the bushings for this engine. We went with 0.187-inch oil holes. This will help send more oil to the main bearings, where it is needed.*

**2**

*With a bushing installation tool that we made in the lathe, we aligned the lifter hole and pressed in the bushings. Be careful not to press the lifter bushing in too far.*

**3**

*Using a small hone, the lifter bushings are honed out to the proper clearance. Use a lifter to fit the bushing. The lifter should slide freely up and down in the bronze lifter bore.*

A small dial bore gauge is use for final sizing.

With all the lifters installed and final honed, we are ready to move on to the next step.

*Camshaft Thrust Plate*

The next performance option is installing the camshaft thrust plate. This is critical when running a hydraulic- or solid-roller camshaft. When running a hydraulic flat-tappet, the camshaft will push back into the engine block. Both hydraulic- and solid-roller camshafts will actually drive forward when running.

To keep the timing gear in place, a camshaft thrust plate is used. There are other ways to do this, such as by making or using a camshaft button. We do not employ this method only because the AMC engine has the camshaft gear bolted on the front of the cam. When the camshaft is able to move, this would affect the pattern on the distributor gear. The camshaft thrust plate is the best option to keep the camshaft in place.

Many newer engines use a camshaft plate to locate the camshaft. With AMC engines, it is important not to alter the oil path when doing this. Using a camshaft plate from a 2.5L GM engine, we took an old AMC timing gear and machined it to use as a template. After marking the screw holes, remove the gear and center-punch the holes. There are a few different locations for the camshaft plate bolts; we prefer the twelve o'clock and the six o'clock positions.

Once the holes are marked, drill and tap holes for the camshaft thrust plate. Take your time drilling. Since this is the front of the engine block,

If you have an old AMC V-8 timing gear, it makes a good fixture for marking the holes for the camshaft thrust plate. With a little machining, the gear makes a great template. The GM camshaft plate for a 2.5L engine is readily available and fits nicely.

When drilling and tapping the camshaft thrust plate holes, mark your drill to the correct length so that you do not drill too deep. Make sure to drill and tap straight. Using a bottom tap will work well to get the threads to the bottom of the hole.

*Test fit the camshaft thrust plate to make sure that the holes are tapped deep enough and that the plate tightens up.*

*The spread between the cylinder head bolts on the outside of the cylinder head is a major problem. Notice the gap between the two head bolts circled in yellow. This is extremely prone to head gasket failure with high-compression engines.*

you only have one shot at this. Take your time and make sure that the drill is straight. Measure the length of the screw, subtract the length of the plate, and mark your drill. You only need to drill about 0.100 inch longer than the screw will go in.

When tapping the holes, make sure that the tap is straight and use some tapping compound. For the final tap, using a bottom tap works the best. Remember to clean the hole with a brush. The 1/4-20 button-head screws seem to work well. They sit as flush as possible.

Remember to use Loctite when installing the button-head screws. When the holes are complete, test fit the camshaft plate to make sure that the screws fully tighten up. As long as your plate tightens, this step is complete.

### Adding Extra Cylinder Head Bolts

When is it needed to drill and tap for extra cylinder head bolts? We have a simple rule: with any compression ratio over 11.5:1, we recommended it. One of the major problems with the AMC cylinder head gasket is the spread between the cylinder head bolts on the outside of the cylinder head.

An engine with a gap between the two head bolts is extremely prone to head-gasket failure with high-compression engines. The gap between the two head bolts repeats for all four cylinders. This gap in head bolts is directly between the combustion chambers. Under high compression and or high boost, this gasket almost always fails.

Stock-replacement head gaskets are especially prone to blowing. So, when running higher compression, switch to the MLS head gasket that is manufactured by Cometic.

Let's get started machining the extra head bolt holes. We drill and install many of these extra head bolts, so we have created some tools that greatly help in their placement. The Indy cylinder heads have a center marked with a machined dimple. We use the AMC torque plate for a drill index. The torque plate locates off the cylinder head dowel pins. That way, each time the torque plate is installed on the block, the bolt holes end up in the exact location.

To make the torque plate our fixture, we located the extra head bolt holes exactly in the center of the two other bolts and drilled these on a CNC machine. That way, we knew that the bolts holes were spaced exactly the same. We also located dowel-pin holes on the other side of the plate so that we could bolt the torque plate to the cylinder head and use it as the template for the cylinder head as well.

### Doing This on Your Own

If you are going to attempt this on your own, let's go over a few items for if you do not have a CNC digital mill. The new bolt holes are 5/16-24 and need to be placed just outside the fire ring on the head gasket. They need to be far enough off the fire ring that they do not interfere with the head gasket sealing.

The other item that is very important is that if the location of these holes is not exactly between the cylinders, the heads will only fit the side on which you drilled them. The hole location will not match the

*Use the torque plate as a template to mark the locations to drill the new head bolt holes. Making our torque plate our template also allows us to install the extra head bolts during the final honing process. This gives the cylinder the same effect as having the cylinder head torqued on.*

*Using the correct drill for a 5/16-24 tap, carefully drill the hole to be tapped. Drill all four holes, then remove the template for final tapping. Always countersink the new hole after tapping so that there are no raised edges. Since there are no head gaskets that come with the extra holes, they will have to be drilled.*

*With the cylinder head bolted on, you can see that the extra cylinder head bolt is aligned with each cylinder. If you can, picture the gap between the original factory head bolts. The extra bolts add the extra clamping force needed with large-compression builds.*

other side unless you locate and drill them with a digital mill.

The other problem with not drilling them with a fixture or a program of some sort is that if a head ever has to be changed or transferred to a new block, the cylinder head will have to be used as a drill index to align them again. Having the torque plate as our fixture, we had the extra head bolt installed during the final honing process. This provides the same effect as having the cylinder head bolted on.

Use the correct drill for a 5/16-24 tap, and carefully drill your hole. Always countersink the new hole after tapping so that there are no raised edges. Drill and countersink all four holes. Then, remove the template for final tapping. Since no head gaskets come with the extra head bolt hole, we have to drill them.

Set the head gasket on the torque plate fixture and sandwich the head gasket between the torque plate fixture (bottom) and a sheet of plywood (top). Then, drill the hole through the torque plate. With the stock head gasket and MLS, if you try marking them and drilling them without sandwiching them, the gasket will usually tear while attempting to drill the hole. The MLS gasket can be just as tricky or worse to drill through because of the multiple layers of steel.

ARP has a selection of 5/16-24 bolts that work well. Measure the cylinder head to figure out the length, and check ARP's bolt chart in the back of its catalog for different sizes. At 5/16 inch, these bolts do not require a lot of torque. ARP has a recommended torque valve for the bolts; we torque ours to 28 ft-lbs. You will most likely break through into the water jackets of the block, so use some liquid Teflon on the threads.

You are now ready for some serious compression or boost pressure without fear of head gasket failure. Some engine builders may recommend use a 3/8-inch bolt to allow for a greater torque value. Years ago, we used a 3/8-inch bolt. However, over time, we discovered that the bolt was very close to the fire ring. With the strength of ARP bolts getting better over the years, we find that the 5/16-inch bolt does the job.

In the past, there were no aftermarket heads from which to choose; we only had the stock cast-iron heads. So, we ran high-compression drag racing engines with cast-iron heads. The stock cast-iron cylinder heads are not solid, so you will break-into the water jacket when drilling the extra head bolt hole. To seal up the water, press in a 1/2-inch valve guide with green Loctite on it. This actually does a good job of sealing the valve guide.

If there are any small water leaks after running the engine, a little Bar's Leaks does the trick. The aftermarket heads are solid in this area and do not break into water.

### Oil System Modifications

The oiling system on an AMC engine is one of the areas that needs the most improvement. The first step is to install an internal oil line in the lifter bore valley. This internal oil line dramatically helps to supply more oil to the bottom end of the engine.

In high-RPM applications, by the time the oil feed gets to the rear of the crankshaft, the oil supply for rod journals number-7 and -8 is inadequate. Plumbing additional oil into the main oil gallery acts as a booster pump for the oil system.

We believe the internal oil line is so important that we will install one even on a stock rebuild. On a completely stock engine build, we recommend the oil line but leave it up to the customer. Over the years, we have seen this internal oil line built many different ways. We have seen a copper line with compression fittings, a hydraulic hose, and a stainless-steel line with AN fittings. One thing that has not changed is the location of the line.

### Locating and Machining the Front Oil Line Hole

The first oil hole is drilled in the front of the lifter valley between the two oil gallery plugs. Start by center punching the start hole directly in the center of the two oil gallery plugs. When looking into the two factory oil gallery holes, an intersection point with be visible. The oil line should feed directly into the intersecting point of the factory holes.

After prick punching the hole, start with an 1/8-inch pilot hole. This ensures that it breaks into the center of the oil gallery. Next, drill the final hole size at 7/16 inch. Once the hole is drilled, you are ready to tap the hole 1/4-inch NPT.

Starting with a new tap will make this job much easier. It is important to keep the tap straight. Once started, continue tapping the hole. Every once in a while, remove the tap, clean the hole, and try your fitting. Do not tap the hole too deep, where the fitting threads all the way in. We like to see the bottom of the fitting just breaking through the inside of the oil hole. Tapping too deep can restrict oil in the gallery.

After tapping, it is very important to deburr the ID of the oil hole. Any burrs left in the block can break off when the line is threaded in for the final time. When installing for the final time, we do not put Teflon sealer on the threads because we want to leave no chance for the Teflon to get into the oil gallery.

## How to Locate and Machine the Front Oil Line Hole

1

*Once your hole is center punched, drill a 1/8-inch pilot hole before drilling your 7/16-inch hole.*

2

*The 1/4-inch NPT oil line should intersect with the center of the factory oil galleries.*

3

After drilling a pilot hole, continue drilling with a 7/16-inch drill.

4

Start the 1/4-inch NPT tap, being careful to start it straight. Once started, tap the oil hole so that the Earl's fitting threads protrude just past the hole. Tapping this hole too deep could cause oil to be restricted in the oil gallery.

The second hole is drilled and tapped on the passenger-side lifter oil gallery. This oil hole should intersect the main oil line. Follow the same procedure as was performed for the front oil hole. Drill your 1/8-inch pilot hole first. At this time, make sure that you are centered with the oil gallery.

While tapping the hole 7/16-inch NPT, the Earl's threads should just protrude into the oil gallery so that the internal oil flow is not blocked.

The second oil-feed hole is located on the passenger-side bank lifter oil gallery. Pictured is the exact location of the hole.

With the Earl's fittings installed, measure for the -6 braided oil line.

*This is the final installation of the internal oil line. This should just be a test fit; this oil line will be installed after the final wash just before assembly.*

Finish drilling the oil hole with a 7/16-inch bit. Apply tapping fluid to the 1/4-inch NPT tap and begin tapping the hole, making sure the tap is started straight. There is only one shot at drilling and tapping a cast-iron block, so double-check everything before drilling.

As with the front hole, make sure not to tap too deep. The threads should just protrude through the hole. The last and final step is to debur the oil hole. Make sure to deburr the inside of the hole.

### *Braided Hose Line Measurements*

Now that the holes are all drilled and tapped, thread in the Earl's fittings. Next, measure for the braided hose. You can use the stainless-steel braided hose; otherwise, the black hose with stainless-steel inner is also popular.

To measure out a length of braided hose, tightly wrap electrical tape where you are about to cut. If using a hacksaw, use a new fine-tooth steel blade. A cutoff wheel also works well but is a little harder to keep straight. Cut a straight line and not to fray the ends.

The hose end needs to sit square in the fitting. Remove the hose end and thread the hose into the outer housing of the Earl's fitting. Next, place a little oil on the ID of the hose and insert the female part of the fitting. Mark the hose so that if the hose begins to push out of the fitting, you will know.

Start threading the fittings together while ensuring that the hose does not push out. Various brands of fittings have various dimensions with which to tighten, but the most popular is a 1/16-inch gap. As long as the hose did not push out, it is done. Repeat for the other side.

Once complete, install the oil line to make sure that it fits well. We will final install the oil line after the block is finish machined and washed for assembly. Only for extreme race

*They do not make a screen kit for an AMC engine, so we use a Moroso big-block Chevy screen kit and modify it to fit. JB-Weld works well. There are two front oil drainback holes that also need a screen installed. Using the leftover screen, form and shape these to fit into the drainback holes. Use the JB-Weld to secure them in place.*

*Using the extra screen, form two screen inserts for the oil drainback holes in the front of the block. JB-Weld secures the screens in place.*

engines would we install oil drainback screens in the valley.

Oil screens can come in handy during a valvetrain failure. This will keep a lash cap or broken rocker arm part from going any deeper into the engine than the lifter valley. We use the big-block Chevy kit from Moroso to do the job because there is no kit available for the AMC engine. It comes with a two-part epoxy, but we use J-B Weld. It seems to work better over time.

There are two oil drainback holes in the front of the AMC engine as well. With the leftover screen, form it to cover these holes and secure it with J-B Weld. Some engine builders have used a normal screen from the hardware store, and there is nothing wrong with that, but we have seen cases where the screen was too fine and it slowed the oil drainback down to the point that the oil pan ran low.

### *Camshaft Bearings*

The front camshaft bearing is not modified. The camshaft bearings are numbered 1 through 5 with number-1 always being the front of the engine. The front camshaft bearing is the widest of the bearings and has only one oil hole in it. It also has a groove 360 degrees around the whole ID of the bearing.

When installing this bearing, align the one oil hole with the oil hole in the block. If you notice that this oil hole is quite large, drill a new oil hole 180 degrees from the original. Drill this modified oil hole in the camshaft bearing positions 2 through 5. The modified oil hole will be only 11/64 inch. This will help keep more oil in the bottom end of the engine.

***The number-1 position camshaft bearing is not modified. This bearing only has one oil hole. The bearing is installed by aligning the oil hole in the bearing with the only hole in the block. If this oil hole is quite large, drill a new oil hole 180 degrees from the original with a 11/64-inch drill bit. This will help keep more oil in the bottom end of the engine.***

### *Oil Galleries*

Another oil modification is to the two 3/8-inch NPT main oil galleries in the front of the engine block. Internally, use a 1/4-inch NPT tap and tap both oil galleries for a 1/4-inch pipe plug. Drill a 0.250-inch hole in the center of the plugs. This will restrict the oil to the top end of the engine when using full roller-rocker arms.

**Oiling Problems and Modifications**

| **Vehicle** | **Street Car with Stock Engine or Mild Camshaft** | **Street/Strip Car with Hydraulic-Roller Camshaft** | **Drag Race/Road Race/Extreme Street Performance** |
|---|---|---|---|
| **Modification** | **Recommendation** | **Recommendation** | **Recommendation** |
| Internal oil line | Not needed/ optional | Required | Required |
| Cam bearing oil hole modification | Not needed/ optional | Required | Required |
| Full groove main bearings or half groove | Recommended | Required | Required |
| Oil gallery modification | Not required | Required | Required |
| Oil pump blueprint/deburr | Recommended | Required | Required |
| External oil line | Not required | Not required | Required |
| Lifter bushings | Not required | Not needed | Recommended |
| Intake gasket style | Valley pan | Valley pan or 2-piece | 2-piece |
| Aftermarket oil pan | Not required | Optional | Required |
| Matched distributor gear | Recommended | Recommended | Required |
| Hydraulic-roller camshaft | Not required/ optional | Recommended | Required |
| Camshaft thrust plate | Only for roller camshaft | Only for roller camshaft | Required |
| Chamfer oil holes on crankshaft | Recommended | Required | Required |
| Aftermarket main bearing caps | Not required | Not required | Optional |
| ARP main bolts/ studs | Not required | Recommended | Required |
| ARP head bolts | Not required | Recommended | Required |
| ARP rod bolts or aftermarket rods | Optional | ARP rod bolts | Aftermarket rods |
| Extra head bolts | Not required | Depends on the compression ratio | Required |

Do not do this on a block with the lifter bushings installed. The lifter bushings have a smaller oil hole drilled in them to restrict the oil, so they are not needed. We have seen this internal oil restrictor done on both sides of the lifter valley, and we have seen it done on only one side. For practical purposes, we do both lifter oil gallery passageways.

Another way that we have seen engine builders restrict oil to the top end is to have custom pushrods made with a smaller oil hole. There are a few modifications that can be done to the front cover as well. On our covers, we make sure that all the passageways are smooth and radiused smoothly.

There has been much discussion that the oil holes on the 401 engines are drilled differently than the 390 and 360 crankshafts. We know this to be true. You can read about AMC oil problems for days on the internet. There is some truth to these articles. We believe that all of these modifications help to some degree with the oiling problems on an AMC engine.

AMC produced a lot of cars, and hundreds of thousands of miles were put on them without any oiling modifications. The oiling problems only come into play when the RPM of the engine goes up.

## Final Block Prep for Assembly

Once the engine block is completely machined, it is ready to be final washed for assembly. The machine shop will run a series of engine brushes through all of the oil galleries. The key here is to make sure that all of the machine chips are removed from the oil galleries. After brushing the engine, it is run through a jet washer that is designed only for the final washing.

*When final washing an engine block for assembly, long brushes are run through all the oil gallery passageways.*

There is a way to perform the final wash without using a jet washer. For years, we washed blocks by hand with a bucket of hot water and Dawn dish soap. Using hot water, begin by rinsing out the oil galleries and handwashing the cylinders with soft rags and Dawn dish soap. Literally scrub all the surfaces by hand. I truly believe that this sometimes does a better job than using our jet washer. Make sure to keep up with the WD-40 on the cylinder walls so that they don't rust.

### *Coat with WD-40*

After rinsing, all of the machined surfaces are coated with WD-40 and wiped clean. Spray the cylinder walls and wipe them with paper towels. The white shop towels that come in a box at most hardware stores work well. The cylinder walls should be wiped until there is no black on your paper towel.

After cleaning, spray the machined surfaces one more time with WD-40. This is very important. It keeps rust from developing, especially in a humid location where the steel sweats.

*The first step to installing freeze plugs is to make sure that their holes are wire wheeled and clean. Using cup-and-core sealant on the freeze plugs, pound them in and make sure that they are installed square.*

*After camshaft bearings are installed, test fit the camshaft to make sure that it turns properly. The camshaft should turn by hand with little to no drag. It is common on AMCs for the camshaft to be tight after the camshaft bearing install. We have a camshaft reamer that we made out of an old camshaft core if needed.*

For years, there were many engine builders who said that there was silicone in WD-40 and that this would delay or even prevent the piston rings from sealing. We even followed this

*This Dura-Bond camshaft bearing has a smaller oil hole drilled in for better oil control. It limits the amount of oil that is used here so that more is sent to the crankshaft.*

*The Dura-Bond expandable camshaft installation tool is used to install bearings. It helps to put a black permanent mark on the camshaft bearing straight out from the oil hole. This will help to center the oil hole in the journal.*

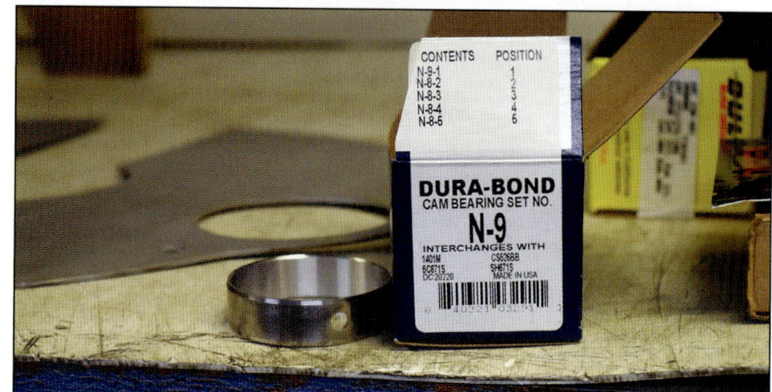


*This is Dura-Bond camshaft bearing set N-9. All five camshaft bearings are numbered with their location to be installed. Position-1 is toward the front of the block.*

and used other brands of anti-rust spray. However, after touring a famous NASCAR engine shop, we noticed that it was spraying the cylinders down with WD-40.

Even in a clean garage, always keep a bag on the engine. You will be amazed at how much dirt flies around in the air. One of the most important factors for a good engine build is keeping it a clean assembly.

### *Freeze Plugs and Camshaft Bearings*

The last steps before the engine is put on an engine stand is to install the freeze plugs, camshaft bearings, and oil gallery plugs.

To install camshaft bearings, start with a set of Dura-Bond camshaft bearings with the oil hole modification already done. Camshaft bearing installation seems easy but can be tricky. If you do not have a specifically designed camshaft bearing tool, do not try to install them yourself.

There are some cheap crude tools available in the marketplace. The most important item is to take care of the ID of the bearing during the installation. The cheap installers do not have any rubber to protect the bearing on the ID. A nice camshaft bearing tool has an expander that fits

*With the Dura-Bond camshaft tool, keep the cone pressed tight against the engine block. Using a hammer, gently tap the bearing to start it and then continue tapping into place. As it gets close, stop and check the placement of the oil hole, being careful not to overshoot the bearing.*

the bearing well and is coated with rubber to protect the bearing.

When installing the bearings, start with the rear and work your way to the front. The Dura-Bond AMC V-8 camshaft bearing set N-9 has all five camshaft bearings numbered with their locations. Position-1 is the front of the block and so forth, with number-5 being the rear bearing.

The installation tool has a cone that fits into the front camshaft bearing bore. Holding this cone tight against the engine block ensures that the camshaft bearings are driven in square. It does not take much for a crooked camshaft bearing to lock up a camshaft.

There are many manufacturers of camshafts, and you must check the camshaft fitment after the bearing install. At times, we have had to turn down the camshaft in our crankshaft grinder to get the proper clearance. This may be an item to leave for the machine shop to install.

### *Oil Gallery Plugs*

When installing the oil gallery plugs, use a liquid Teflon to seal them. Some machine shops do not put sealer on the plugs that are internal, and this is okay, but we prefer to seal all the plugs. Don't forget to install the small oil control plugs behind the front 3/8-inch oil gallery plugs. Do not put sealer on these plugs.

Two oil gallery plugs are in the valley. Install two 3/8-inch NPT plugs in oil gallery holes. When installing the freeze plugs, we prefer brass over steel. For the small additional cost, it is worth it.

Using Loctite cup-and-core plug sealant, coat the plug generously before installation. Even though it might seem tedious, install the freeze plug with the words straight up and down; the small details are important. When installing the freeze plugs, make sure to install them evenly. If they are installed crooked, the chance of a leak increases.

The last plug to install is the camshaft plug in the rear. Test fit the camshaft before installing this plug just in case it has to be removed. You are now ready to put the engine on a stand. Mount the engine lower on the stand so that it is easier to spin over once the cylinder heads are installed.

*The front two oil gallery plugs are 3/8-inch NPT. Install them with just a little bit of liquid Teflon. These are internal plugs, so they do not need much.*

*Don't forget the internal 3/8-inch NPT oil gallery plugs in the lifter valley. These plugs are unique to the AMC and are often overlooked.*

# Crankshaft

When rebuilding a donor engine that was purchased at a swap meet or on the internet, check the stroke of the crankshaft. Just because the advertisement may have stated that the block and crank were for a 401 doesn't mean that it is correct. At least the AMC engine blocks have the logo on the outside of the block for displacement (cubic inches), which makes it easy to determine the size of the engine block.

*To check the stroke of a crankshaft, bridge the two main journals and measure down to the lowest point of the connecting-rod journal. Document this number. Then, repeat this for the highest point of the rod journal. Once you have both of these measurements, subtract the highest measurement from the lowest measurement; the difference is the crankshaft stroke.*

## Crankshaft Stroke

Measuring the stroke of the crankshaft provides a definite answer as to which crankshaft is installed. Always use the same journal when measuring. We recommend checking all of the connecting-rod journals, especially if the crankshaft was previously ground. Since these engines are old, you never know what someone else did to repair a crankshaft.

A journal shop may cheat the stroke on the crankshaft during grinding to save a crankshaft. It is always helpful to know this going into the project rather than when you are halfway in. The main journal dimension on 290, 304, 343, 360, 390, and 401 engines all have the same main journal diameter of 2.7474 to 2.7489 inch. The connecting rod journal diameter for engines 290, 304, 343, and 360 are the same 2.0948 to 2.0955 inch.

The AMC 390 and 401 engines have the same connecting-rod journal diameter of 2.2464 to 2.2485 inches. Depending on the producer of the rod and main journal diameters, there are some print differences out there. This final dimension and the bearing clearances should be left to the machine shop.

## Crankshaft Modification for a TorqueFlite Transmission

The type of transmission affects which crankshaft flange is used and whether machining of the rear of the crankshaft is required.

BorgWarner automatic transmissions were used from 1965 to 1971. The big cast-iron BorgWarner M11-B and M-12 series were used until 1971 on 343, 360, 390, and 401 applications. Beginning in 1972, AMC used a TorqueFlite 727, which was a far superior transmission. The Torque-

**Solid Engine-Transmission Combination**

Note that the 904/998 is a great low-end transmission with a lot of torque and works very well behind a 360 or 401 engine. ■

Flite later developed its name as a very fast performance transmission.

The 1968–1971 BorgWarner transmissions have a tag attached to the case above the pan that carries the vendor number and the AMC part number for the application. The 6-cylinder engine and smaller V-8 engines (the 290 and 304) used the light-duty aluminum-case transmission, while the 343, 360, 390, and 401 used the cast-iron-case transmission.

One exception was the 1968–1969 AMX with the 290 4-barrel V-8, which used the big AT. The 1972–1974 360 and 401 automatic transmissions were TorqueFlite 727s with the numbers located on the left side of the pan. The 258-6 (Javelins) and 1972–1974 Javelin and AMXs with 304 V-8 engines used the light-duty 904 and 998 TorqueFlite transmissions.

## Crankshaft Flange

The 1968–1970 crankshafts have a different rear flange and flywheel setup compared to the 1971-and-up models. The 4-speed manual transmission was BorgWarner T-10. Yes, it is different than the more-popular T-10s that other manufacturers used, but it's not much different. The T-10s usually have a tag attached to one of the bolts in the tailhousing. This tag has the vendor numbers and the AMC part number.

*The flat crankshaft design was used in all 1969-and-older AMC V-8 engines. We have also seen a few engines (mainly the 390 engine) dated 1970 with this crankshaft.*

*This crankshaft flange was used in all 1970-and-newer AMC V-8 engines.*

*McLeod SFI aluminum flywheels are only available for purchase as internally balanced. Ideally, this flywheel should only be used on internally balanced crankshafts.*

*This is an externally balanced SFI flywheel with six pieces of heavy metal installed. The flywheel needs to be installed on the crankshaft during balancing. When a mechanical part is SFI certified, you are not allowed to drill or modify it. For most performance applications, the crankshaft is (or should be) internally balanced.*

*These bushings are pressed into the rear of pre-1970 crankshafts for use with a 727 transmission. The OD of these bushings is the same, which allows you to change transmissions by just changing the adapter.*

To determine if the transmission is a wide- or close-ratio transmission, the last letter of the vendor number indicates this. A sample of an AMX might read "AS1 T10V." The last letters indicate the series.

The early crankshafts had a flat flange with a small pilot bearing. The manual flywheel was designed to locate on the OD of the crankshaft flange. The flexplate has a small-diameter hole to locate off of the pilot bearing. All AMC crankshafts are external balanced from the factory. The flywheel has a counterweight designed in it, while the flexplate has a series of holes drilled on one side.

The aftermarket SFI flywheels have holes drilled on one side. Otherwise, we have also seen heavy metal (tungsten) installed. The popular transmission (and the stronger of the automatic transmissions) is the 727. The crankshaft flanges on 1968 an 1969 models will not accept the 727 torque-convertor snout. The rear of the crankshaft can be machined to accept the newer-style pilot bearing. This process is a lot easier to do during the rebuild.

## Bushing Adapters

If a customer is not sure which transmission to use, we can machine the rear of the flange during the rebuild. Two different bushings adapters can be installed: one for the original pilot bearing and one for the 727. That way, if you decide to go back to the original 904 transmission, it is as simple as changing the adapter.

To machine the rear flange of the crankshaft, we use our driveshaft lathe. It has a 24-inch chuck on it. If all you have is a small engine lathe, it probably will be beneficial to farm out this job to a tool and die shop.

*To machine the rear of the crankshaft for the transmission conversion bushings, gently chuck on the snout and use a steady rest in a very large lathe.*

## Inspection and Magnafluxing

The first step to inspect the crankshaft begins with a hot-tank cleaning. Next, perform a visual inspection of the crankshaft by looking for obvious discoloration or spun bearings.

Now, check the overlooked places that will bite you later if you don't check them now.

*Visually inspect the crankshaft. Look for obvious discoloration or spun bearings. Heat discoloration is shown on this journal. It's a journal to pay attention to in the magnaflux machine.*

### Crankshaft Snout

If the original balancer was removed from the engine, how easily was the balancer removed? If the balancer slid right off, then mic and inspect the snout thoroughly. Are there any grooves in the snout, or is the machined surface damaged? While checking this, look at the threads for the balancer bolt. On many occasions, we've seen a crankshaft come in with the bolt snapped off, and the customer never said anything. If the threads need to be repaired, now is the time.

### Crankshaft Thrust Bearing and Flange

When checking the rear flange, inspect the threaded flywheel bolt holes. The crankshaft thrust bearing is very important to check. If the thrust bearing is damaged, this can be ground oversized as long as an oversized thrust bearing is available. If damage is beyond grinding, it can be welded and repaired.

The thrust bearing often can tell the history of the crankshaft. An AMC engine's thrust bearing is located on the center main journal—not the rear. This is a common mistake, and common phone call that we receive starts with, "My thrust bearing does

*Before installing the crankshaft in a magnafluxing machine, it must be completely clean. The large loop is a magnet that passes over the crankshaft.*

*This is a closer look at the large magnet ring that passes over the crankshaft for magnafluxing.*

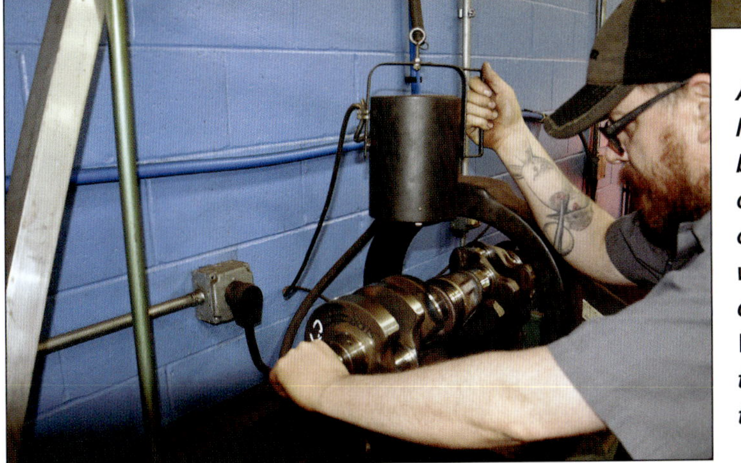

*An ultraviolet light is used after brushing the liquid chemical on the crankshaft. This works well if it is done in the dark. We have a tarp that swings over the area.*

not fit . . ." That's when we know that the builder has previously only assembled a Chevy engine.

If only the rear of the thrust bearing is worn or damaged, the crankshaft had (at one time or another) a load pushing it from the rear. A common problem that causes this is a clutch application that was set up wrong, which puts constant pressure on the rear of the crankshaft. Another cause is when a torque convertor had no clearance between the mounting pads and the flexplate. This will also happen when a torque convertor has a ballooning effect.

A crankshaft does not usually fail on its own. Most likely, there is another reason that it fails. Regrinding the crankshaft does not mean that it will not happen again. Finding the cause of the problem is very important. We have a rule: you cannot put it back together unless you understand why it failed.

### Magnafluxing

Crankshaft magnafluxing is very important, especially if the crank has seen a bearing failure or another form of failure. Most of the time, crankshaft cracks go unseen. There are usually no major warning signs until it breaks in half.

Magnafluxing uses an ultraviolet light to see cracks. A chemical solvent is brushed on the crankshaft before an ultraviolet light is shined on it. Working in a dark location is the best environment to see the cracks.

The old-timer machinists used to say, "Does the crankshaft ring out?" This was only true on steel crankshafts, but it actually works. Take a steel hammer and lightly hit the counterweights. Steel cranks make a particular ringing sound. When a crankshaft is cracked, tapping the counterweight will produce a dead ring that just stops.

I do not recommend skipping the magnafluxing phase of the process, but if a cracked crank is found, give it a try. Back in the early 1970s, we did not have a magnaflux machine, and I remember my boss hitting a crank on each counterweight, hearing it ring out, and saying "It's all good; $30."

### Performance Grinding Options

The AMC crankshaft holds up well to some serious horsepower. All of the AMC crankshafts were forged steel from the factory. Thanks to the larger connecting-rod journal diameter on the 401 (2.246 inch), we can offset grind these crankshafts to gain some stroke.

When offset grinding the

*Here, we're offset grinding the AMC crankshaft down for a 2.100-inch small-block Chevy connecting-rod journal. This configuration will net 421 ci.*

*Before beginning to offset grind the crankshaft, check it for straightness and magnaflux it.*

crankshaft, the journal size comes down to 2.100 inch, which is small-block-Chevy size. With a 2.100-inch journal diameter, just about any rod length configuration can be used. Even when not offset grinding, the rod journal can be ground down to 2.100 inch. We don't recommend it, but we have ground the rod journal down to 2.00 inch for a few high-RPM drag engines. This is the old 327 Chevy rod-journal size, which is often referred to as the "small" journal.

Offset grinding provides more room to add stroke to the crankshaft. The extra stroke makes a great torque monster, but this torque may work against you if you are building a higher-RPM drag engine.

When grinding a crankshaft down more than the 0.030 inch, get the crankshaft nitride treated (reheat) treated. The small-block Chevy connecting rods are thicker than the original AMC rods. The Chevy rod thickness measures approximately 0.015 inch thicker per rod. Always measure the connecting rod because every manufacturer differs slightly. The crankshaft grinder will need to open up the width of the crankshaft journal to accommodate the extra width. This will restore the connecting-rod side clearance.

Another option for the wider Chevy connecting rod is to machine 0.007 inch off each side of the connecting rod. Although this also would work, it changes the balance of the connecting rods and crankshaft. We prefer to open up the width of the connecting rod journal instead of narrowing the rod.

In the past, we cross drilled the main bearings for extra oiling. Today, with the design of full- or half-groove main bearings, we'd rather leave the strength in the crankshaft. The only cranks that we have seen develop cracks have been cross drilled.

## Grinding and Polishing

The first step to get a crankshaft ready to grind is to check the crankshaft for straightness. This is usually done after magnafluxing, but if any straightening is needed, magnaflux the crankshaft after the straining process.

Our machine is pretty basic for crank straightening. The crank sits in a set of V-blocks on the two outer mains. With an indicator, check for runout and mark the crank with a marker. Depending on the use of the engine, we will let 0.002 inch slide through, especially if we are grinding the crank. After grinding the crank, it will be perfectly straight. Anything that is 0.003 inch and over should be straightened.

The straightener has a hydraulic ram with a large radiused arm that drops onto the main journal. With the high side up, put pressure on

*Put the crankshaft in V-blocks and check the runout with a dial indicator. Make sure to pay attention to the burnt or spun bearing locations, but also check the whole crankshaft.*

This crankshaft is indicated in and ready to start grinding.

Crankshaft grinding to today's specifications for good oil control is one of the most technical and advanced duties in the shop.

the crank with the hydraulic ram, leaving the indicator on to see how much the crank is moving. Straining a crank is an art form.

Our crankshaft grinder works well, and with a chisel and sometimes some heat, we can repair a crank that is bent 0.025 inch. Obviously, we only straighten a crankshaft from this far out if another one can't be found. A crank should always be re-magnafluxed after this process.

Sometimes the snout of the crankshaft can be bent, or a crankshaft can be bent really badly but only from the last main to the end of the crank. These types of bends are a lot riskier to repair. It is common that after heating the crank (to either weld a journal or straighten it), we want to slow cool the crank. So, we wrap it in specially designed heat blankets.

Only about 50 percent or fewer machine shops have a crankshaft grinder. Many small shops do not have one. To pay for the machine, a crankshaft grinder needs to be turning cranks. It is hard for a small shop to keep the crankshaft grinder running. Do not be afraid if your machine shop does not grind cranks. It will rely on another shop to grind your crankshaft, and it will be a shop that your machine shop trusts.

### Grinding Specifications

The specifications that are used to grind a crankshaft are published in most engine bearing catalogs. They provide a high and a low limit. To determine the proper bearing clearance, a machine shop has to do some extra work. After the machining is complete on the engine block, install the main bearings and torque the main caps on. We set up the dial bore gauge to the middle of the crankshaft specification.

The bearing clearances that are determined are for the crankshaft to be ground in the middle of the specification. If we determine that this clearance is not enough, we can proceed to grind the crankshaft to the low end of the specification. If the clearance needs to be tightened, grind the crankshaft to the high side of the specification.

Unfortunately, the consistency of the bearings is not as good as it once was. A quick check is to ball mic the bearings to determine how consistent the thickness is. This procedure provides the best results for the correct bearing clearances but will leave small lines in the bearings from the dial bore gauge. We always explain this to customers so that concerns aren't raised during assembly.

After installing the main bearings and torquing the main caps in place, run the dial bore gauge through to determine the sizes for grinding the crankshaft.

### Connecting Rods

Repeat this procedure for the connecting rods. Many rod-bearing options are available for Chevy connecting rods. There are many

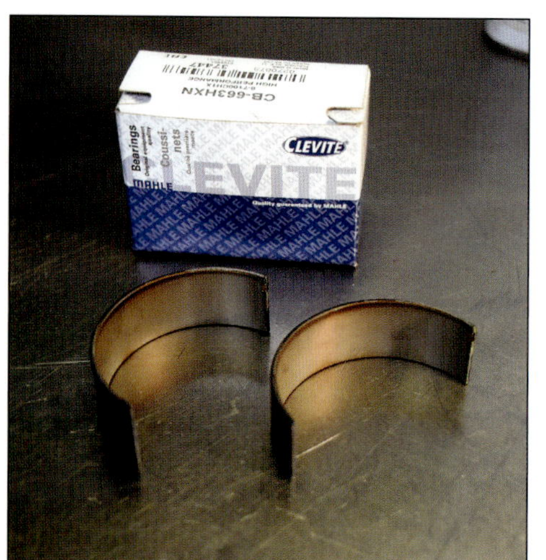


*Mahle Clevite offers connecting rod bearings for a small-block Chevy in many varieties. The benefit of using small-block Chevy rods is that various bearing sizes are available. Mahle Clevite offers bearings with an STD clearance of plus or minus 0.001 inch, coated, and the popular H-Series.*

*Once crankshaft balancing is complete, micro-polish the crankshaft. This is done with a series of three different belts. It is the last step before assembly.*

performance options and various vendors. Bearings are available that add 0.0005 to 0.001 inch of extra clearance or bearings that tighten the bearing clearance.

If the AMC bearings are kept, the choices are limited. The main bearings are limited to the AMC lineup, and these usually hold up well, even in the performance applications. There just are not as many performance or clearance options for AMC main bearings. Another bonus to using the Chevy rod bearings is the price; it's all about supply and demand.

### Polishing

After grinding, the crankshaft needs to be polished. Always balance the crankshaft before the final polishing takes place so that any marks from installing the bobweights can be addressed. As easy as this sounds, there is science behind it. Understanding the peaks and valleys for oil control is important.

A crankshaft is always polished in the correct direction of rotation. The finish of the polish job is also very important. The goal of a properly polished crankshaft is to improve the life of the bearings. This is what is called "micro-polishing" the crankshaft.

Believe it or not, most machine shops will polish these cranks the opposite direction. After polishing, the crankshaft is thoroughly cleaned in a parts tank. Brush and rinse out all oil holes. The crankshaft is now ready for the assembly room.

## External and Internal Balancing

All V-8 AMC engines are externally balanced except for the 327 V-8 engine (this engine is from a different family) and the 290-ci engines in 1966. We have seen one 290-ci engine externally balanced, but we are not sure if it had mismatched parts. The Hines balance catalog states that the early 1966 290-ci engines were internally balanced and that the late 1966 engines were externally balanced. We have not found any other information from reliable sources to confirm this.

### External Balance

External balancing is when a counterweight is machined into the balancer, or if it is an aftermarket balancer, the weight usually bolts on. The original harmonic balancer on AMC engines was externally balanced. The large cutout signifies that this is externally balanced.

The 1970-and-older harmonic balancers were three-bolt; the 1971 and newer were four-bolt. Both of these balancers bolt up to all V-8

*The cutout signifies that this is externally balanced. The crankshaft key locates the harmonic balancer and makes sure that the counterweight is located in the correct location.*

***The 1970-and-older harmonic balancers (left) were three-bolt. The 1971-and-newer balancers (right) were four-bolt. Notice the difference in counterweight removed from the two balancers. Both of these balancers bolt up to all crankshafts but are balanced in extremely different ways.***

crankshafts. Look closely to see the difference in the counterweights.

In the past, harmonic balancers were switched out regularly. Running the wrong harmonic balancer will cause the engine to be out of balance. We had an engine come in with the wrong harmonic balancer installed. Luckily, we made the customer balance his engine (this crankshaft was out 180 grams in the rear and 125 in the front). When talking to the customer, he stated that the car shook at idle so badly that he thought it had a misfire. When rebuilding an engine, always balance it.

Another problem with the harmonic balancers is that they are all rubber lined. These balancers are 45 to 55 years old now, and rubber dries out over time. It is common for the balancer to slip and turn on the old, dry-rotted rubber. Once this happens, the engine is out of balance and the timing marks are no longer accurate. This plays a large problem when trying to time an engine.

### *Water Pump*

The crankshaft key locates the harmonic balancer and makes sure that the counterweight is in the correct location. Related to the three-bolt and four-bolt harmonic balancers, we need to discuss the various water pumps that are available. Not only are the pulleys different but they also each take their own different water pump.

The only water pump that is being reproduced is the newer, longer water pump for the four-bolt pulley setup. The older, shorter water pump was only available as a remanufactured item and recently has been difficult to find.

***This is an aluminum, high-flowing GMB water pump (part number 110-1040P).***

An aluminum, high-flowing water pump is sold by GMB (part number 110-1040P). However, a stock cast-iron water pump for the four-bolt pulley setup can be purchased from NAPA and other parts houses. We have not found an aftermarket manufacturer for the shorter water pump with the three-bolt pulley that was used prior to 1971.

When we need the cast-iron pump for a numbers-matching build, we send out the water pump to be rebuilt. There are a few rebuilders remaining, including NAPA and a few that are listed in *Hemmings* magazine. If you do not need the old cast-iron water pump, the new pump by GMB bolts onto the older engines with no problems.

When using the new pump on an older engine, use the new-style four-bolt balancer as well so that the small-block Chevy pulleys align. Many Chevy pulley options are available.

## Flywheels

An AMC externally balanced flywheel has a counterweight on the rear. This is easy to identify by its size and shape. This counterweight signifies that the flywheel goes to an externally balanced crankshaft. To prevent mistakes, AMC designed its flywheels to be bolted on in only one position. This always locates the counterweight in the correct location.

Flywheels and flexplates are engine specific, due to the balancing. There are only two different rear crankshaft flanges and a few various-sized engines, so it is easy to

*This is an AMC externally balanced flywheel. This counterweight signifies that it is external. Flywheels can only be bolted on an AMC crankshaft in one position. This locates the counterweight in the correct position during installation.*

bolt up a misbalanced flywheel or incorrect flexplate.

The following table, which was provided by Eddie Stakes at Planet Houston AMX, provides flywheel casting numbers:

| AMC Standard Flywheels | | |
|---|---|---|
| Year | Engine | Part Number |
| 1977–1979 | Four | 325-0437 |
| 1967–1971 | Six | 317-2415 |
| 1972–1979 | Six | 321-2623 |
| 1967–1969 | 290 | 317-9069 |
| 1970–1971 | 304 | 319-6927 |
| 1972–1978 | 304 with 3s | 321-2651 |
| 1979 | 304 | 323-3955 |
| 1967–1969 | 343 | 318-1609 |
| 1970–1971 | 360 | 319-6929 |
| 1972–1974 | 360 | 321-2653 |
| 1968–1969 | 390 | *319-1662 |
| 1970 | 390 | 319-6929 |
| 1971 | 401 | 321-0496 |
| 1972–1974 | 401 with 4s | 321-2655 |

*AMC Dealer note: replace with 319-1661 or 319-1661-C.

TECH TIP

## Flywheel 319-7219 Versions

Three distinct versions of the flywheel are available with part number 319-7219. If you have one of these flywheels, place your flywheel flat on the bench with the casting number facing up and at 12 o'clock (like you're reading a clock).

| Version 1: 319-7219-C | |
|---|---|
| Crankshaft flange recess measurement | 4.500 inches |
| Counterweight position | at 7:30 |
| Application | Stock 1970 390 4-speed car |

| Version 2: 319-7219-C | |
|---|---|
| Crankshaft flange recess measurement | 4.500 inches |
| Counterweight position | at 4:30 |
| Application | Stock 1970 360 4-speed car |

**Version 3: 319-7219***

| | |
|---|---|
| Crankshaft flange recess measurement | 4.650 inches (approximately 5/32 inch larger than the above two versions) |
| Counterweight position | at 9:30 |
| Application | Unknown. Believed to be out of a 1972-and-up 360 or 401 (304s do not have a counterweight) |

*Does not have the "-C" after the casting number but does have "E-25" (or other letter/number combo) cast in just above the counterweight.

All cast-in counterweights are 1 square inch with the exception of Version 3, which is ¼-inch shorter (length 1 inch, width 1 inch, depth 3/4 inch).

The 1970–1972 flywheels (360/390/401) with castings 3197219 have *more* than the three counterbalance weights in different areas than mentioned above. There are about five to seven different ones known to exist.

Original 290 and 343 flywheels are basically obsolete. The 390 flywheels are extremely difficult to locate. The 360 and 401 flywheels are more plentiful, and a number of aftermarket companies reproduce them, such as Schieffer and Hayes. ■

### Pistons

The first step to balancing the pistons is to weigh them, noting the lightest piston. Once the lightest piston has been determined, the rest of the pistons need to be matched to the weight of the lightest piston. Most aftermarket pistons are all CNC-made now, and the quality of the aluminum has improved over the years. We rarely have to even touch the balance on good aftermarket pistons because aftermarket piston companies have started checking that themselves.

Once all of the pistons are weighed, add in the piston pin and the pin clips if being used. This will provide a total weight for the piston. Original or even new cast pistons usually need balancing. The connecting rods can be weighed similar to the pistons. The only difference is that the small end (pin end) and the big end (journal end) will be weighed separately. The connecting rods are balanced within a gram or less.

Creating a bobweight requires one connecting rod bearing and one piston ring set. Weigh these items and document them on a balance card. Piston pins are needed, and if the pistons are aftermarket, the pin clips are also needed for the total weight. This is how a bobweight is calculated.

This example is from our AMC 401 drag race build. The bobweights are actual weights that are attached to the crankshaft's rod journals to simulate the weight of the connecting-rod and piston assembly.

These bobweights are assembled with lead shot. Each one is filled with 1,873 grams. Once they all weigh the same, they are installed on the crankshaft.

TECH TIP

**Calculating the Bobweight**

Piston + pin + clips = 635 grams
Piston rings = 53 grams
Reciprocation rod (small end) = 195 grams
Rotation rod (big end) (2 x 450) = 900 grams
Rod bearings (2 x 43) = 86 grams
Oil = 4 grams

Total bobweight = 1,873 grams

## Harmonic Balancer and Flexplate

After all the bobweights are installed, install the harmonic balancer and flywheel or flexplate. We always check the press fit on the harmonic balancer, especially if using a brand-new aftermarket balancer because it is common practice for them to leave it on the small side. You can always remove material to install it, but if it did not have enough press fit, there is no way to add material.

*When weighing the pistons, include the pin and piston-pin clips if they are used.*

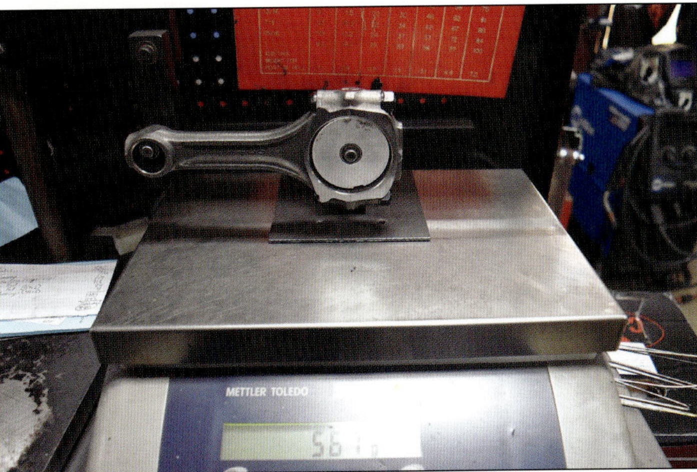


*The first step to checking the weight of the connecting rod is to weigh the big end (journal end) of the connecting rod.*

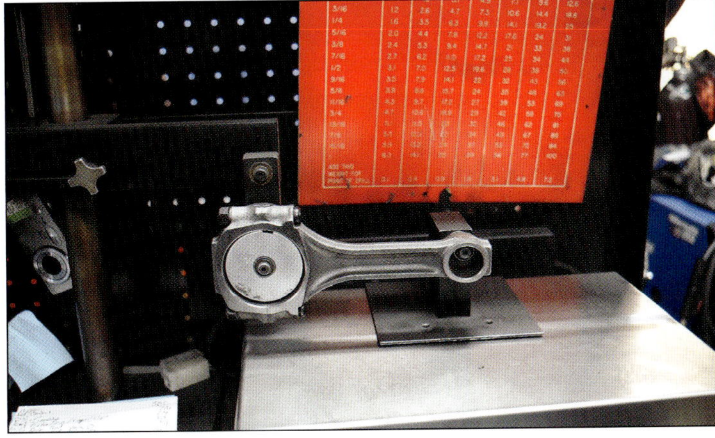

*The second step is to weigh the small end (pin end) of the connecting rod.*

*After bobweights are weighted correctly, install them on the rod journals.*

### *Balancers*

Most balancers have instructions with them that state how much press fit they need. Most machine shops will do this for you, even if you are assembling your own engine. When the engine was balanced, the machine shop would have installed the balancer on the crankshaft. So, when you see an additional charge on your machine shop bill for honing the harmonic balancer, don't get excited; the machine shop really had to do this.

Most crankshaft balancers spin the crankshaft up to about 500 rpm. Many different theories exist about balancing, but we leave that to the experts. Our shop's balancer is a Hines, which balances electronically through harmonics. The balancer shows us the exact location to remove or add weight. If adding a lot of weight, there is a correct way and a not-so-correct way. Heavy metal is installed into the counterweights, and this adds a lot of weight quickly to the crankshaft.

### *Heavy Metal Balancing*

Heavy metal needs to be pressed into the crankshaft vertically so that when the crankshaft is spinning at 8,000 rpm, there is no chance of the metal being thrown out. If you are building a street engine that only needs a few grams added, you can add weld to fill a counterweight hole.

When welding on a true cast-iron crankshaft, use a stick welder with nickel rod. Even though the heavy metal is pressed in, tungsten inert gas (TIG) weld both sides of the metal to make sure that it does not come loose. The reason that we TIG weld is because it will produce a nice, smaller bead that will not stick up and interfere with the connecting rod.

***Hang the crankshaft over the side of the mill table and clamp it in. Both heavy metal holes are drilled and prepared for final reaming.***

***See how close the reamer is to the rear flange on the crankshaft? If we were pressing in 1-inch tungsten, we would have to notch the flywheel flange just to get the reamer past.***

Some people ask, "Is it okay to modify the harmonic balancer, flywheel, or flexplate to balance the crankshaft?" The answer is that yes, you could. However, the proper way is to only add and remove to the crankshaft. Look at it this way, the balancer and flywheel are balanced to this crankshaft and only this crankshaft. If, for any reason, you have to change the flexplate or balancer, the new ones would have to be matched balanced to the old ones.

Here is another common question: When changing the flexplate, do I need to remove the crankshaft for you to rebalance my crankshaft? The answer is that no, you do not. Just bring the new flexplate into the machine shop and have it match balance them. When dealing with an internally balanced engine, these items are neutral balanced and can be changed out without any balancing.

***Run the reamer through with cutting oil to give the heavy metal just a little bit of press fit. Using a drill bit does not provide an accurate-enough hole for pressing in the heavy metal.***

***With the crankshaft upside down in the press, prepare to press the heavy metal into the counterweight. Even though the metal is pressed in, we will tungsten inert gas (TIG) weld the metal in on both sides of the counterweight as well.***

# Connecting Rods, Pistons, and Rings

This chapter focuses on stock and aftermarket connecting rods, pistons, and rings for AMC engines.

## Stock Connecting Rods

Let's break down when to use stock connecting rods. AMC connecting rods are some of the strongest OEM rods in existence. Most AMCs have forged connecting rods. After some performance modifications, these rods support about 500 to 600 hp. We have seen them take more, but we tend to stay on the safe side.

### Rebuilding Connecting Rods

1

*The first step to reconditioning the stock connecting rods is to hot tank them and magnaflux them for cracks. Magnetizing the connecting rod is shown here.*

2

*With the connecting rod magnetized, pass the rod through the magnet. With magnaflux solution and the black light, the cracks show up as small lines. When we magnaflux, we turn the lights off and drape a tarp over the top to help us see the cracks.*

**3**

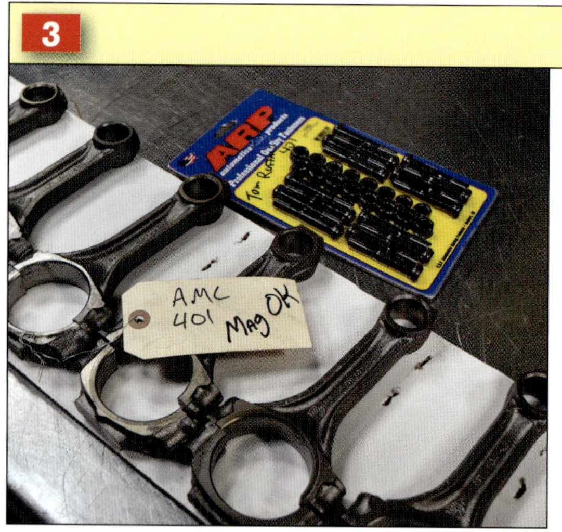


*Now that we have a good core set of connecting rods to rebuild, remove all the old rod bolts and prepare them for shot peening.*

**4**

*Using a small press, remove the old bolts by pressing down on the connecting rod. While standing the connecting rod on a piece of brass, the bolts should come out without a problem.*

**5**

*The connecting rods are wired in a steel shot-peen machine. They are run for about 10 to 15 minutes.*

**6**

*Cutting the connecting rod in the cap grinder, remove as little as possible from the connecting rod until the flats clean up.*

**7**

*Install the new ARP rod bolts in the rods. Make sure to align them correctly for pressing them in.*

**8**

*The bolts are pressed in using a rod bolt press fixture.*

9

*Torque the new ARP connecting rod bolts in a rod vise.*

10

*To hone the connecting rod to size, we use a Sunnen rod hone with an automatic power stroke mandrel.*

11

*Here, we use a Sunnen rod dial bore gauge to check the connecting rod for roundness, taper, and final size.*

12

*Gently kiss the side of the connecting rod on the belt sander to square up the connecting rod. This is more of a cosmetic thing. It puts a nice touch on the rod, deburring it.*

### Checking for Cracks or Defects

First, magnaflux the stock connecting rods to check for any cracks or defects. Next, check the piston pin bore. We find that you can only press pistons on a couple times before running out of piston pin press. This will get you every time if you do not check it. We often see a piston pin walk out and destroy the bore.

When ordering new forged pistons, we always order a set of 0.001 oversize piston pins from Trend. After a few swipes on the Sunnen rod hone, we have restored our proper piston pin press. Lastly, we install a set of ARP connecting-rod bolts and recondition the connecting rods. This sums up the performance options on stock connecting rods.

As we stated, stock AMC rods are very strong and will suit most performance builds. The first step to rebuilding the stock rod is cleaning, magnafluxing, and then shot peening the rod. Before magnafluxing the connecting rod, we magnetize it. The connecting rod is passed through the magnetic field using the same machine that we used to magnaflux crankshafts. Using magnaflux solution and a black light, any cracks will show up as fine lines. Now, we have a good set of connecting rods to begin our rebuilding process.

First, remove the stock rod bolts. Use a small hydraulic press and a piece of brass under the connecting-rod bolts to do this. They press out relatively easy that way. Sometimes using a brass hammer to tap them out is just as easy. Be careful when tapping the bolts because you do not want to put any nicks in the connecting rod. This is why it is important to use a brass hammer.

### Shot Peening

The final prepping step is to shot peen the connecting rods. Shot peening is different than shot blasting,

### Keith Black Pistons

The Keith Black pistons all use a small-block Chevy wrist pin. This requires the installation of a pin bushing that is supplied by Diamond Pistons. Wait, you might ask about installing a pin bushing and running a floater pin. You are correct! We can bore the stock AMC pin bore out and install a big-block Chevy pin bushing.

After installation, the pin bushing needs to be pin bored and then honed to fit properly. In our opinion, if you are in need of a full-floater connecting rod with ARP rod bolts installed economically, it is more reasonable to install an aftermarket small-block Chevy connecting rod. ■

which is a surface-finishing technique that involves rapidly impacting the surface of an object with a controlled stream of abrasive material.

Shot peening is a process to prevent fatigue failures that originate on the surface of the part and induce compressive stresses by bombarding the surface of the parts with uniform small steel balls. The process is similar to repeatedly and evenly hammering a surface with a ball-peen hammer so that the small indentations or dimples form on the surface and the metal immediately below those indentations tries to resist further compression, creating what's known as residual compressive stress. The fatigue cracks generally do not initiate in a compressively stressed area, so the connecting-rod life is extended.

With the rod bolts removed from the rods, we can now cut the connecting-rod flats. Remove as little as possible from the connecting rod; only remove until the flats clean up.

The next step is to cut the rod bearing cap in the cap grinder. The objective is the same: remove as little as possible. Keep in mind that cap cutting (removing material) from the connecting rod is actually shortening the connecting rod.

Install the new ARP connecting-rod bolts in the connecting rods. Make sure to align the bolt, as this will make pressing in the bolt a lot easier. Using a rod bolt installation fixture, press the new ARP rod bolts into the connecting rod.

Now that the new bolts are assembled, reassemble the connecting rods. Make sure that the caps are assembled correctly with the numbers matching each cylinder. Once the connecting rods are reassembled with the caps torqued on, they are ready to be honed to size.

Use the Sunnen rod hone to carefully hone to size. While honing the connecting rod, check the rod size precisely with the Sunnen gauge. Gently kiss the connecting rod on the belt sander. This is more cosmetic than anything; it squares up the side of the rod, removing any burrs.

## Aftermarket Connecting Rods

Not as many options are available for aftermarket stock AMC performance connecting rods for as there are for a manufacturer such as Chevrolet. Some aftermarket connecting rods are available that keep all the stock AMC sizes, but be very careful of the cheap offshore rods. In our opinion, you have invested too much time and money to stick a set of offshore connecting rods in your engine.

### *K1 Technologies*

K1 Technologies offers three different connecting-rod part numbers for AMC V-8 applications. The K1 Technologies rods are forged H-beam steel that is made from the billet 4340 steel H-beam design. They all come with high-quality ARP 2000 fasteners with a shot-peened finish for longer life. All K1 Technologies rods come with premium bronze wrist-pin bushings (instead of being press fit).

The rods are finished in the United States and held to very tight tolerances. Bores finished to plus/minus 0.0001 inch and weight to plus/minus 1 gram per end. We have used these connecting rods and have determined that they are a really good option. Unless you find these connecting rods on the shelf at a vendor, they usually take about a month to receive.

### *Molnar Technologies*

Molnar Technologies offers AMC 360, 390, and 401 connecting rods. Its AMC H-beam rods are machined from billet 4340 steel and then heat treated to provide improved strength. To make the rods even stronger, they are shot peened to increase fatigue life. All Molnar connecting rods are fitted with highly durable premium bronze bushings for use with floating pin–type pistons.

Each rod set for the AMC engines includes ARP fasteners, lubricant, and installation guidelines. Molnar's rod selection consists of 360-, 390-, and 401-ci engines with a stock-stroke crankshaft. Molnar also offers a stroker rod with a 6.000-inch length available in both a 2.00- and a 2.100-inch crankshaft rod-journal diameter.

All Molnar rods are finished in the United States at the Molnar Technologies shop in Michigan. Critical rod dimensions are held to very precise tolerances of plus/minus 0.0001 inch, which is the tightest tolerance that is found in the performance and racing aftermarket.

*Small-Block Chevy Rods*

Next is the option of running a small-block Chevy connecting rod, which has many different bore and stroke combinations available. To run this type of connecting rod, there are many machining steps that are needed. Details are described in the Chapter 4.

The small-block Chevy wrist-pin diameter is more than adequate for high-horsepower applications. This makes ordering custom pistons a lot easier. When it comes to making some serious horsepower, every strength category of rod is available, including aluminum.

The first option is a stock connecting rod with ARP rod bolts for any 500-hp-and-under street/strip application. Everything higher than 500 hp uses an H-beam connecting rod that is produced by any of the aftermarket rod companies, such as K1 or Molnar. For extreme race applications and boosted engines, a good brand-name billet small-block Chevy connecting rod is the best choice.

## Pistons

For a stock restoration, some manufacturers still make cast pistons. We really don't use a stock cast piston for any type of rebuild any more. The reliability of an aftermarket piston is worth the extra expense.

*Forged*

With the fuel octane numbers on the pump not always accurate, the insurance of having a forged piston is a good thing. A little too much timing paired with low-octane fuel could lead to detonation that can destroy a stock cast piston.

*This is what a piston looks like with severe detonation. It takes a lot of heat to destroy a piston.*

*This aftermarket piston was custom made by Diamond Pistons with a small-block Chevy wrist pin.*

Federal-Mogul (the old TRW) still produces a forged piston for the AMC 401 engine. Pistons are available in 0.020 and 0.030 inch oversize. Overall, this piston is not a bad option; it is strong but a bit heavy. It uses the original ring package of 5/64, 5/64, 3/16 inch. Sometimes it can be hard to find this piston in stock. Federal-Mogul only runs it a few times a year, and when it sells out, you have to wait for the next run. It wouldn't surprise us if this piston was discontinued in the future.

*Keith Black*

Keith Black came out with a few pistons for the AMC 390 and 401 engines quite a few years ago. These pistons were designed to be an off-the-shelf replacement so that you would not have to wait for manufacturing. The 401 pistons KB354 and KB392 were drop-in pistons that used a normal ring package with only one dilemma: they used a Chevy pin diameter.

The KB392 piston is a flat-top design for more compression and uses a 1/16-inch ring package. The compression ratio for this piston with a 51-cc head is 11.8:1 and with a 58-cc head is 10.9:1. The 1968–1969 390 engines use one of the two 401 pistons. For this combination to work, the 401 connecting rod or a 5.85 Chevy rod must be used. This combination allows the deck height to be where it needs to be.

The 1970 390 has the same deck height as the 401, but the difference is the stroke of the engine. Piston number KB394 uses the 5/64-inch stock ring package with a Chevy pin. Because of the unique thermal conductivity and ring location, it requires a modified piston-ring end gap. Following these directions is essential. Otherwise, you will butt the piston rings and break a piston. Follow Keith Black's instructions when installing this company's pistons.

### *Custom Pistons*

Any aftermarket piston company will make a custom piston for a higher price. After many years of purchasing AMC pistons, we settled in on a few manufacturers. For higher-horsepower boosted and nitrous-oxide applications, we use Diamond Pistons.

Diamond has many options, including a 1/16, 1/16, 3/16 inch ring package for less ring drag. For our boosted and NOS applications, Diamond offers a great selection of wrist pins and coatings.

For stock rebuilds, street cruisers, and street/strip applications, RaceTec offers a great piston at a reasonable price.

Another good AMC piston is available from Wiseco, which actually has pistons with part numbers that they are trying to keep on the shelf. Wiseco offers forged AMC 360 pistons and AMC 401 pistons. These are premium-quality forged AMC piston kits. Incorporating suggestions from many of today's leading AMC performance engine builders, Wiseco is manufacturing flat-top and reverse-dome oversize 360 pistons and 401 pistons. These pistons include thicker decks and performance-optimized piston ring lands.

The Pro Tru AMC pistons come with anti-friction skirt coatings, plasma-moly piston rings, heavy-duty wrist pins, and pin-retention clips. The pistons have symmetrical valve pockets that can accommodate oversized valves and high-lift camshafts. This Wiseco kit comes complete with piston rings. The only thing you have to watch is that the Wiseco pistons come with a 1.000-inch wrist pin.

As previously stated, if using press-fit connecting rods, the stock pins were 1.0007 to 1.0008 inches. After AMC rods are pressed on and off, the rod starts to lose some of its press fit. If the new pins are already 0.0007 inch smaller, this is a problem. We have seen many pins walk out into the cylinder wall. This is why we purchase oversize pins from Trend that are 1.001 inches. It's hard to explain to a customer why we have to purchase two sets of pins, but it's better than having a pin come out. Wiseco is not the only one doing this; 1.000 inch is a common piston pin size, so it is easier to just use them.

### *Piston Rings*

There are many different piston companies that can make a great piston; these are just a few that we have settled into using. For pistons rings, everything from Hastings to Federal-Mogul are great piston rings. Total Seal is our choice of ring for all high-performance builds. The stock ring combination is 5/64, 5/64, 3/16, and for performance builds, we like to use a thinner-option 1/16, 1/16, 3/16. Of course, there are much thinner options out there. Piston rings are had to find for some bore sizes. Before ordering a custom piston, make sure that there is a ring made for that combination.

## Installing Pistons on Connecting Rods

Now that the connecting rod is complete, the piston is ready to be installed on the connecting rod. Check and repair the piston pin press or bushing clearance. A Sunnen rod oven makes this job easy. As the pin bore heats up, it creates just enough clearance for the pin to slide through.

There are a few different ways to assemble pistons on connecting rods, and most involve some way of heating the small end of the connecting rod. I have seen good garage mechanics heat the rod with a torch

***Set up the piston pin stop to keep the wrist pin centered.***

***A Sunnen rod oven makes installing a press-fit piston easy.***

***The connecting rod is pressed onto the piston. Notice that the other connecting rods are being heated as we install the first rod on the piston.***

and push the pin in successfully. However, I don't recommend this. If too much heat is used, you can ruin the press fit on the pin.

We like to keep the connecting rods numbered, so when installing them, there are four left pistons and four right pistons. If using stock replacement pistons or Federal-Mogul pistons, the front is stamped with either an arrow or an F. Aftermarket pistons with valve reliefs have to be installed with the intake and exhaust pockets aligned.

When using a floater piston pin, there are a few options. Some piston manufacturers use a single or double circlip to keep the pin in place. The newest option is a single circlip in a form of a snap ring. Always use some assembly lube when installing the pin through the piston and connecting rod.

When installing the piston clips, make sure that they are all seated in the groove. Bad things can happen if the clip comes out. The last and final check is the straightness of the connecting rod. The piston has to be on the connecting rod for this. If there is any misalignment, we can straighten the rods only for small alignment issues.

### *Piston Ring Installation and Fitting*

Even for stock rebuilds, the piston-ring end gap should be checked. Often, even for a stocker, we will have to open up ring end gaps a few thousands of an inch. For performance builds, rings will normally come 0.005 inch oversize for custom grinding to your application. Stock ring packages can follow the factory specifications for ring end gap.

All performance ring companies supply a specification sheet with their recommendations for ring end gap per application. Cylinder heat affects ring end gap. That is why all boosted and nitrous-oxide applications require additional clearance.

*Follow the piston-ring manufacturer's recommendations on how to check the piston-ring end gap. When installing the ring in the bore, it is essential that the ring is square. Often, a machine shop will use a fixture for this purpose.*

**TECH TIP**

**Ring End Gap Tip**

When a manufacturer provides a range for ring end gap, remember that too tight is disastrous, but an engine will rarely notice if it is a few thousandths of an inch too loose. ■

For example, take a racing application, such as a dirt Modified. By the end of a feature race, the engine may be pushing 240 degrees or more. This is where the piston ring gap needs to be on the high side. In a perfect world, max-performance race engine rings are at a 0 gap when fully at temperature.

When it comes to some series engine building, some builders tighten up the piston ring gap until the rings just start to show signs of the piston ring butting. Some newer-technology pistons rings are Total Seal's zero-gap rings.

Keith Black was one of the first piston companies to offer a hypereutectic piston for AMC engines. This piston was pretty popular when it first came out. It is one of the only companies to offer an off-the-shelf piston for 1968–1969 AMC engines.

There are some pretty important specifications that must be followed. We have seen AMC engines come in with piston tops that were damaged from not following these guidelines.

## Suggested Piston-to-Wall Clearance

Keith Black pistons can be installed tighter than other performance pistons. A close-fitting piston rocks less, supports the rings better, and seals the engine for maximum power. When a loose-fitting engine is desired, the rigid skirt design of the Keith Black piston allows the builder a choice without fear of piston damage. See the Auto Applications Clearance table for minimum and realistic maximum loose fit clearance for Keith Black pistons.

The Keith Black piston material does not grow as much as a forged piston. This makes the piston-to-wall clearance on a hypereutectic Keith Black piston a lot tighter. The theory behind a tighter piston, especially for a street application, is less piston rock. The less the piston is able to rock, the better the piston ring seal is. This type of piston also has less piston slap noise, especially when the engine is cold.

To correctly measure the Keith Black piston, measure about 3/8-inch down on the piston skirt. This should put you even with the balance pad. The clearances that Keith Black recommends is pretty tight, and some machine shops may want to put a little more clearance in the bore.

| Auto Application Clearances | | | | | | |
|---|---|---|---|---|---|---|
| | Hypereutectic | | | Forged | | |
| Application | Ring End Gap Factor | Suggested Piston-to-Wall Clearance | | Ring End Gap Factor | Suggested Piston-to-Wall Clearance | |
| | | Bore to 4.100 inches | Bore 4.100 inches and up | | Bore to 4.100 inches | Bore 4.100 inches and up |
| Street—Naturally aspirated | 0.0065 inch | 0.0015 to 0.0020 inch | 0.0020 to 0.0025 inch | 0.0040 | 0.0035 to 0.0045 inch | 0.0045 to 0.0055 inch |
| Street—Towing | 0.0080 inch | 0.0015 to 0.0020 inch | 0.0020 to 0.0025 inch | 0.0045 inch | 0.0040 to 0.0050 inch | 0.0050 to 0.0060 inch |
| Street—Nitrous or supercharged | 0.0080 inch | 0.0020 to 0.0025 inch | 0.0025 to 0.0035 inch | 0.0050 inch | 0.0045 to 0.0055 inch | 0.0055 to 0.0065 inch |
| Drag—Gasoline | 0.0075 inch | 0.0015 to 0.0045 inch | 0.0020 to 0.0045 inch | 0.0040 inch | 0.0050 to 0.0070 inch | 0.0060 to 0.0080 inch |
| Drag—Alcohol | 0.0065 inch | 0.0015 to 0.0045 inch | 0.0020 to 0.0045 inch | 0.0040 inch | 0.0040 to 0.0070 inch | 0.0050 to 0.0080 inch |
| Drag—Supercharged or nitrous gas | 0.0095 inch | 0.0020 to 0.0045 inch | 0.0025 to 0.0050 inch | 0.0050 inch | 0.0060 to 0.0090 inch | 0.0070 to 0.0100 inch |
| Drag—Super-charged alcohol | 0.0085 inch | 0.0015 to 0.0045 inch | 0.0025 to 0.0045 inch | 0.0050 inch | 0.0050 to 0.0070 inch | 0.0060 to 0.0080 inch |
| Drag—Super-charged fuel | 0.0115 inch | 0.0030 to 0.0050 inch | 0.0035 to 0.0055 inch | 0.0060 inch | 0.0070 to 0.0100 inch | 0.0080 to 0.0110 inch |

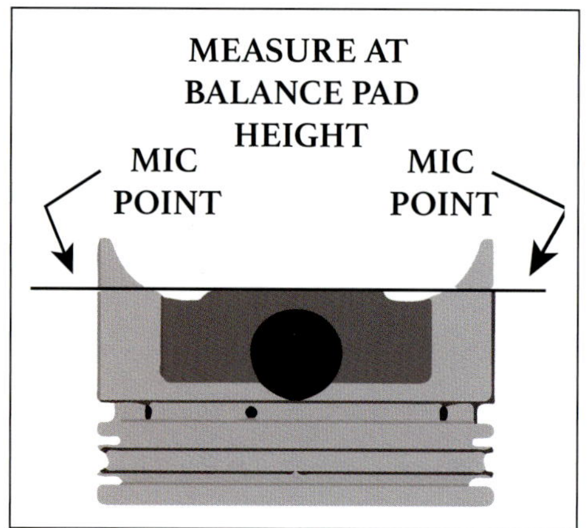


***Keith Black pistons are made of a hypereutectic material. This material does not increase in size like a forged piston would. Due to this, the piston-to-wall specifications are kept a lot tighter on hypereutectic Keith Black pistons. The idea behind this material is to keep the piston tight in the bore at all times to prevent piston rock. The more that a piston can rock or tip in the cylinder bore, the greater the risk is for losing the piston ring seal.***

Remember that this piston does not expand with heat like other pistons would, so we recommend staying within the suggested clearance.

## Piston-Ring End Gap

When checking the piston-ring end gap, install the ring about 1/2 inch in the bore. It is very important to make sure that the ring is square in the bore. Most machine shops use a special tool for this. Check the clearance with a feeler gauge to make sure that it meets the specification. Using a Goodson ring filer machine, the rings are file fit to the proper clearance.

It is probably a little bit overkill, but we always file fit rings to each cylinder. The only time that this will make a difference is when the cylinders are different sizes. Good machining practices keeps you out of trouble.

After deburring piston rings, install them on the pistons. Always keep the top rings separate from the second ring because mixing these two rings up would be an issue. They are designed for different purposes. Dots or markings on the piston rings are always assembled facing up.

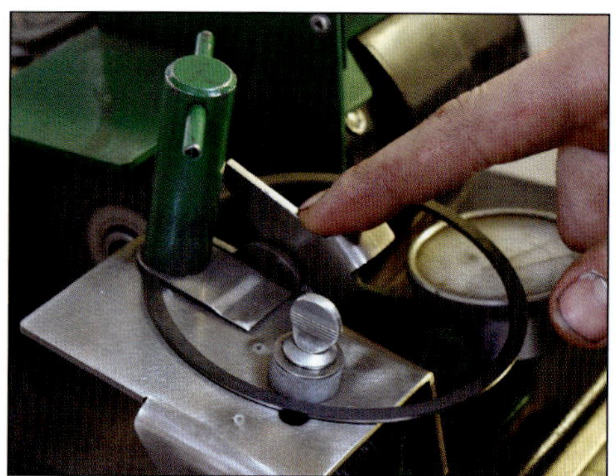

***File fit the piston rings with a Goodson ring machine. After correct gap is achieved, deburr the ring using a small jeweler file.***

***After rings are deburred, install them on the pistons, making sure to follow the markings on the rings. The dots always face up. Always keep the top rings separate from the second ring so that they do not get mixed up.***

CHAPTER 6

# Camshafts, Lifters, and Timing

We discuss camshafts, lifters, and timing for AMC engines in this chapter.

## Camshaft Types

We will keep this section about camshafts simple but go over all of the different options. All of the V-8 AMC engines were offered with a hydraulic flat-tappet camshaft from the factory. This type of camshaft was the norm for all American car manufacturers at the time. However, General Motors offered a few applications with a solid flat-tappet camshaft.

For production, AMC never produced a solid-tappet camshaft. Factory camshafts were offered with a few performance options; one was called the Machine camshaft. This was an option that many owners changed after purchasing a AMC vehicle. Another option was the camshaft that was available from the dealer in the Group 19 book.

### *Hydraulic Flat Tappet*

Most factory camshafts were vacuum friendly with mild duration numbers. For the novice engine builder, a hydraulic flat-tappet camshaft uses a lifter that needs the correct preload. On this style of camshaft, the lifter is designed to rotate as the camshaft turns. It has two different rocker-arm configurations: one that is adjustable and a nonadjustable valvetrain. We will go into more detail about rocker options in Chapter 8.

A hydraulic flat-tappet camshaft requires a special break-in procedure and engine oil requirement. It is the most affordable camshaft option to run, but it also has a very high failure rate. This failure rate is mainly due to the lack of zinc in today's oil.

Another factor is the increase of valve-spring pressure over the years. Our build ratio of hydraulic flat-tappet cams compared to hydraulic-roller cams is about 1 out of 75 engines. If we build a flat-tappet engine, we do not allow it to go out the door without running it and breaking in the camshaft.

### *Solid Flat Tappet*

The old-school drag race and performance option was installing a solid flat-tappet camshaft. The difference between a solid over a hydraulic is the solid lifter does not have any

*This is a solid flat-tappet camshaft. A hydraulic flat-tappet and a solid flat-tappet are nearly impossible to differentiate with the naked eye. These cores are usually made out of cast instead of billet. To differentiate between a solid flat-tappet and a hydraulic flat-tappet, look at the valve lifter. The hydraulic one has a spring in it under the C-clip so that the plunger has travel.*

preload. Rocker arms are set with a valve lash instead of the preload. With this style of camshaft, a more-aggressive camshaft with higher valve lift can be used. Due to the lifter being solid, the higher valve-spring pressure will not overtake the lifter.

We have not built an engine with a solid flat-tappet camshaft in more than 20 years. There are so many benefits to running a hydraulic roller and a solid roller that the solid flat-tappet camshaft is pretty much outdated.

### Hydraulic Roller

Hydraulic-roller camshafts are the future. Nearly every engine manufactured after 1995 has a hydraulic roller. The only disadvantage to using one is the cost. After purchasing a camshaft, lifters, rocker arms, and pushrods, the cost for this conversion may be as high as $1,600.

We feel that this cost is well worth the investment. If there is camshaft failure, it usually takes the whole engine out. Running a hydraulic-roller camshaft is like buying an insurance policy on your engine. However, this is often a hard sell for the customer. Look at it this way: it is only a little bit of extra money to spend when compared to the cost of rebuilding the engine twice.

There are many performance benefits to using a hydraulic-roller camshaft. Hydraulic-roller lifters have come a long way since their original design. This advancement allows us to run cams with a lift as high as 0.650 inch. A hydraulic flat-tappet camshaft could never run with this lift. With a roller cam, the lobe lifts can be much more aggressive as well.

Bullet Racing Cams grinds all of our AMC cams and has many different profile camshaft cores that are available for grinding. There are many quality hydraulic-roller lifters available. This is not an item to cheap out on.

We use Johnson hydraulic-roller lifters when running this style of camshaft. Some cheap lifters have the oil hole in the wrong location. Some lifter designs that are run with large lift camshafts will actually travel past the oil band on the lifter and bleed out oil pressure at high RPM. It is common to spend $600-plus on a set of lifters.

Other items that are needed a roller camshaft include shorter pushrods and at least a roller-tip rocker. However, we usually choose a full roller-rocker arm.

### Solid Roller

The final camshaft option is a solid roller. This camshaft is mostly used for racing applications. However, some of our customers have built a solid-roller camshaft engine and still drive it on the street.

Solid-roller camshafts are designed to very aggressive with high lift, long duration, and high RPM. These cams are normally designed to be used with high-compression and high-flowing cylinder head combinations. We have seen camshaft lifts as high as 0.800 inch with extremely high-flowing cylinder heads, such as the ones made by Indy Cylinder Head.

*This is a billet AMC camshaft core. Telling the difference is rather easy because of the shiny camshaft lobes and the bronze color between the lobes. This style of camshaft core is sometimes used to grind a hydraulic roller and is always used when grinding a solid-roller camshaft.*

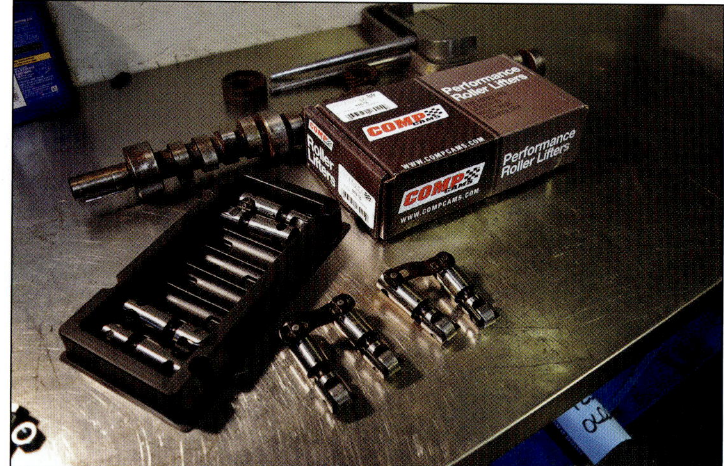


*When running a solid-lift camshaft with a small-block Chevy lifter, the lifters need to be ordered with a custom link bar for the different lifter bore spread on an AMC engine. These lifters are not be available off the shelf to buy and take a few weeks to arrive in the mail, so plan accordingly.*

The downside to running a solid camshaft is evident when driving it on the street or at low RPM. A solid-roller camshaft is designed to run with high spring pressure on the seat. It is common to see a closed spring pressure of 250 to 350 pounds. This puts a substantial amount of pressure at full lift on the needles in the lifter.

When this style of camshaft is run for long durations at a low RPM, it shortens the life of the lifter considerably. The camshaft lobes are only oiled by splash from the crankshaft. At low RPM, very little oil is splashed on the camshaft and lifters. In addition, low idle speeds slow down the camshaft and allow the high valve-spring pressure to impact the lifters. Think of it this way: you do not want to store a solid-roller engine for an extended period of time with some of the rockers at full lift. This will ruin a good set of valve springs really quick. This is why most engine builders recommend removing (or at least loosening) the rocker arms during storage.

There are many questions and options that must be considered when selecting a camshaft. Rely on your engine builder for this. Depending on your complete combination and the vehicle's intended use, the camshaft design can vary considerably.

## Lifter Bore and Block Inspection

Lifter bore inspection may be the most overlooked item when rebuilding an engine. Unless you are the original owner of the vehicle, you do not know the engine's history. We often have customers bring in a car with what they believe is the original engine, but, after disassembly, we find that the crankshaft has been turned 0.010 inch and the bores are 0.020 inch over already.

During disassembly, pay attention to the lifter bores. As you remove the lifters, look for any loose bores, especially if the lifter was damaged. If the engine has had any lifter failures, mark these bores and notify the machine shop when you bring it in. If any bores are in question, the machine shop can dial bore gauge them.

### *Block Damage*

After removing all of the lifters, inspect the top and bottom of the block for damage. If your engine had a lifter failure earlier in life, it will leave signs of damage. While it is not common, we have actually seen three engine blocks that had 0.010-inch oversize lifters in one bore. These bores all had "O" stamped next to the lifter bore. On the assembly line, when a lifter bore had a machining problem, this is how they would save the block instead of scraping it.

Saving the block is a good thing until the engine gets to the rebuilding stage. You can't buy a 0.010-inch oversize lifter just anywhere. This is why you never throw out any old parts until your engine has been completed. We went back through the old lifters and found one lifter body that was 0.010-inch oversize. This lifter was sent out to a lifter rebuilder and be rebuilt. Another way to repair lifter bores is to install a bushing.

### *Lifter Inspection*

Camshaft inspection usually is just looking at the camshaft and noting any major problems. This is an item that is almost always replaced during a rebuild. If the camshaft is a hydraulic flat tappet, we always replace it.

If you are freshening a previously rebuilt engine and plan to reuse the camshaft and lifters, make sure that all of the lifters are numbered for their location. If, for some reason, the lifters get mixed up, don't even try to figure out where they go—just replace them. You do not have to keep track of where hydraulic-roller lifters go.

If your heart is set on reusing the flat-tappet camshaft, inspect the lifter lobes for any irregular wear marks or pitting. It is common that these engines are stored more than they are running. Often, the lobes will have a light coat of rust on them. Sometimes a light polish or Scotch-Brite pad can be used to remove the surface rust. If the rust left any sort of pitting, a new camshaft should be used.

Only once have we seen a block come in that had 0.020-inch oversize OD camshaft bearings in it. Unfortunately, we did not find this until all of the machining was complete. We had to have a custom-made set of camshaft bearings made to save that block.

## Camshaft Selection

In the past, drag-racing applications mainly used a solid flat-tappet camshaft. However, today, most street and street/strip engines use a hydraulic-roller camshaft. A solid-roller is mainly used for drag and road racing applications.

When selecting a camshaft, bigger is not always better. Ask your machine shop for its expert recommendation.

### *Brake Vacuum*

If the plan is to use power brakes, you will need enough engine vacuum

## Camshaft Selection

These are some questions to ask when selecting a camshaft:

- How will the car be used (street cruiser, drag race, street/strip, Power Tour)?
- Do you plan on having power brakes?
- Do you have an automatic or manual transmission?
- What is the rear-end gear ratio?
- What is your desired horsepower?

to operate them. We find that duration at 50 is around 0.230 and is where you start to lose vacuum for the brakes. There are other options, such as a vacuum canister and a vacuum pump that can add engine vacuum.

### *Too Large of a Camshaft*

The biggest mistake regarding camshaft selection is selecting a camshaft that is too large. If running a stock cylinder head, there is an RPM limit. There is no reason to pick a camshaft that is designed for an RPM that is way higher than the intake and cylinder heads can flow.

Picking a proper camshaft is a science in itself. Over the years, we have used so many different camshafts that we know what works and what does not. There are many good camshaft companies out there that will custom grind a camshaft. It is always good to run your combination by an expert who designs camshafts for a living. We use Bullet Racing Cams because we have established a good relationship with them over the years. A camshaft recommendation form is available on bulletcams.com. Although the information on the form is extensive, the more information is provided, the better the recommendation will be.

### *Preparation*

Most camshaft companies have a specification form on their website. Print this form, fill it out, and review it. It will help you prepare for the questions that they will ask when you call. I often receive phone calls to help customers pick out a camshaft for an AMC engine. We have used many camshafts for AMC engines, so we have a good idea of what works, but I still ask a lot of questions about what the customer is looking for and the application for the vehicle.

The following is an example of how a camshaft will only perform well if the information provided to the engine builder is accurate: We built a really nice AMC drag engine for a customer who said that he wanted to run a 200 shot of nitrous oxide at the drag strip. We selected a camshaft that was suited for the 200-hp shot and ordered a convertor that was built, knowing this was a NOS engine. After completing the engine, the customer called back and said that the engine seemed very lazy off the starting line. After talking to the customer, we realized that he was not spraying the engine at all. The customer decided not to install the nitrous and run the car without it.

### *Comp Cams*

Comp Cams offers several camshafts for the AMC V-8 engine from mild street performance to aggressive racing profiles. These camshafts are available in the old hydraulic flat tappet and the more-popular hydraulic roller.

One of the most popular customer requests is for the car to make "that old muscle car sound when I am at a stop sign." The Comp Cams Thumpr camshafts were designed for this and actually perform well. Just remember that these camshafts were designed for the purpose of creating that loping muscle car sound, and none of them use very high valve lifts to get that.

Comp Cams offers three different versions of this camshaft for AMC V-8s. These camshafts have a unique way of providing that special exhaust tone. The first one has a 279-degree intake duration and 296-degree exhaust duration with only 0.491-inch lift. This camshaft is a good starting point for an engine that will not need as many valvetrain modifications due to only having 0.491-inch valve lift. You will not need high valve-spring pressure for this camshaft.

The Comp Cams Mutha Thumpr camshaft performs from 2,200 to 6,100 rpm while keeping the valvetrain on the less-expensive side. The Mutha Thumpr duration is increased to the 287/304 range. This camshaft has valve lift that is under control at 0.500 and 0.486 inch. The compression ratio needed for a camshaft like this is still on the lower side at 9.1. Most camshafts of this size will ask for a little larger stall (about 2,500 rpm) and will perform a little better with more rear-end gearing. The idea of more rear-end gearing is that you will accelerate to the stall RPM quicker with more gearing.

If you are looking for that more aggressive package for some street and a little drag strip action, the Comp Cams Big Mutha Thumpr camshaft has an RPM range of 2,500 to 6,400. It still has reasonable valve lift of 0.512 and 0.497 inch. The duration is where this camshaft brings on the radical idle and extreme loping sound. With duration numbers as high as 295 and 314, this camshaft is aggressive and has no engine vacuum. The convertor needed for this application is 2,800 to 3,000 rpm.

These camshafts will fit all V-8 AMC engine blocks, including all of the various sizes. All of these camshafts are designed to be hydraulic-lifter versions.

Comp Cams also has many other AMC camshafts available, including offerings in the Magnum series. This series has camshaft and lifter kits available in 270, 280, 292, and 305 degrees of intake duration. The High Energy series camshafts are offered in 252, 260, and 268 durations, and the Extreme hydraulic camshafts are available in 262 and 274 durations.

Additionally, solid-lifter camshafts are offered in the Hi-Tech series in 290, 300, and 304 durations. The Hi-Tech series also has hydraulic camshafts for 312 and 320 durations, and there is a 316 intake-duration profile for roller-lifter applications.

AMC roller lifters are also available to use with this camshaft. If using small-block Chevy lifters, you need to order them with a special link bar to fit the AMC lifter bore spread because it is different than the Chevy block.

#### *Lunati*

Lunati is another quality source for AMC camshafts and valvetrain components. One of the most popular grinds that we use is from the Voodoo series. This camshaft has 256/262 degrees of duration and 0.484/0.507 valve lift.

We usually combine this camshaft with good air-gap intake and headers. When these items are used together, they make a nice street-performance engine that is very streetable without problems. These camshafts only get larger from here with duration numbers starting at 250/256 and going all the way up to 276/284 degrees of duration.

If the engine is designed for some mild drag strip running, Lunati offers a larger camshaft with 285 intake duration and 300 exhaust duration. These camshafts keep the valve lift on the lower side under 0.550-inch lift. These camshafts offer good performance but also keep the valvetrain costs in check. It's no big secret that we are using valve lifts as high as 0.650 inch in hydraulic-roller applications. This kind of build is not for everyone, so keep it in check when picking your camshaft.

### Camshaft Thrust Plate Installation

The machining of the camshaft thrust plate detailed in Chapter 3. The camshaft thrust plate is only installed on blocks with a hydraulic-roller or solid-roller camshaft. The way that the lobes are designed on a flat-tappet camshaft, the camshaft will walk backward, so there is no need for a thrust plate.

On a roller camshaft, the camshaft will try to walk out of the block during rotation. You could design or modify a camshaft button that presses off the from cover. This also works to keep the roller camshaft from walking out. We have also seen someone install a longer camshaft bolt with washers and just let it rub off the front cover.

The thrust plate option is the best. It gives you the reassurance that the camshaft is not going to walk forward, and it is much more professional. The camshaft thrust plate that we use is from a 2.5L Chevy engine. Center the plate over the camshaft when locating the mounting holes. The screws are a grade-8 button-head. Always use red Loctite on these screws.

### Timing Chain Options

For stock applications, timing chain options are one from Cloyes or any other brand that uses S.A. Gear products. The stock timing sets were all single rollers.

*The camshaft thrust plate is installed using two button-head screws. It is important to use Loctite on these when installing them. Button-head screws are used so that there is no interference with the timing chain.*

### *Comp Cams*

Comp Cams offers three different timing sets for 290 to 401 AMCs. Hi-Energy single-wide chain kits use cast-iron gears and are ideal for stock or mildly upgraded performance engines. Magnum timing sets are designed for street and mild performance use and feature a cast-iron camshaft gear, a double-row timing chain, and a billet-steel crankshaft gear that has three keyways. The keyways allow for 4-degree advanced or retarded timing adjustability.

A Hi-Tech Roller Race timing set is offered using the same gears as the Magnum set. However, the chain is a pre-stretched, heat-treated, double-roller design with heavy-duty oversized pins. Hi-Tech timing sets can be used in both street and performance engines. Even for stock rebuilds, the Rollmaster double roller timing chains are a good choice.

### *Rollmaster*

As far as we know, the Rollmaster timing chain is the only one that offers nine different keyways for timing adjustability. We like using these kits because it eliminates the use of the old-fashioned camshaft bushings. Back in the day, drilling out the camshaft gear and installing a bushing was very popular. With the Rollmaster, that is pretty much eliminated with the nine different settings.

*Rollmaster offers a few different part numbers for the AMC double-roller timing chain. There is a billet steel version and a billet steel version that is nitrided for better wear over time. Both timing sets are available in various undersizes for align-honed engine blocks. The standard nitride chain that is shown is part number CS7111.*

*After removing the Torrington bearing from the camshaft gear, measure the thickness of the camshaft thrust plate. This is the amount that needs to be removed from the gear. For the ID clearance of the plate, machine the camshaft gear to give yourself about 0.005 to 0.010 inch clearance on the ID. This provides room for a little misalignment.*

*Machine the crankshaft gear about 0.020 inch to realign the timing chain. These dimensions may change, depending on which timing-chain kit and camshaft thrust plate is used.*

*If there is not a clear path for the oil feed, this can be fixed by using a Dremel tool or a small dye grinder. With a small stone or carbide tool, the slot for the oil feed can be machined to allow a clear path for the oil to get to the distributor gear.*

According to Rollmaster, the company designed the nine-keyway crankshaft gear out of billet steel. This is the only way that the gear would hold up and not break with all the keyways in it. In high-performance applications, we have even seen the three-keyway cast gears break. The billet-steel gear gives you the confidence that it will not break. The more the valve-spring pressure increases, the more strain that it puts on the timing set. There is a limit to the more-stock cast-iron kits.

We have had problems with cheaper chains when using aftermarket sets. The chain on these sets was designed by Iwis and is produced in Germany.

The AMC engine does not have as many choices when it comes to timing kits. Other makes of engines have multiple choices when it comes to quality timing sets. Finding a reliable company that produces a billet kit for an AMC was difficult.

## Rollmaster Timing Chain Modifications

There are some machining steps needed to use the Rollmaster set with a camshaft thrust plate. Nick Alfano of Alfano Performance designed the anti-walk kit for AMC V-8s. These kits use a Rollmaster timing set and a GM-style camshaft thrust plate. We start with Rollmaster part number CS7111.

First, remove the Torrington bearing from the camshaft gear. The back of the camshaft gear will need to be machined so that the thrust plate fits over the ID of the camshaft gear. A few thousands of an inch for clearance is all that is needed. It is very important to mount the camshaft thrust plate on the center of the cam. After measuring the camshaft thrust plate thickness, remove this dimension from the back of the camshaft gear.

To realign the timing chain, the crankshaft gear also needs to be machined. The normal amount removed from the back side of the crank gear is 0.020 inch. With a die grinder and a small carbide ball, open up the slot for the oil to get to the front distributor gear. After these machining steps are complete, the timing set should mount up perfectly aligned.

## Distributor Gear Installation

The AMC engine is one of only a few engines where the distributor drive gear is removable from the camshaft and mounted in the front of the engine. Both the eccentric for the fuel pump and the front distributor gear bolt to the front of the camshaft using a special washer and bolt.

If your original distributor gear that bolts to the camshaft is damaged, it needs to be replaced. These are getting harder to find because some manufacturers have stopped making them. Both the distributor gear and camshaft gear need to be replaced together. It is common for these gears to fail if they are not heat treated correctly or the same.

If a stock distributor gear is used on the distributor, a replacement kit by Enginequest (EQ-CE124N) is available. When using an MSD distributor, use both MSD gears together. Another company that makes both gears is Bulltear.

## Oiling

The key to long gear life is using matched gears and making sure that the gear receives proper oiling. The front camshaft distributor gear gets oil through an oil hole in the front of the camshaft. This stream of oil is distributed through a groove that is cut on the inside of the camshaft gear all the way to the front distributor gear. It is very important to follow the oil feed hole and make sure that it extends all the way to the distributor gear.

Aftermarket camshaft companies sometimes take it upon themselves to make this hole smaller in diameter. When this oil feed hole is made

*The camshaft gear is unique to the AMC engine. The distributor drive gear is not attached to the camshaft; it is bolted to the front with the fuel pump eccentric. When installing this gear, cover it with a camshaft break-in paste.*

*This is the oil feed hole responsible for getting oil all the way to the front distributor gear. We have actually seen aftermarket cams without this oil hole.*

smaller, it does not align with the large chamfer and groove in the camshaft gear. This burns up a distributor gear almost immediately.

Over the years, companies have taken it upon themselves to reengineer the timing chain. Not that this is a bad thing, but some changes have negative implications. This is why it is so important to trace the oil path all the way to the gear.

This oil problem is so evident that some people have routed an external oil line and plumbed it into the front cover to spray on the gear. While this is a great idea, if you make sure that the gear is getting oil, you will not have this problem. During the final assembly, we will once again go over the assembly of the timing chain and oil path to the front distributor gear; it is *that* important.

## Harmonic Balancer

There are two different harmonic balancer designs: a three-bolt pulley and a four-bolt pulley. The new aftermarket balancers come with the four-bolt pulley design.

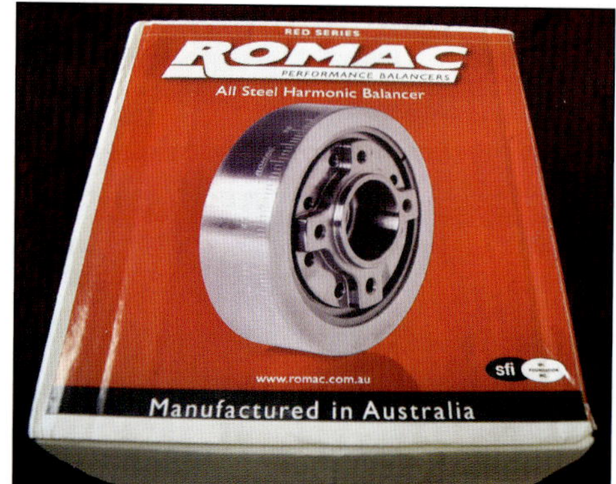


***Always check for proper clearance when installing a new harmonic balancer. Any machine shop can hone this. Just bring them the balancer with the crankshaft snout dimension. Follow the manufacturer's recommendations for clearances.***

### *Three-Bolt Pulley*

The harmonic balancer with the three-bolt pulley was used on the V-8 engines that were produced before 1970. There is some speculation that some of the 1970 engines had the three-bolt pulley harmonic balancer on them as well. This idea is popular because the engine was from the prior year if the car was built in the early months of January or February. The three-bolt harmonic was also externally balanced.

The three-bolt balancer in stock form is not being reproduced. It is possible to switch to the four-bolt balancer because it will press right on. The only problems will be having to switch all of the pulleys over to the four-bolt balancer and having the water pump at a different height. We have done this, and with a mixture of some aftermarket small-block Chevy pulleys, it is possible.

As far as we know, the only aftermarket balancer being made in a three-bolt form is from BHJ. These have to be special ordered, but they are available. These are an aftermarket-looking balancer that is SFI rated, which is probably a little much for a stock restoration, but it will work.

### *Four-Bolt Pulley*

The harmonic balancer with the four-bolt pulley is the most popular, and it covers all 1970-and-up V-8 engines. When building some serious horsepower, either internally balance the crankshaft or use an aftermarket internally balanced crankshaft. Both Romac and BHJ offer internal models for the AMC V-8. All factory balancers were externally balanced for AMC V-8 engines.

Usually, the original harmonic balancer has rubber that is dry rotted and cracked. If it is in too bad of condition, it must be replaced. There are a few companies that produce new balancers, including BHJ and Romac, which both offer precisely made balancers. Off-shore companies make cheaper balancers, but we have seen the balance weight be off substantially on them.

***To hone the harmonic balancer, we use a Sunnen rod machine. Selecting the proper stones gives the ID of the harmonic balancer a smooth surface for pressing on.***

For most of our builds, we use a Romac harmonic balancer (part number 0288). Most new harmonic balancers need to be honed to fit. Follow the manufacturer's directions for proper press fit.

All balancers should have a slight interference fit onto the crankshaft that matches the factory shaft diameter or with a plus tolerance of 0.0005 inch. Romac produces balancers with undersize bores to suit applications where the crankshaft snout may be undersized. Undersized balancer bores are indicated after the part number. For example, part number 0202–001's balancer has a 0.001-inch-smaller bore diameter. Romac also produces balancer bores 0.005 inch under for preferential honing.

If assembling your own engine, measure the crankshaft snout diameter and bring this measurement with the balancer to the local machine shop. It will hone the balancer to the proper press fit. When installing the balancer, use a little bit of silicone in the keyway groove to prevent oil from following the crankshaft key groove.

# Front Cover, Oil Pump, and Oil Pan

*The front cover on the AMC V-8 engines is unique because it doubles as the timing cover and houses the oil pump. The water pump bolts on to the front cover with the bolts going through the pump, timing cover, and into the engine block.*

*There are a few companies that make replacement covers for the AMC V-8 engines. Only a few of these covers are being made properly. One of the best covers on the market is made by Bulltear. In some of the other aftermarket covers, the distributor hole is not machined in the correct location and will cause premature gear failure. (Photo Courtesy Bulltear)*

AMC's front-cover/oil-pump design was different than any other conventional V-8 design. The front cover that housed the oil pump was designed to be removable. The oil pump housing was built into the front cover. This design made the oil pump gears and bypass valve accessible from the outside of the engine.

This is different from GM-designed V-8 engines, where the oil pump is housed inside the oil pan. The downside to this design is that if the oil pump fails or takes in foreign material, it destroys the whole front cover.

This front cover houses the distributor, water pump, and oil pump. Several dimensions on this front cover must be perfect, including the distributor's location and angle.

## Front Cover

Some brands that we use for remanufactured covers are OEM, Silver Seal, and Bulltear. The AMC V-8 timing cover by Bulltear is a great replacement that meets OEM standards and is a direct replacement for an AMC V-8's oil pump. These timing covers fit 290 through 401 engines.

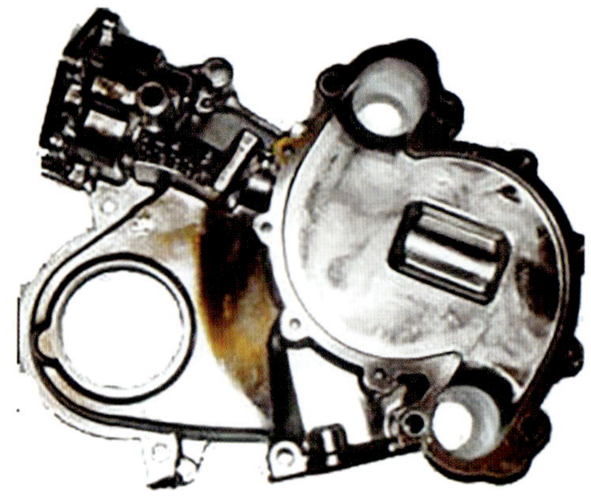

*Bulltear's HD timing cover is nickel-plated for extreme duty and abrasion resistance, which results in a long-term oiling solution on stock motors and racing engines. The cover comes with HRC gears and a new front main seal. (Photo Courtesy Bulltear)*

All timing covers are test fit with pins, the OEM engine block, and on CNC equipment. These covers have a closer tolerance than an OEM cover. The Bulltear nickel-plated (HD) timing cover is for extreme duty, and its abrasion resistance results in a long-term oiling solution on stock motors and racing engines. Bulltear sells its cover with its HRC gears. These gears have hydro relief grooves that extend the life of the distributor and camshaft gear. This also helps to protect the oil pump housing bore.

Due to the problems with the stock AMC front cover, there is a demand for aftermarket covers and new oil pump designs. Several companies have tried to design a new front cover, but many of the cheaper versions have failed. We have seen cheap front covers with the oil pump cavities machined wrong, incorrect distributor hole locations, and even missing bolt holes.

With the flood of aftermarket covers being manufactured, there has been a wave of different designs for oil pump configurations. We have seen everything from taller gears, spacer plates, differently designed bypass valves, and even eliminating the pump altogether and using a belt-drive oil pump instead.

For most stock and mild high-performance builds, the stock cover works adequately with minor oil modifications. The engine oil modifications discussed in this book help considerably with the stock oil pump suppling good pressure.

### *High-Horsepower Front Cover*

Indy Cylinder Head offers a front-cover setup with its billet oil pump attached. This is the best of all the systems, but it is probably only needed in extreme high-horsepower applications. However, if you want the best piece available and want to spend money, it sure looks cool. Other options include a Jessel front-cover system used with an external belt-drive oil pump.

When refurbishing an OEM front cover, it is common to do a lot of thread repair. If you have a good OEM core front cover with a nearly perfect oil pump cavity, it is worth repairing a bunch of threaded holes to keep the OEM cover. Before companies were making new front covers, we did whatever it took to repair these front covers.

## Oil Pump

Prepare to rebuild the stock oil pump by hot tanking the front cover. After inspection, we determine the condition of the oil pump housing and decide if it is worth rebuilding.

## Rebuilding the Oil Pump

**1**

*After the front cover is washed and glass beaded, stone all of the surfaces to remove any high spots.*

**2**

*Before installing the gears, stone the gear surface slightly to remove any high spots.*

**3**

*Install the oil pump gears into the housing and check the clearance between the gear and the housing. This helps to assess how worn the housing is.*

**4**

*Check the gear protrusion to select the correct gasket thickness. This is very important to achieve the correct oil pressure.*

**5**

*Measure the protrusion of the spur gears. For most cases, you will have a protrusion (the gears are higher than the housing). Document these measurements. There are different thicknesses of gaskets, and we have stacked two gaskets in rare instances. Once you have the gasket thicknesses, subtract them from the protrusion. The factory specification is 0.006 to 0.008 inch.*

**6**

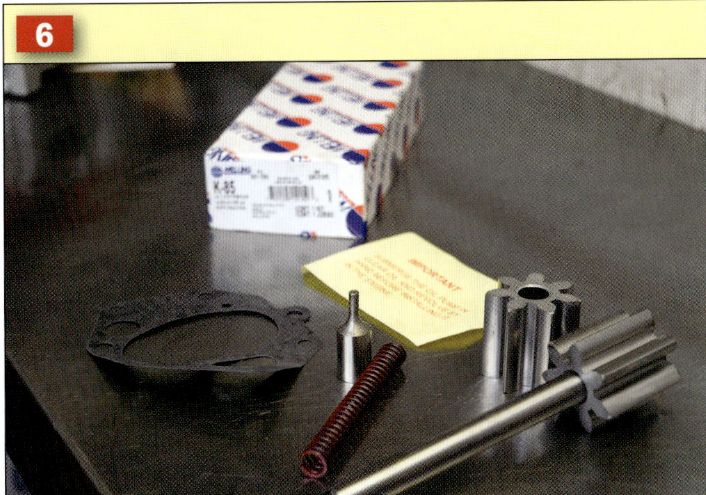

*Lay out the Melling oil pump kit for inspection.*

**7**

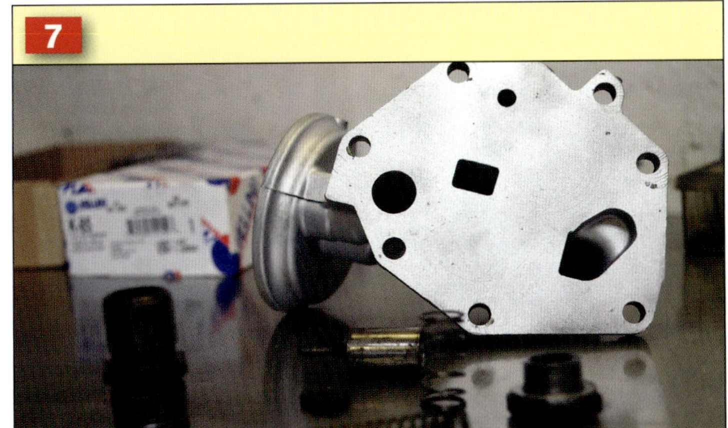

*The oil filter housing/oil pump cover plate are ready to be assembled after cleaning.*

**8**

*To rebuild the oil pump pressure relief, the first step is to put a light coat of oil onto the plunger and install it into the housing. The plunger should move freely in the chamber.*

9

*The next step is to install the bypass spring. The bypass spring controls what pressure the relief releases. We have installed a small washer to act as a shim to prevent the bypass from opening to soon. We can control the oil pressure a little bit that way.*

10

*The final step is to install the threaded plug. This is the original plug from the cover. The cap and sealing washer do not come with the new oil pump kit, so do not throw anything away during disassembly. If they are needed, a local parts store or hardware store will have a copper sealing washer.*

The first step will be to glass bead the complete cover. Be very careful while beading the internals of the oil pump housing. Holding the bead nozzle too close damages the oil pump cavity. After blasting, install any Heli-Coils needed in the housing. With one final blowing out, the cover is ready to install the oil pump kit.

The first step is to preassemble the spur gears into the housing. Make sure that the drive gear rotates freely in the housing. Inspect the shaft on the old gear to determine if it is worn. This will provide clues as to the condition of the bore on the housing.

Next, inspect the housing bore on the cover. It is important that the housing bore is not worn. Measure the protrusion of the spur gears. Most cases will have a protrusion (the gears are higher than the housing), which needs to be documented.

The gaskets have different thicknesses, and in rare occurrences, we have needed to stack two gaskets. Once the gasket thickness is known, subtract it from the protrusion. The factory specification is 0.006 to 0.008 inch. Just from experience, we like to set up ours at 0.006 inch. Preferably, you only want to use one gasket to achieve this.

There are many different manufacturers for pump gears and new casted housings. With different manufacturers, you are bound to come up with the wrong dimensions. If there is not a protrusion, we have milled the housing to get our protrusion. If there is too much protrusion, you have to face the gears. These gears are heat treated and are very hard, so we normally grind them.

We always use a Melling oil pump kit to rebuild the pump. Melling used to include two different springs in the pump kit. However, recently, it has only come with one.

The next step is to measure the radial clearance between the gears and the housing. If the clearance is 0.003 inch or more, the housing is no good. These measurements are key to an AMC engine having proper oil pressure.

The bypass valve is next. The oil pump kit comes with a new spring and plunger. Make sure that the plunger slides back and forth without getting stuck. If using a used cover, check that the bypass plunger does not have too much clearance. The bypass spring included in the Melling kit is what we use. There is a crush washer on the plug, and we always replace it; this washer does not come with the pump kit.

***Performance Options***

Indy Cylinder Head offers an adjustable billet oil pump (part number 401-01-22). This oil pump

*The Bulltear oil pump plate allows the use of an external oil pump pickup, oil coolers, and remote oil filters. The internal oil pump pickup must be plugged when using an external pickup.*

is high volume, and the pressure is adjustable. This billet oil pump must be used with the Indy cast-aluminum front cover (part number 401-T1-21).

Many companies offer a mid-plate kit that installs between the pump gears and the housing cover. With this mid-plate, the oil pump gears ride on steel and not the aluminum. The idea with this is that the steel plate does not expand like the aluminum, which creates more stabilized pressure. The wear plate usually has a smaller hole that will limit the amount of oil going through the bypass. This pumps a larger amount of oil through the engine.

This plate also helps if a pump cover is worn with gear marks. When installed, this plate is sandwiched between the oil filter adapter and the timing cover. These kits fit all stock covers.

Bulltear also offers an oil filter relocation block. This kit replaces the oil filter adapter. The oil filter bypass is eliminated with this kit, but it still uses the pressure bypass spring and the plunger. This kit enables you to run a remote oil filter.

The Bulltear kit (number 534) is a plate that allows you to use an external oil sump line or a dry sump. The oil pump pickup hole is plugged internally with a pipe plug. This kit can also be plumbed through oil coolers and remote oil filters.

## Oil Pan and Pickup

For stock and mild performance builds, the stock-designed oil pan is adequate. However, the stock oil pan may have seen a lot of abuse over the years. In addition, the weather seems to get the best of the oil pan, especially in the Midwest. In most barn-find restorations, the oil pans are so rusted that they need to be changed. It is not worth blasting the pan up real nice only to find it has a little rust pinholes and leaks.

A few companies restamp oil pans. A lot of Jeep followers like to install AMC V-8 engines, so these oil pans can be found for sale from the 4WD companies. The only difference is that the Jeep pan has a slight angle in the front of the pan for clearance. The average person usually can't tell the difference. If your build is a stock numbers-matching car that is going to be judged, then do not use the Jeep pan.

Milodon has a few performance oil pans from which to choose. Pan number 30260 is a deep oil pan with holes for external pickup. This pan is great for all-out racing applications. We are using this pan with a single pickup line, and it is plumbed into Milodon's oil pump adapter plate. This engine now has an external-pickup oil system.

Milodon has slinging pickups as well. Part number 24050 is the single pickup and part number 24070 is for the double pickup. These systems are advertised to increase oil volume up to 7,500 rpm. We have safely used these above 8,000 rpm. They also offer an oil system (part number 24055) for pro touring, autocross, and street/strip cars.

Canton Oil Pans also has a few oil pans that are great quality.

***Bulltear offers this nice oil filter relocation block. This allows you to relocate the oil filter to a convenient spot to service. Notice the plate sandwiched between the housing and the oil filter relocation plate. This is where the oil inlet line feeds into from the oil pan. The new external oil pickup line eliminates the internal screwed-in pickup.***

***This is a good example of Milodon's single swinging pickup assembly. The installation of this unit is very similar to the double-pickup version, which we will walk you through.***

## Assembling the Oil Pickup System

1

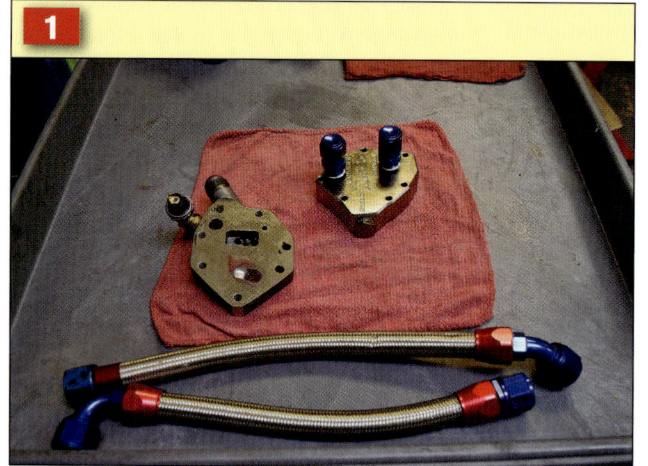

This is Milodon's double swinging pickup assembly. Preassemble the complete system to resolve any minor clearance issues and build the oil line assemblies. When laying out the oil system, make sure that everything is clean and deburred.

2

Start by drilling two holes for Milodon's dual-line with swivel pickup (part number 20470). Our Milodon oil pan did not have the predrilled holes, so we marked the two pickup holes and drilled them to the appropriate size. Remember when drilling holes that the pickup screen should be about 3/8 inch off the bottom of the oil pan. When complete, preassemble the pickup screen into the oil pan. During final assembly, pay attention to the bulkhead fittings, as an oil leak will occur if they do not seal. Always fill the oil pan with mineral spirits or water for a leak check when installing.

3

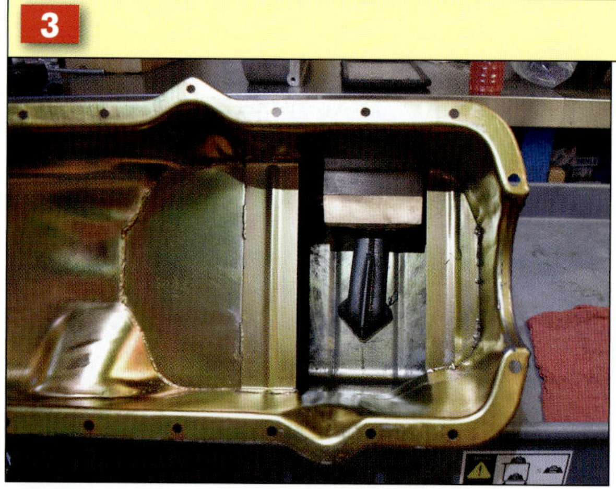

After the pickup screen is assembled, the inside will look like this. The pickup screen should not sit on the bottom of the oil pan and should swing freely from the front to the back of the pan.

4

Next, install the front cover on the dowel pins. We use two bolts to hold the cover in place.

5

The oil system gear selection and fitment was completed earlier in the chapter. We already know our gasket thickness from the earlier measurements. The oil pump mid-plate with the oil fitting are installed with the gasket we already determined.

6

With the gasket installed first, now install the mid-plate with the oil-supply fitting. The AN fitting needs to clear the edge of the engine block. It is common for a little clearancing to be done here. We use two bolts just to hold it in place.

**7**

*The last step to installing the oil pump plates is to install the cover plate. The two fittings on the bottom go to our remote oil filter location. With a second gasket, install the cover plate in the correct location. The pressure relief was rebuilt earlier in the chapter.*

**8**

*Notice the threaded hole just behind the timing cover next to the oil pan rail. This hole is a blind hole from the factory and is not drilled through into the oil gallery. The single-pickup version does not require this modification. The dual-feed pickup screen system requires drilling an oil hole into the oil gallery below it. This hole should be drilled starting with smaller drill bits and increasing in size. Once you are close to size, switch over to a die grinder to do the rest. This ensures that you stay within the oil gallery. Also, debur the oil hole as it is completed. Next, tap this hole with a 1/2-inch NPT tap and install a -12 AN fitting for the second oil pickup line.*

**9**

*We are now ready to install the oil pan on the engine. Check the clearance next to the AN fitting that was installed into the oil pan rail. Often, this fitting makes contact with the oil pan. Minor clearancing of the pan is usually needed. Once the oil pan fits freely, build the oil lines.*

**10**

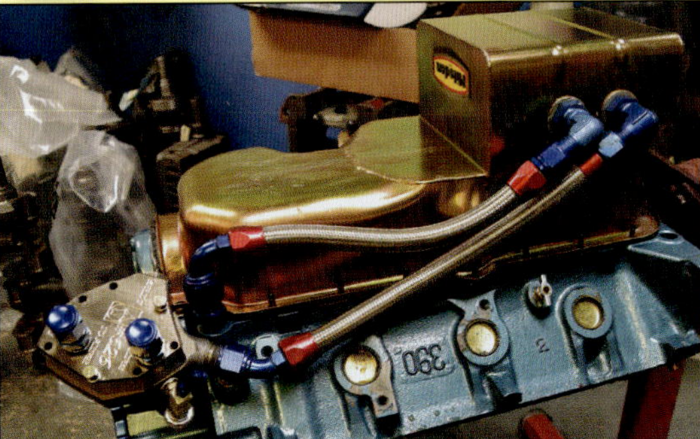

*The supplied oil lines from the Milodon kit work most of the time. The major thing to note is the header location. Build the oil lines to hug the oil pan rather than stick out. With the oil lines fabricated, our preassembly and clearancing are complete. Now, we can disassemble everything and complete the machining. That way, when our assembly begins, we won't have to worry about clearance issues and keeping everything clean.*

# Cylinder Heads

*The two different exhaust-port configurations are the pre-1970 rectangular port (left) and the 1970-and-later dogleg port (right).*

A nice aspect of the AMC family of cylinder heads is that they are basically the same design. With very few modifications, they can all bolt up to an AMC block. The engine family that we are talking about is every engine except the 327.

## Differences and Specifications

The major cylinder head differences are the exhaust port design, valve size, combustion chamber size, rocker-arm design, and head bolt diameter. It sounds like a lot of differences, but all of the engines have the same head bolt pattern.

The two most desirable types of AMC V-8 heads are the 1970-to-early-1971 heads with 51-cc chambers (casting number 319-6291) and the mid-1970-to-mid-1973 58-cc heads (casting numbers 321-2993 and 321-3948). Both heads have the superior dogleg exhaust port and studded rocker-arm mounts. The only real difference between them is a thicker layer of metal inside the combustion chambers. When comparing the two side by side, it is very noticeable, especially between the valves.

### Pre-1970 versus Post-1970

Cylinder heads produced from 1970 have a dogleg exhaust port. Pre-1970 cylinder heads have a rectangular exhaust port. The later heads have 1/2-inch head bolts and the early heads have 7/16-inch head bolts. The deck height on the pre-1970 engine block is 9.175 inches, and the deck height on 1970 and later is 9.208 inches. There are two different intake manifolds for these cylinder heads.

It is common to bolt the 1970-and-later cylinder heads on the older blocks using the Edelbrock 9693 head bolt bushing kit. The 1970 heads with 51-cc chambers paired with 1970 pistons have a compression ratio of 10.25:1.

In the Midwest, we have been dealing with reformulated fuel, which seems to have a detonation problem—even with 93-octane fuel. The 58-cc cylinder heads combined with a later-design piston keeps the compression around 9.5:1. You may want to keep some race fuel around and keep the engine timing reasonable. This is workable on a street/strip car that does not need octane booster with every tank of gas.

### Pistons

TRW makes a forged version of both piston types (all factory pistons were cast). The TRW piston was a very common upgrade back in the day.

*Federal-Mogul is the old TRW that we all remember from the 1970s to the 1980s. The company still offers a forged piston for the AMC 401. The AMC 390 engine has been discontinued.*

*Notice that the rocker-arm stud has a shoulder just below the threads. This shoulder is so the rocker-arm nut can have a positive stop. When the rocker-arm stud is torqued down to a specific torque value, there is no rocker-arm adjustment. With a nonadjustable valvetrain, the pushrod length must be correct in to have the correct lifter preload.*

The 401 version by Federal-Mogul is still being made but is sometimes difficult to find. In today's world of aftermarket forged pistons, the Federal-Mogul (TRW) piston is very heavy in comparison.

All Edelbrock heads have the larger head bolt holes. The Edelbrock busing kit allows you to bolt on these heads. The dogleg cylinder head is the more-common head. It has been known to flow a little better than the rectangular-port head. The dogleg cylinder head also has many more header choices from which to choose. AMC manufactured a 1969 390-ci engine and a 1970 390-ci engine.

### 1970 AMC 390 Engine

In 1970, AMC changed the design of the 390 cylinder head. This engine was only manufactured for one year and had a normal dogleg-style exhaust port. These were the same cylinder heads that were bolted on to the later 401 engines. This cylinder head was the only 390 with 1/2-inch cylinder head bolts.

Due to the fact that the deck heights also changed, the 1970 version of the 390 intake manifold was also different. The 390 engine became the pattern of future for AMC engines. This was the last year for the 390 engine, and the 401 took its place in the performance division. Of course, there were still the smaller-valve heads produced for the 304- and 360-ci engines.

The cylinder heads manufactured after this all had dogleg exhaust ports and 1/2-inch head bolts. The intake manifold also stayed the same for the rest of the manufacturing years. The only major design changes in the cylinder heads from here were the valve sizes and the valvetrain going from a stud rocker arm to a bridge design.

The original 1970 cylinder head came with the smaller 51-cc cylinder heads. As regulations and the octane level of available fuels were changing, the last AMC head had 58-cc combustion chambers.

### Deck Heights

The deck heights are different for these two engines as well as the intake manifolds. This makes the 1970 390 engine the rarest, and it is getting difficult to find. If you are doing a proper number-matching build for a 1970 390 engine, there is only one year from which to choose an engine.

Another major difference in the cylinder heads is the valvetrain. The newer cylinder heads (mid-1970s and up) went to a 5/16-inch rocker-arm bridge. For stock applications this is fine, but even mild performance builds need the heads to be converted to a normal rocker-arm stud that is adjustable.

The early years had a 7/16-inch stud with individual stamped rocker arms. This setup is okay but was also nonadjustable. The rocker arm studs have a shoulder on them for a positive stop to torque the rocker arm down. There are two different combustion chamber sizes also. The higher-compression engines had 51-cc chambers, and the lower-compression engines had a 58-cc chamber.

## Aftermarket Cylinder Heads

With various manufacturers jumping on the bandwagon, some cylinder head choices are available.

*Edelbrock aftermarket AMC cylinder heads are a great choice for a street/strip engine build.*

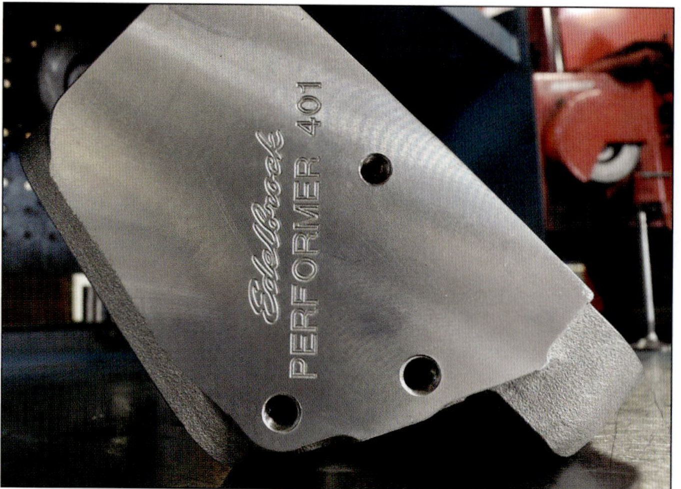


*Customers have asked us mill off the Edelbrock logo on the ends of the cylinder heads and paint them AMC blue to hide the fact that they're aftermarket cylinder heads.*

### Edelbrock

The Edelbrock cylinder heads are designed to be a bolt-on replacement. These are considered to be a slight performance upgrade for any 1967–1991 343, 360, 390, and 401 engine.

The cylinder heads come with adjustable rocker-arm studs and guide plates. Edelbrock mentions in the instructions that these heads are set up for small-block Ford adjustable 1.6-inch rocker arms. We prefer to use AMC rockers from Harland Sharp, but both work well.

The stock rocker ratio from the factory is 1.6:1. The intake flange is drilled to accommodate the 1968–1969 and the 1970-and-up intake manifolds. Both the intake and exhaust ports are located in the stock location to make bolting on all accessories very easy. All part numbers of these cylinder heads include 1/2-inch head bolt holes.

The Edelbrock RPM Performer heads (part number 60119) have no exhaust heat crossover. The company offers a few different part numbers with different valve-spring options. Flat-tappet and hydraulic rollers are the valve-spring options that are available.

If installing these heads on the older blocks with 7/16-inch head bolts, the Edelbrock bushing kit must be used. Included with the heads are step dowel pins that are also needed to bolt these heads onto the early engines. The intake valve angle has been changed to 45 degrees; this improves flow over the stock 30-degree angle.

Part numbers 60129 and 60139 have a machined heat crossover for emissions. We very rarely use the heads with the exhaust crossover. Customers have asked us mill off the logos on the heads to hide the fact that they are aftermarket.

**Edelbrock Cylinder Head Specifications**

| *Item* | *Specification* |
|---|---|
| Combustion chamber volume | 54 cc |
| Intake runner volume | 185 cc |
| Exhaust runner volume | 70 cc |
| Intake valve diameter | 2.02 inches |
| Exhaust valve diameter | 1.60 inches |
| Valve stem diameter | 11/32 inch |
| Valve guides | Manganese bronze |
| Deck thickness | 5/8 inch |
| Valve spring diameter | 1.55 inches |
| Valve spring maximum lift | 0.580 inch |
| Rocker stud | 3/8 inch |
| Guide plate | Hardened steel |
| Pushrod diameter | 5/16 inch |
| Valve angle | 18 degrees |
| Exhaust port location | Stock |
| Spark plug fitment | 14 mm x 3/4 reach, gasket seat |

### Indy Cylinder Head

The other main supplier of aftermarket cylinder heads is Indy Cylinder Head from Indianapolis, Indiana. It has two cylinder head applications that are available: the 401-SR and the 401-1K.

#### *401-SR*

The 401-SR is a replacement aluminum cylinder head for the 360 to the 401 ci. This head features combustion chambers that have a modern high-quench, heart-shape, 61-cc chamber. The intake runners are 235 cc. The nice aspect is that all the stock intake manifolds bolt right up to these cylinder heads. This head is a great choice for street, strip, and drag race applications.

These cylinder heads can also be drilled for the extra 3/8-inch head bolts. Depending on the camshaft, there are different part numbers for the type of camshaft that you are using. Intake valves are 2.100 inches and exhaust valves are 1.650 inches. This is a great choice for a head that still has all the stock accessory bolt holes and increases performance. The stock AMC headers also bolt right up with these cylinder heads.

#### *401-1K*

Indy also offers a trick high-flowing cylinder head (part number 401-1K). This cylinder head uses the 0.800-inch offset Indy shaft rocker kit. This is the same rocker kit that is used on the 440 Chrysler setup. Jesel also offers a shaft-rocker setup for this cylinder head.

While the valve angle was kept at 18 degrees, the intake valve was moved 0.045 inch toward the cylinder wall. The exhaust valve also moved 0.045 inch toward the cylinder wall. The exhaust is the other major change in this head; it has the same layout as a 440 Chrysler, which uses a normal Chrysler header. With numbers as high as 245 cc and larger for the intake-port volume, this cylinder head is a heavy hitter. It must be used with Indy intake manifold 401-3X.

We recommend using all Indy components, including valves and gaskets. The cylinder head was designed for high compression, and the extra head bolt location is marked for you. This makes drilling the extra head bolt an easy task. Combustion chambers are 58 cc but can be milled to 51 cc. This provides room to fine-tune the compression ratio.

## Inspection, Cleaning, and Magnafluxing

As always, the first step to working on anything is determining if it is worth it. If rebuilding a numbers-matching restoration, the stock cylinder heads must be used, so let's get magnafluxing.

#### *Inspection*

Before disassembly, a quick inspection can provide information about the history of the engine. In our case, a visual inspection showed that all of the rust was in two of the cylinders. This rust indicates that there was standing water in the engine, which is a good indication of a problem.

After disassembling the heads, they get jet washed in the hot tank. Our heads had so much rust and crust on them that we had to steel-media blast them before magnafluxing. Normally, we magnaflux first, but with all the rust, it would have been hard for the cracks to show up. Always try to do things in order to save steps and money. If the heads would have turned out to be cracked, we would have wasted the time and money to blast them.

#### *Cracked Heads*

The first item to inspect is the outside of the head by the lower head bolts because these cylinder

*The first step to cylinder head inspection is to disassemble the cylinder head for hot tanking.*

*After magnafluxing, the yellow highlighted crack just above the head bolt hole is easy to see. This is a very common place for the cylinder heads to crack. These cylinder heads are very thin in this area.*

heads have a cracking issue in that location. When these heads were fly cut to allow room for the head bolt, the two outside corners are very thin and sometimes, if not cracked already, will crack when the cylinder head is retorqued on. For this reason, we only torque the two outside lower head bolts to 65 ft-lbs.

Before spending a lot of time on the heads, clean this area with brake cleaner and magnaflux it to see if they are cracked. We have seen these heads crack all the way around the corner of the head. An estimated 60 percent of the heads that we see are cracked.

If the heads are cracked all the way around the corner, find new castings. If they are only cracked in the fly-cut groove (usually about 1 inch long), drill both ends of the crack, machine it out, and braze the crack. After machining, do another pressure test to make sure that there are no leaks.

Very seldom do we see these heads crack anywhere else. Once we know that we have two good castings with which to work, we can progress with the cleaning. Most of the time, we install all new 45-degree stainless-steel valves in the heads, but to save some money it is possible to glass bead and reuse the original valves. Once the valves are clean, polish and mic the valve stems. The valves are ground in the valve grinder. This will also rule out any bent valves. All valves that are bent or have pitting should be replaced.

## Valve Options: Stock versus Performance

AMC used a 30-degree intake valve in all its cylinder heads. A 30-degree intake valve restricts the airflow quite a bit. It is common to update the heads with a 45-degree intake valve.

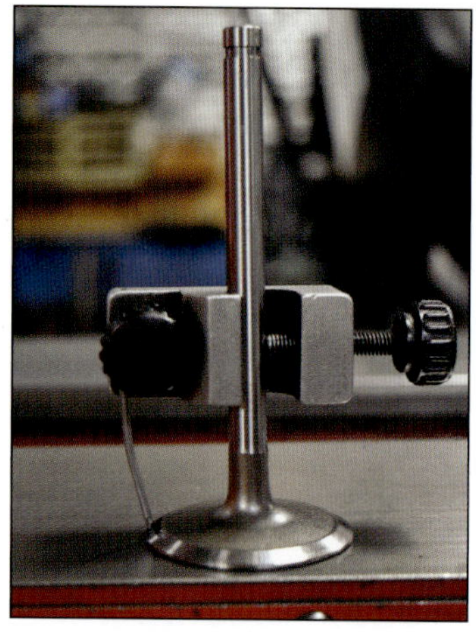

*This is a stock replacement valve. The factory intake valve angle is 30 degrees. For performance applications, change out these valves for the better-flowing 45-degree valves.*

*Manly offers a complete line of valvetrain parts, including many different grades of small-block Chevy valves. The added benefit of running a popular valve in the AMC cylinder head is the variety of lengths and valve head diameters available.*

Early on, not many options were available for valves besides the stock replacements. Today, there are valve companies that custom make any type of valve that is needed. The stock valves have a 3/8-inch stem diameter with a three-groove valve keeper.

In the early years of rebuilding these heads, it was common to change the guides over to 11/32-inch stem diameters. This opened the valve selection to include small-block Chevy valves. Since the small-block Chevy is so common, there are many different valves available.

With the AMC valvetrain being nonadjustable, valve length is critical. Instead of trying to find an exact-length replacement valve, it was easier to switch the valvetrain to adjustable studs. Using Chevy valves also allowed us to change the intake valve angle to 45 degrees to improve flow. With a little valve bowel blending, the Chevy valves work well.

*For stock-application replacement valvetrain parts, SBI manufactures everything from replacement valves to valve springs, rocker arms, and pushrods.*

There are Chevy valves for every application from stainless steel to titanium. This covers everything from a hydraulic flat-tappet to high-lift, solid-roller application. The biggest mistake in the valvetrain area is underestimating the spring pressure of a solid-roller spring. If not using a severe-duty valve in this application, it will fail. Remember to listen to your engine builder; they will lead you in the correct direction for valves.

There are a few companies that make stock replacement valves. One of the leaders in this area is SBI Valves. SBI has a good listing in its catalog for each of the AMC engines. When rebuilding a stock engine, it is important to use a correct replacement valve to keep the valve length the same.

A few small aftermarket companies sell replacement valves and performance valves. We have had a few valve failures with the small companies that sell two-piece valves. When a valve fails, it usually causes major destruction. It is not worth the failure rate to use poorly made valves. The AMC valve lineup is pretty much the same for all the engines and years except for the valve diameter.

## Cylinder Head Machining

Regarding new Edelbrock cylinder heads, cylinder head machining can be a little overwhelming. Let's start with the basic machining for cast-iron heads.

Make sure that the heads have been magnafluxed and are ready to start machining. Valve-guide work will be our first machining operation. There are many ways to check the valve-guide clearance. Most seasoned machinists check guide clearance by feel. If you would like to do a quick check before taking the cylinder heads to a machine shop, make sure that the valve guide is clean and that the valve stem does not have excessive taper.

Slide the intake valve into the guide. Hold the valve by the head and try to wiggle it from side to side. The intake valve should rock very little. Next, do the same to the exhaust valve; the exhaust valve will have more clearance than the intake valve. The exhaust valve runs with more heat than the intake valve, which will cause the exhaust valve to grow more than the intake valve. This will just give a general idea if the guides are really bad.

The machine shop will check the valve-guide clearance with micrometers and pilots. Our preferred option for guide repair is to install bronze valve-guide liners. Most shops install a bronze valve-guide liner even though the guide might not be worn too badly. Most feel that the valve-guide liners are more durable. K-Line makes a few different kinds. One style will have a spiral groove on the ID of the guide.

The thought is that a valve guide with the spiral on the ID will hold oil for cooling and lubrication. The other style has a smooth bore on the ID. Depending on the application, we use both. When we have an application that might run more combustion-chamber heat, the liner with the oil groove works well. K-Line supplies a special tool kit for installing these liners.

The valve guide is bored out with the supplied reamer, then the installation tool installs the liner into the bore. After the liner is pressed in, it will need to be broached. This process expands the valve guide so that it stays in place. After broaching, the liner is trimmed to length. Some final honing to size is performed, and then we have the perfect clearance. If a valve guide is really worn, the cylinder head is bored out, and a cast-iron replacement valve guide is installed.

## Machining the Valves

1

*This is an example of a K-Line installation kit. Included in the kit are the step reamer, liner installer, and various-sized broaches.*

2

*The K-Line liner kits come in many different valve-guide diameters. The 3/8-inch kit is used for stock AMC valves, and the 11/32-inch kit is for when the guides and valves are changed. These kits come with all of the appropriate reamers, drivers, and broaches to install and fit the liners.*

3

*The first step is drilling out the original valve guide. This is done with a stepped reamer and a centering cone that centers off of the valve seat.*

4

*Using the installation driver, the liner is pressed into the bored-out valve guide. The liner should be installed flush with the cylinder head.*

5

*Valve-guide broaches come in different sizes. These broaches help wedge the liner to the cylinder head so that it does not become loose while the engine is running.*

6

*Flip the cylinder head over to trim the excess liner material off with the cutter.*

7

*The valve-guide liner is now ready to be final sized. This process is done with an adjustable diamond hone.*

## Valve Job

After the valve-guide work is done, move on to a nice three-angle valve job. A popular question among customers is: Should I harden the exhaust-valve seats? Early on, when fuel had lead in it, the lead protected the exhaust seat from wearing away. Automotive manufacturers did not start heat treating the exhaust seats until the mid-1970s.

Over the years, we have learned which manufacturers' heads have soft seats and which ones hold up. When it comes to soft seats, the Chevrolet and Ford heads are the first to start sinking if you do not use a lead substitute in the fuel. The AMC heads hold up well, and we have stopped installing hardened valve seats in these heads.

Over the years, we have noticed that the valve seats on AMC heads do

*A modern-day valve-seat cutting machine can approach $100,000 or more.*

*Valve seats are cut by cutters that have three angles at a minimum: the top cut, the seat angle, and the bottom cut. There is a large range of performance cutters that can have radiused angles for bowel blending.*

*Cylinder head CCs are used to calculate the compression ratio of the engine or determine the piston to be used to hit a desired compression ratio. After doing a valve job and any cylinder head combustion chamber porting, match the CCs to all the chambers.*

not sink. The only time that we install seats is if we have a damaged valve seat. A good three-angle valve job is one of the most important machining operations when rebuilding an engine.

Valve jobs today are done by precision machines that cost $75,000 to $100,000. The quality of the valve jobs with these machines is considerably better than what was available in the past by using a hand grinder and changing out different-angle stones.

#### *Valve-Stem Heights*

If using all the stock nonadjustable valvetrain components, the machine shop must be critical about all of the valve stem heights. When the valvetrain is nonadjustable, the correct valve heights control how much preload the lifter has.

The wrong lifter preload can be the cause of a noisy valvetrain or even hold a valve open. When converting the valvetrain over to adjustable components, it is still important to keep the valve-stem height the same. This also controls the valve-spring installed height. It is easier to set up the valve-spring pressure if the heights are really close.

For aftermarket valves, converting from the 30-degree stock valve angle to the 45-degree valves requires some blending of the bowels. If going with this option, remember to ask the machine shop to do some bowel blending.

### CCing the Combustion Chamber

Now that the valve job is complete, we can CC the combustion chamber to see where we land. Sometimes the design of the valve can substantially change the CC. Obviously, the valve job will also affect the CC. This is a good time for this step because the next step is to resurface the cylinder heads, and we can tighten up the CCs if needed by surfacing the cylinder head.

Here's a general rule that will get you close: 1 cc usually equals about 0.007 inch removed from the deck. This is just a rough estimate because the design and size of the chamber changes this.

Always start surfacing with the worst head first. The goal is to keep the CCs the same when the process is complete. If you are trying to drop

*Cylinder head finish is controlled for better head-gasket sealing with more automated surfacers and CBN cutters.*

the compression ratio, there are a few options: unshroud the valves to increase the CCs or run a 0.010-inch thicker head gasket. Keep in mind that the closer to a zero deck that you keep the piston, the more efficient the chamber will work.

## Cylinder Head Surfacing

Finally, we are ready to surface the cylinder head. As we discussed from CCing the chambers and calculating the compression ratio, this will provide a start as to how much is needed to mill off the surface. When it comes to head gaskets, there are only a few choices: the original steel-backed Fel-Pro gasket and the Cometic MLS gasket for performance applications.

Years ago, heads were surfaced with a wet grinder, and the surface finish was not as good as it is today. These machines have come a long way. A surface finish as smooth as glass is needed, especially for an MLS gasket. It is important to machine both heads so that the combustion chambers are the same size (CCs).

Some people request to have their engine blueprinted. When we make sure that all of these chambers have identical CCs, this is a form of blueprinting. From the factory, you might have different CCs from end to end in one chamber or from one head to the other.

## Adjustable Valvetrain

Even on stock rebuilds, it is advantageous to machine them to have an adjustable valvetrain. This is the more modern way, and it will eliminate future problems. The older cylinder heads already had 7/16-inch rocker stud holes drilled and tapped in the heads. An ARP rocker stud can be installed right into the head, and it will work.

## Hardened Guide Plate

We prefer to install a hardened guide plate with the new rocker arm stud. To install a hardened guide plate, first drill out the pushrod hole because this will no longer need to locate the pushrod. The guide plate's sole purpose is to locate and keep the pushrod in line.

Measuring the thickness of the guide plate and the thickness of the rocker arm stud base determines what needs to be machined off the rocker boss. Normally, around 0.300 inch is milled off the rocker stud pad.

After milling this dimension, always run a bottom tap into the stud hole to make sure that it is tapped all the way to the bottom. This will save you from headaches in the future. As the years went on, the new style of cylinder heads went to a 5/16-inch threaded hole with a rocker-arm bridge. These also can be converted over to a 7/16-inch stud with a guide plate.

On the newer heads, we have broken into water on a few, so we are conservative on how much we machine off the rocker pad. After machining the pad, drill and tap the 5/16-inch holes out to 7/16 inch for the stud. Once this is done, don't forget to drill out the pushrod holes again.

## Valve-Guide Seal

As long as we have the cylinder head mounted in the machine to do the guide plate install, now is the time to machine down for the new-style valve-guide seal. The old, hard plastic valve-guide seals don't last long, and anyone who has ever disassembled an older engine has noticed that seal pieces can be found in the engine (most of the time). The old seal floated on the valve. The new-style seal presses onto the valve guide and stays stationary as the valve opens and closes.

The Viton seals are available in a variety of valve-guide OD sizes as well as valve stem diameters. Absolutely a more positive valve stem seal will produce better oil control. The seals are made out of a high-temp Viton material that has a spring that keeps tension on the valve. Machining down the

*Valve-stem guide cutting tools are available from many manufacturers, including Comp Cams. The cutters are available in a couple different valve-guide OD sizes.*

*Ditching the old, original valve seal for a new-style positive seal that presses onto the valve guide is the way to go. The old, hard plastic seals were known for breaking apart after a while. Note the new Viton positive-press seal in the center.*

***For larger camshafts, make sure to have enough retainer-to-seal clearance. Using the camshaft valve lift, this is carefully calculated.***

valve guide for this style of seal also increases the retainer-to-seal clearance.

### *Retainer-to-Seal Clearance*

To check the clearance, slide a valve in and install the retainer and valve locks. Use an indicator to open the valve to the desired camshaft lift. Measure the distance between the retainer and the valve seal. This clearance needs to be at least 0.100 inch.

If the retainer hits the seal, it will be destroyed immediately. We provide little extra clearance here in case you want to install a larger camshaft or install a different rocker ratio. That way, the owner can rest assured that there will be enough clearance.

### *Valve Pocket*

Lastly, for heavy-hitting valve springs, the valve-spring pocket may need some machining to accept a larger-OD valve spring. When installing a double or a triple valve spring, the pocket will likely need to be machined. There is a limit as to what can be machined depth-wise out of the pocket.

There is water underneath this pocket. If more valve installed height is needed, a longer valve might be the better way to go.

## Selecting Valve Springs, Retainers, and Locks

In most cases, the camshaft size and type dictates the valve springs, retainers, and locks during the build. The various camshaft designs require different valve-spring pressures. The four different types of camshaft are hydraulic flat-tappet, solid flat-tappet, hydraulic roller, and solid roller.

Most camshaft manufacturers offer recommendations for the necessary valve-spring pressure. For stock hydraulic applications, a single spring with stock retainers and valve locks is all that is needed. For slightly larger camshafts, move to a double roller; move all the way to triple springs for solid-roller cams. As the performance goes up, stronger parts are needed.

The valvetrain pieces are very important. Think about the consequences if a valve is dropped. Most of the time, dropping a valve due to a retainer or a valve lock failure will destroy a whole engine. This is why we recommend staying with name-brand valves, spring, retainers, and locks.

As the spring pressure increases, more strain is placed on the valve. Stock valves for low spring pressure are available. Then, they step up to stainless valves and go on to severe-duty and titanium valves.

## Cylinder Head Assembly

Assembling cylinder heads sounds pretty easy, but there actually is a lot involved. Selecting the correct parts is only half of it. Setting up the valve-spring pressure correctly for the camshaft and selecting the correct valve seal are just as important.

### *Cleaning*

Whenever assembly is discussed, we will talk about cleaning. After all of the machine work has been completed, the cylinder heads need a good brushing and cleaning. Most shops have a separate jet washer for final washing. Our machine shop has an industrial-grade degreaser that works well for removing machining chips and oils.

All of the valve-guide holes should be brushed before washing. Then, a short 15-minute wash is adequate. With one final inspection of the heads, we can begin assembly.

A machine shop will begin to set up the valve-spring pressure by measuring the installed height. Most of the time, the camshaft manufacturer will recommend a desired spring pressure. After doing this for years, the shop will have a pretty good idea of where it likes to set up the springs.

It may seem like you can just throw the heads together at home with just a valve-spring compression tool, but there are precision tools that are needed. I recommend leaving this up to the machine shop if you are not a seasoned professional.

Coil bind and retainer-to-seal clearance are also important items during assembly. Options that are available to get spring pressure correct are the valve locks that are +0.050 inch and -0.050 inch. In addition, hardened valve-spring shims are available in different thicknesses.

When setting up a nonadjustable valvetrain, it is very important to have the valve stem height the same across the board. Otherwise, you may end up with an engine that has multiple-length pushrods to get the lifter preload correct. This is a little more forgiving when setting up for an adjustable valvetrain. Although, you will want to keep this as accurate as possible anyway. Once all the measuring has been figured out, it is time to assemble the heads.

*To press on the valve stem seal, put a little bit of assembly lube on the ID of the seal and carefully align the seal with the valve guide. Using a seal installer, lightly tap the seal into place. Always make sure that the spring did not get removed or damaged during installation. For the do-it-yourselfer, a socket that fits the seal will work well.*

*Once the valve-spring pressure is determined and the appropriate valve-spring shims are installed, it is time for final assembly. Using a valve-spring compressor, compress the spring and install the valve keepers.*

### Installing the Valves

When installing the valves into the valve guides, place a small amount of assembly lube on the valve stem. Next, install the valve stem seals. The stock application seals are a hard plastic material that will press over the valve stem. From the factory, the intake and exhaust had the same seal. When rebuilding the cylinder head, we always machine the valve guide down for a positive valve stem seal that presses onto the valve guide. Even on a stock rebuild, this is the best option.

The aftermarket seal is a steel band with Viton rubber that uses a small spring to hold tension to the valve stem. With a little bit of assembly lube on the ID of the seal, press it onto the guide. Be careful not to damage the rubber portion of the seal or the spring.

Now it is time to install the valve springs, retainers, and valve locks. Carefully install a valve spring and retainer over the valve. Using a valve-spring compressor, carefully compress the spring, being careful not to damage your valve-stem seal.

Once the spring is compressed, the valve locks (commonly called valve keepers) are installed. Slowly release the compressor, making sure the keepers stay in place. This will complete the cylinder heads; they are now ready for assembly onto the short-block.

## Rocker-Arm Options

Stock-application rocker arms are a 1.6:1 ratio for all AMC engines. Factory-stamped steel rockers are not adjustable, so the rocker arm nut is just torqued down. These rocker arms held up pretty well, considering that it was a stamped-steel rocker. For very mild builds, the stock rocker does just fine.

In the later years, the rocker arms changed to bridge rockers. This style of rocker arm used a bridge for each cylinder. The threads in the cylinder head were downsized to 5/16 inch. This setup was known to break bridges under stock applications—let alone a performance build.

Most engine builders convert these heads by machining out the rocker threads to 7/16 inch. There are many companies that offer roller-tip rocker arms as well as full roller rocker arms. A roller-tip rocker uses the same-style ball and fulcrum but has a roller tip that rides on the valve. This was considered a mild step up from a stock rocker arm.

The body usually is a stronger design, and the roller tip was claimed to be a horsepower gain. In some of the roller-tip rockers, we have seen some heat issues with the fulcrum.

If you are going to spend the money to update to a roller rocker, you may as well go all the way to a full roller. Remember that whether the camshaft is a hydraulic roller or not, the roller rocker arms are noisier than the stock-rocker design. Comp Cams uses the 1.6:1–ratio Ford rocker arm for AMC applications.

One of the longtime companies that has made AMC rocker arms is Harland Sharp. This is our rocker arm of choice for mild to race applications. Most full roller rocker arms have a problem clearing the stock AMC valve cover. The stock covers were very short so that the compressor of some air-conditioned cars cleared the top of the valve cover. Even the tall aftermarket valve covers had to make sure that the rockers cleared the covers. When a rocker arm is just barley hitting the cover, it sometimes sounds like something major is broke.

Jessel offers a custom shaft rocker-arm system for high RPM and valve-spring pressure applications. Without a doubt, the most reliable valvetrain in a race application is a rocker shaft assembly. When using the 440 Chrysler design AMC head from Indy Cylinder Head, there are more performance options for shaft rockers. Just remember that this cylinder head from Indy uses a true 440 Chrysler-designed header. Sometimes, finding the correct header to fit your car is not easy.

When using different rocker arms, always check the pushrod geometry. Aftermarket custom-length pushrods are usually available in every 0.050-inch lengths. In Chapter 10, pushrod geometry is covered in depth.

# INTAKE MANIFOLD

*The 1967–1969 intake part number was 448-6228 and the 1970 version was part number 448-8411. The intake here was available as a Group 19 performance item from performance dealerships.*

All production-made V-8 engines came with a cast-iron intake manifold that had either a 2-barrel or 4-barrel carburetor flange. Of course, the Group-19 specialty intakes were also available, such as the Edelbrock-designed cross-ram intake and the ever-popular R4B.

Just like all muscle cars, the intake manifold is one of the first items to be changed. The AMC engine has only two different intake-manifold bolt patterns. The only factory-designed gasket available is a valley-pan gasket to seal the intake manifolds to the heads. These were challenging to seal in the past.

Just like all engines, many different manufacturers jumped in the design process and produced various intake manifolds. Throughout the 1970s, many designs were produced for both dual-plane and single-plane intakes, along with the popular 4150 flange and the Dominator 4500 flange.

As the aftermarket intakes picked up, it didn't take long for manufacturers to offer a conventional two-piece intake gasket to eliminate the one-piece valley pan.

## Pre-1970 Intake Manifolds

The easy way to differentiate the early engines from the late engines is the exhaust port. Early heads have a rectangular exhaust port, and the later heads have a dogleg port. The early engines have a shorter deck height, and the center two bolt holes on the intake are different.

The Edelbrock cylinder heads come with both bolt patterns on the cylinder heads. That way, they only had to manufacture one part number that worked on the various years. The intakes are different and cannot be swapped around due to the different deck heights.

The older or newer heads can be drilled for the different intake bolt holes to make the heads work on either application. Most aftermarket intake gaskets come with both bolt patterns as well. Edelbrock offers a part number for an intake that will fit the early 1968 and 1969 engines.

## 1970-and-Newer Intake Manifolds

The 1970-and-newer intake manifolds are the most popular. All V-8 engines within this time span take the same intake manifold. Edelbrock has the most-popular aftermarket intake manifold. Buyers have a few choices, including an RPM performer. This intake has a more stock appearance and is a good choice when hood clearance is a problem. This is the only aftermarket intake that we know will fit the old snorkel air cleaner assembly.

***This is Edelbrock's RPM Performer AIR-Gap intake manifold. The divider between the intake runners classifies this intake as a dual plane, although this intake is much more advanced than the older dual-plane intakes. Allowing the airflow between the intake and the runners keeps the fuel charge cooler.***

***This single-plane intake was designed by Indy Cylinder Head. The open plenum allows the air-and-fuel mixture to directly flow to all the runners.***

## Dual Plane versus Single Plane

The single-plane intake manifold may seem very basic in that the plenum is completely open. In other words, there is no divider in the manifold. The open-plenum concept provides a direct flow of the fuel into the runners of the cylinder head. With this intake, it is possible to look into the carburetor flange and check the port alignment without anything restricting the view.

The dual-plane intake has separated runners that run above and below. One side of the runners goes to the left cylinder head and the other goes to the right cylinder head. With this design, the airflow has many corners to move around, which makes it harder to check the port alignment.

When both intake manifold designs are next to each other with the carburetor removed, it is easy to see the difference. However, actually understanding the differences and how each type of intake flows air and fuel is a different story. Just like when buying a carburetor, the intake manifold that is advertised to make more horsepower is not always the best choice.

### *Dual Plane*

The dual-plane intake manifold became the most commonly used intake on production-based vehicles. Over the years as engineering and technology progressed, the development of the single- and dual-plane intakes evolved.

As vehicles grew larger and were generally heavier, it was determined that low-end power and torque was needed to get the vehicle moving. This led to most production vehicles running the dual-plane intake due to the fact that it made more low-end power and torque. The powerband of these engines was generally lower, and that is where the dual-plane intake made most power and torque.

Due to the different hood clearance required on the AMC cars, this limited the height and design of the intake manifolds. The shorter the intake, the harder it was to make the air flow into the cylinder head runners. The taller intake allowed the runners to stand more upright, which allowed the airflow to have a more direct path to the valves.

The shorter and typically lower runners result in all the characteristics of the lower powerband. This technology has changed dramatically in the last decade. The development of the Edelbrock AIR-Gap intake manifold is a dual-plane manifold on steroids. This intake was designed as a dual-plane manifold but is about 2 inches taller in design, which creates a hood-interference problem in some models. It also flows numbers as well as the old single-plane manifold without giving up as much low-end torque.

When selecting an intake manifold for a street car, the dual-plane manifold more than likely will be the best choice. Most street-driven cars stay around the low- to mid-range

RPM levels. This is where a dual-plane intake shines. As we tell our customers, on the very low end, it is torque that accelerates the car rather than horsepower. There are some tricks that can be done with carburetor spacers to change the powerband a little.

The new AIR-Gap intake manifolds have a notch in the divider on the dual-plane intakes. A common modification in the past was to notch the divider about a 1/4 to 3/8 inch down for just about the full length. This slightly raised the powerband. The carburetor spacers also do about the same thing.

The taller the carburetor is spaced, the higher the powerband goes. Obviously, on a mild build these changes are relatively small. This topic can get very detailed and scientific when it comes to runner length and carburetor spacers.

### *Single Plane*

The single-plane intake manifold is simple in design. When looking straight down into the carburetor mounting pad, it just looks like it would flow more air. Why wouldn't it make more power? It looks like a big open hole with a wide-open shot to all of the cylinder head runners.

Set the intake manifold on the heads and look straight down the runners to see how the ports align. You can even see the valves. This is all good, but remember that this design takes power away from the low end and brings the powerband up higher.

The direct path of the intake runners is what makes a high-RPM engine work well. Add in a carburetor spacer, and this will only add to the high-RPM power.

Engineers figured out that the single-plane intake made more horsepower and torque higher up in the RPM range. The single-plane intake manifold gave up some low-end torque but raised the powerband. This style of intake works well on lighter cars, such as the S/C Scramblers and AMXs. The better the cylinder heads flowed, the more power the single-plane intake would make.

When looking at the design of the short-runner, dual-plane intake, the air and fuel have to round corners before making it to the cylinder head, which can only rob power. The design of the single-plane intake has one purpose: deliver air and fuel in the most direct path possible. This is where a sheet-metal intake came in for extreme high-RPM horsepower.

The key to this design is the amount of the intake valve that is visible. The more of the back side of the intake valve that you can see from the carburetor flange, the better it is.

## Hood Clearance

When selecting an intake manifold, hood clearance is one of the most important items to consider, especially if you are not willing to modify the hood. If this is the case, the intake options are limited, and it will also dictate the engine build.

There is no reason to build a high-RPM screaming engine if the intake manifold has to be limited. If the goal is to take it to the drag strip once or twice a year, then you are mainly building a street car. You will be happier with a dual-plane intake.

If the build is trying to look as stock as possible, we recommend a stock cast-iron intake manifold. There are some port-matching tricks to help the stock intake flow a little better.

For clearance measurements, the best way is to measure the stock intake height and then double-check that measurement against an Edelbrock book because Edelbrock offers measurements for all its intake manifolds.

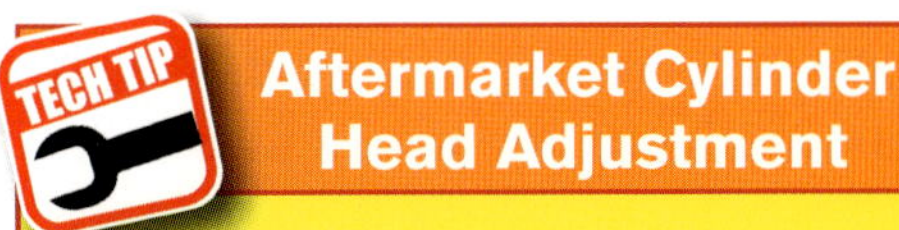


**Aftermarket Cylinder Head Adjustment**

We have taken one of Edelbrock's intakes and milled the top of the carburetor mounting flange down to fit a particular vehicle. Just make sure that the carburetor mounting holes are tapped deep enough. Another trick is to mill off the Edelbrock name on the intake manifold and paint it to appear like a factory manifold. ■

## Aftermarket Intake Manifold Options

All companies that manufacture aftermarket manifolds offer technical support for selecting the best manifold. They almost always list the desired RPM level of the intake manifold. This is one of the most important factors.

If a camshaft is designed to make power from 2,000 to 6,500 rpm, do not select an intake that advertises an RPM level of 3,200 to 8,000. If there is one way to kill power, this will do it. The engine builder or machine shop is a good place to get advice on an intake manifold choice. Otherwise, give these aftermarket companies a call, but have as much information available as you can.

### *Edelbrock Performer*

The industry-standard intake manifold that has been around for a long time is the Edelbrock Performer. This is a low-RPM performance dual-plane intake manifold. We use this intake as a stock replacement, although it flows better than the cast-iron intake.

For the newer Jeeps that still had the AMC V-8 engines in them, this intake was advertised as an E.O. legal replacement intake. Besides performance reasons, this intake also does a great job of taking a few pounds off the engine and helps dissipate heat better than its cast-iron counterpart.

#### Edelbrock Performer RPM

One of our favorites for AMC builds is the Performer RPM intake. This intake still is a dual-plane design, which makes it a good street-driven choice.

The technology of this intake does a much better job at a higher RPM than the stock dual-plane intake. The intake runners are designed with a clearer path to the cylinder head than the other dual-plane intakes.

This intake provides the best of both worlds. It is one of those intakes that progressed as the engineers studied the effects of more direct-path runners. The intake manifold is higher than the stock unit by only 3/4 inch, but the benefits of this intake over the normal performer are significant. Remember when I wrote that we'd trim the carburetor flange to keep hood clearance? This is the intake manifold that we'd commonly cut down.

#### Edelbrock AIR-Gap

The most newly designed intake manifold on the market is the AIR-Gap intake. Several manufacturers are making slightly different versions of this manifold. The main concept is to allow air to flow between the intake runners and the carburetor-mounting flange. This helps keep the heat out of the intake manifold and the carburetor. If the vehicle has had fuel vapor lock in the summer months, this intake helps considerably with that issue.

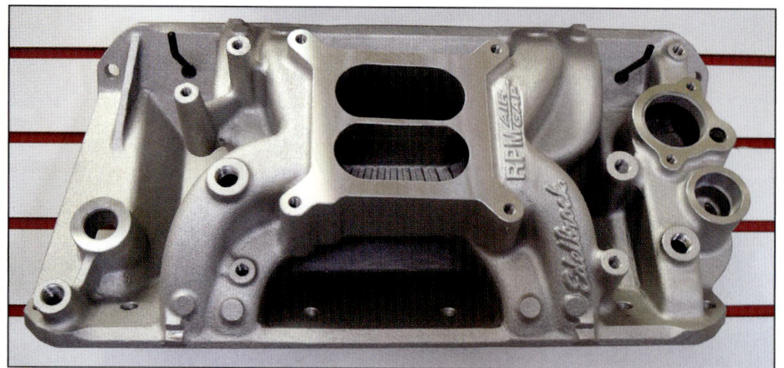


*Edelbrock's AIR-Gap is probably known as the best all-around intake available for street/strip applications. This intake is a dual-plane design that produces power not far from the open-plenum designs.*

This intake manifold was one of the first dual-plane intakes to separate the runners from the manifold. We have seen this intake add 20 to 30 hp on our chassis dyno when compared to a stock intake. This intake not only shines on the lower end with great torque numbers but also performs as well as some single-plane intakes on various combinations. The only problem with this intake is its height. Many times we would love to run this intake, but it poses a hood-clearance problem on many AMC cars.

*Edelbrock's Torker was one of the first intakes released. It has an open-plenum design but a short intake that allowed for hood clearance. Notice that the carburetor sits just slightly turned with this intake.*

#### Edelbrock Torker

The Edelbrock Torker intake manifold was an early design single-plane intake that was kept short to not interfere with hood clearance. This intake was one of the first designed open-plenum intakes. This intake was a favorite among AMC owners because it fit under just about all AMC hood packages. The carburetor-mounting surface set the carburetor at a slight angle on the intake manifold. This intake was only available with a 4150 flange.

#### Edelbrock Victor Jr. 4150

The Edelbrock Victor Jr. intake manifold was the company's first designed 4150 single-plane intake manifold. The Victor Jr. was mainly designed as a higher-RPM intake that was best suited for racing applications, especially drag racing, where higher RPM were needed.

Although this intake was designed mainly for racing, quite a few of these are running around on the street. This intake made far-better horsepower numbers than any dual-plane intake at the time.

Depending on the camshaft and cylinder heads, the AIR-Gap gives this intake a run for its money. If an engine is designed with a higher RPM solid-roller camshaft and some good-flowing cylinder heads, there is no doubt that the Victor Jr. will make more power than the other intakes, especially at higher RPM.

This intake sits a lot higher than the stock intake and will make hood-clearance issues, just like the other tall intakes. We have used this intake on some mechanical fuel-injection units such as the Rons fuel injection. The intake is well suited to drill and tap for injectors. This is also a common intake that we use for plate-style nitrous oxide systems.

***Baffle Pan***

Edelbrock does not reproduce the steel baffle pan on the underside of the intake. The manifolds are set up to use them, and they have the rivet holes already drilled.

Usually, it is not a problem to remove this baffle tray from the old stock intake manifold and reuse it. The problem arises only when you don't have a stock intake. We usually do not use the whole tray anyway. We remove only the portion of the baffle that covers the PVC hole.

Carefully cut this piece off the tray and install it onto the new Edelbrock intake. This is important only if using a PCV valve in the stock location. If you do not have a baffle, the PCV will suck oil right out of the engine. On race engines, it is possible to install a freeze plug in this hole instead of running the PCV. When using this setup, we do not use the stock valley tray gasket. Use either Fel-Pro or the Mr. Gasket individual intake gasket.

***Indy Cylinder Head***

Other aftermarket intakes that are available include those from Indy Cylinder Head. When using its race head, which was designed after the 440 Chrysler, Indy has its own intake that must be used in tandem. Indy Cylinder Head also offers an intake manifold designed for its AMC dogleg-exhaust-port head. Some of the older intakes are the nostalgia offset dual 4-barrel intakes. These intakes don't make the most power, but they are cool looking.

Factory and most aftermarket intakes have an oil-fill tube in the front. This tube presses into the manifold and is topped off with a breather cap. This was the only form of a breather designed on an AMC engine. The valve covers did not have any oil-fill or breather ports on them. For a stock engine, this single breather and a PCV was adequate.

Once you start building a performance engine with more compression, the crankcase pressure needs a place to escape. The single oil-fill tube breather is not enough. If a breather of some sort is not added, oil leaks will develop.

## Intake-Port Alignment

For any engine build, intake-port alignment is very important. Most aftermarket intakes need to be milled to align the bolt holes and the runners. They purposely make these intakes tall so that they can be surfaced to fit. It goes back to the concept that you can't add material, but you can always remove it.

When rebuilding an engine, surfacing the deck and the cylinder heads changes the intake height. Once the heads are installed, we

*Aftermarket intakes do not come with this stock valley pan. This one was removed from a stock intake. If using the stock PCV port on the aftermarket intake, cut this piece off of the stock tray to reinstall it over the PCV opening.*

*Most aftermarket intake manifolds need to be surfaced in to align the bolt holes and the intake runner.*

secure the intake gaskets to the cylinder head using some painter's tape. Be careful not to cover up the runners so the runner alignment can be inspected. Then, set the intake manifold onto the engine.

The first thing to do is center the intake on the bolt holes. Inspect the bolt holes and maybe try to install a bolt into both sides. It is common that only half of the bolt hole will be visible on each side.

Once this is determined, the machine shop will help you figure out what needs to be surfaced to align the bolt holes. At this time, inspect the runner alignment, even though the intake needs to be milled to bolt it up. Most of the time, the runners align when the bolt holes are aligned. There are times that the runners might look good, but the bolt holes are off just enough to make it hard to bolt on. In this case, open the intake bolt holes slightly.

Remember that it is better to surface the intake twice rather than have the machine shop remove too much.

A machine shop usually will remove some material from both ends of the intake. Before installation, set the intake back on and measure the gap on both ends. This will help determine how big of a bead of silicone will be needed when installing the intake.

One time we had to run a double intake gasket to save an original factory aluminum intake. It was definitely not something that we like to do, but it was our only option in that scenario. If you are doing some gasket matching on the intake to the cylinder head, always make sure that the cylinder head is larger than the intake opening. One of the worst things is for incoming airflow to hit the cylinder head.

## Intake-Manifold Gasket

As was mentioned previously, all AMC V-8 engines used a thin steel valley-pan gasket. The Fel-Pro valley pan gasket (part number MS96011) fits both of the bolt patterns. The center four-bolt holes are slotted on the gasket for both applications.

These are some of the more challenging gaskets to install. They need to be slightly formed and test fitted before gluing. Once the gasket is preformed, install Permatex high tack on both sides. The hard part is getting this gasket to stay in place while installing the manifold. I have seen some engine builders use 3M weatherstrip adhesive to glue the intake down to the heads. The other choices for intake gaskets are the non-valley-pan style.

### *Mr. Gasket*

Mr. Gasket offers two different intake gaskets. The only difference is the material from which they are made.

Just like the valley pan, these gaskets have the center bolt holes slotted to fit both 1968–1969 and 1970-and-up intakes. When using these gaskets, apply some RTV around the water ports, but do not use any around the intake runners. The ends do not use the rubber end seals; most engine builders do not use these because they have a tendency to squeeze out.

When test fitting the intake, measure the gap on both ends. This will be the size of the silicone bead that is needed. Always go a little bigger than measured so as to not to leave an air gap and have oil leaks.

*Look closely at this valley pan to see how easy it is for these to fail if they are not sealed with brush tack.*

*Here are Mr. Gasket intake gaskets 800G and the Ultra Seal 5835. The only difference is the material.*

## Carburetors

There are three different bolt patterns that are available for carburetors: the Holley 4150, Carter 4150, and Holley Dominator 4500.

### *Holley 4150*

Most aftermarket manifolds are designed with what is called the standard Holley 4150 flange. This has also been called square bore. There is no doubt that the Holley 4150 flange carburetor is the most popular aftermarket carburetor that is available. The Carter AFB carburetor (which the Edelbrock carburetor is designed after) will also bolt up to the 4150 flange.

### *Carter 4150*

Only the very early Carter carburetors have a smaller bolt pattern. Every once in a while, we will get one of these intakes in, and it is easily noticeable that the flange is smaller. Many of the intake manifolds made with the 4150 bolt pattern also will be double drilled with both bolt patterns on them.

### *Holley Dominator 4500*

The only other popular carburetor bolt pattern that is available is the Holley Dominator 4500. This carburetor is a purpose-built high-horsepower race car–orientated carburetor. This style of intake manifold has a huge, open plenum that is designed to flow huge air numbers at a high RPM.

The 4500 carburetor was never used on a factory AMC engine or actually on any production-based engine made. Although this carburetor is designed purely for race applications, occasionally one can be seen on a street car. When it comes to hot rodding, there are no rules.

*This Quick Fuel carburetor is by far the most popular aftermarket carburetor manufactured. This carburetor is commonly referred to have a 4150 flange. The 4150-style carburetor covers most street and race applications up to about 800 hp. Although, you will see specially designed 4150 carburetors handle much more than 800 hp, it just takes a lot of modifications.*

*This is the popular 4150 flange pattern. It has two different bolt patterns, which allow the Carter or Edelbrock carburetors to bolt up along with the popular Holley versions.*

*The Dominator (commonly referred to as the 4500 carburetor) was designed purely for all-out competition engines. Comparing the overall size of this carburetor idicates how much fuel this carburetor can deliver. When the design of the Dominator carburetor came out, a whole new line of intake manifolds was needed to fit this new carburetor flange.*

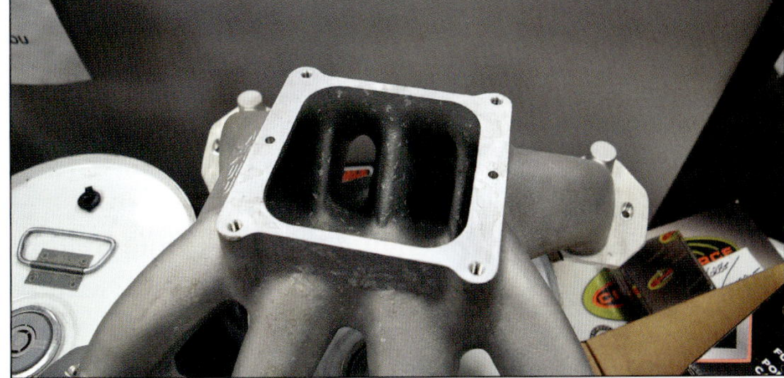

*Notice the size of the opening on this Dominator intake manifold. The 4500 flange was truly only designed for making a large amount of horsepower. The design of the open plenum being this large supports horsepower being made at much higher RPM levels than the 4150 could ever produce.*

# Engine Assembly

*The engine block is final washed and installed on an engine stand. After final prep, it will be ready to start assembly.*

Our block has been prepped with camshaft bearings, oil plugs, and freeze plugs, which have been discussed in earlier chapters. Now, it's time to install the engine on an engine stand for assembly. If doing this assembly yourself, it is important to do this in a clean environment away from dirt and wind.

When not assembling the engine, keep a clean bag over it at all times. Remember that when using engine assembly lube, dirt and debris will attach itself quickly. We have a rule that if you need to blow off parts or use compressed air, do so in a different room.

## Assembly Preparation

Once the engine is secure in a clean environment, wipe out the cylinders one more time. It is important to be organized during assembly. It can be easy to miss items if you are not organized.

To get ready further, the crankshaft needs to be washed and brushed really well. Run a series of small engine brushes through all of the crankshaft oil passages. Use mineral spirits or brake cleaner while brushing.

After we are sure that the oil passages are cleaned, blow air through all the holes until they are dry. Always make sure that both the harmonic balancer and the flywheel threads are clean. After the crankshaft is installed, you do not want to be repairing any threads.

Set up a clean table and lay out the pistons and rod assemblies. Always set rod assemblies out in numerical order; this will help prevent assembly mistakes. Gather the new piston rings and lay them out in groups (the top ring, second ring, and oil rings). Other items that are needed to assemble the short-block are the main and rod bearings, camshaft, and timing chain.

### *Assembly Lube*

At this time, all items need to be clean and blown dry. Assembly will be one of the most important things to guarantee a long-lasting build. Years ago, we used the same assembly lube on the whole engine. Today's technology has taken us to different types of assembly lube for each step.

If running a flat-tappet camshaft, a form of camshaft assembly lube is needed. Driven has a great flat-tappet assembly lube. To install the crankshaft and the roller camshafts, we use Michigan 77 assembly lube. Other lube that is needed includes ARP bolt lube and liquid Teflon. When it comes to Loctite, we use the service-removable blue kind on some bolts.

Now that everything is laid out, you are ready to begin the assembly. Assembling an engine takes great patience, and with great planning, you can concentrate on the assembly.

## Camshaft Installation

Everyone will assemble an engine in a different order. There probably is no wrong order in which to assemble an engine, but we will explain the benefits to following our order. The camshaft is the first item to be installed.

A flat-tappet camshaft should be lubed with Driven camshaft paste. If installing a roller camshaft, use either the lube that is supplied or Clevite 77 assembly lube. Bearing Guard was developed by Clevite 77 and is now more commonly known as Mahle Clevite. What better company to produce an engine lubricant than a bearing company?

*Carefully install the camshaft with assembly lube. Install the camshaft slowly so that the camshaft bearings are not scratched.*

*Most camshaft manufacturers include lubricant to install on the camshaft during assembly. There are different lubricants for various styles of camshafts and mechanical moving parts. As long as you use the proper lubricant, you will be okay. We assemble many different engines, so we purchase the Driven assembly lube in bulk. It also comes in smaller tubes for single engine assembly.*

*There are many great companies that make engine bearings and roller-camshaft lubricants. We settled in on using Michigan 77 Bearing Guard. This product is available in bulk for engine builders and in smaller bottles also. This lubricant works well on roller camshafts, lifters, pushrods, engine bearings, and rocker arms.*

### *Camshaft Test Fit*

Most machine shops will test fit a camshaft after the camshaft bearings have been installed. Different camshafts vary in size. If the camshaft was not tested, make sure that it slides in very easily and turns with little-to-no resistance. If the camshaft is tight and difficult to spin, this must be addressed now. This is the reason that the camshaft is the first item to install.

Recently, we have had to install the camshaft in the crankshaft grinder and grind 0.00 inch from it. Sometimes there may be just one bearing that is tight. To determine the problem, turn the camshaft, even if a wrench is needed to turn it. This will leave marks on the tight bearings. Remove the camshaft and determine the tight spots. Sometimes, if a camshaft bearing is installed crooked, it can create a tight spot.

Let's assume that the machine shop installed them properly. If you have just one tight spot on one bearing, install a used camshaft and strike a brass drift on the camshaft right beside the tight spot. This might take a couple of tries, but if it is just a little tight, this usually will work. Now, if you have tight spots on all of the bearings, make a trip back to the machine shop to have it check the tight spot with all of the correct tools. At this time, when the camshaft turns freely, you can move on to the next step.

### *Camshaft Thrust Plate*

Install the camshaft thrust plate at this time. A camshaft thrust plate

*Once the camshaft is installed, install the camshaft thrust plate. Note that a camshaft thrust plate is only used on roller camshafts.*

*With the main bearings installed, make sure that the oil holes are aligned one more time. Then, add assembly lube to the main bearings. Notice that the thrust bearing is located in the center main.*

only needs to be used when using a roller camshaft.

## Crankshaft Installation with Bearing Check

The most important part of installing the crankshaft is to make sure that the bearing clearances are correct. Most likely, the machine shop has checked this already. When bringing an engine block into the machine shop, ask the shop to check for you.

If they are align honing the main housing bore and grinding the crankshaft, the shop can put the bearing clearances exactly where they need to be. The first step is to install the upper main bearings. The most common mistake is installing the thrust bearing on the wrong main. An AMC thrust bearing is on the center main as opposed to most engines (especially Chevrolets), which have the thrust bearing on the rear main.

When installing the upper bearings, make sure that the oil holes line up. Install the upper half of the rear-main seal. Some builders stagger the split on the rear-main seal, and some leave it on the parting line.

When installing the rear-main seal, the open part of the lip must face the inside of the engine. Picture how this seal works: the crankcase pressure puts pressure on the lip seal and holds it against the crankshaft. If this seal is installed backward, it will have a huge oil leak.

*To check the main bearing clearance, the main bearings are installed in the block and caps. After torquing the main bearing caps, set up the dial bore gauge to the crankshaft size. This will determine the bearing clearance. For checking bearing clearances at home, the old-fashioned plastic gauge method works just fine.*

*Don't be afraid to grab a buddy for some help to set the crankshaft in the block. It is extremely important that the crankshaft is not nicked during assembly.*

#### *Placing the Crankshaft*

Generously place some assembly lube onto the upper bearings. It is now time to install the crankshaft. Grab a buddy and have him or her help you install the crankshaft. With each of you grabbing an end of the crankshaft, slowly lower it into the engine block. Once the crankshaft is sitting in the block, rotate it a half of a turn. You will notice that the assembly lube coated the crankshaft.

Install the other half of the rear-main seal into the cap. Using anerobic sealer, lay a thin line from the parting line of the rear-main seal to the outside of the main cap. This prevents oil from following the parting line and leaking. All the main caps will be numbered.

#### *Installing Bearing Caps*

Carefully install the lower bearings in the main caps. When installing the caps from front to back, all bearing notches should be aligned. All main caps must go into their correct locations and direction.

***With the main caps snugged up, install a dial indicator on the front of the crankshaft to check end play. Once the indicator is installed, lightly press the crankshaft forward and backward, reading the indicator.***

When installing the main bolts or studs, use ARP moly paste on the threads and on the heads of the bolts. This is a friction preventer for torquing. Once all of the caps are installed, run the bolts or nuts down just snug. Now, check the thrust clearance.

#### *Thrust Clearance*

Placing an indicator on the front of the crankshaft, check the front-to-back movement of the crankshaft. A stock engine's crankshaft movement of 0.004–0.007 inch will work. On a race engine, especially one with a transmission brake, we will run as much as 0.010 inch. For recommendations on the proper clearances, ask the engine machine shop.

To set the thrust, use a large, flat-blade screwdriver and move the crankshaft forward. Loosen the middle thrust cap and, using a rubber dead blow hammer, hit the front snout of the crankshaft. This action will square up the thrust. Tighten the main bolts or nuts and recheck the thrust clearance.

When checking the thrust, if you pry hard enough, the crank will move more. The correct thrust is the amount the crankshaft moves without holding pressure on the crankshaft. After the proper thrust is achieved, final torque the main caps. Once torqued, grab the snout of the crankshaft and spin it. This is one final check to make sure that the crankshaft spins with little to no effort.

### Piston and Rod Installation

Before installing the piston rings on the pistons, check the piston-ring end gap. If using stock replacement piston rings, the ring end gap will be good most of the time. All piston-ring manufacturers supply instructions for ring end gap.

***To check the piston-ring end gap, install the rings into each cylinder bore. The bores probably are machined to the same size, but we still install each piston ring into each bore.***

***Using a squaring device, make sure that each ring is perfectly square in the bore. It's customary to check the ring end gap about halfway down in the bore.***

Years ago, there were pretty standard ring gaps. Today, each manufacturer has different ideas on piston-ring gaps. Normally, the instructions contain recommendations for ring gaps for stock, race, and boosted applications. Remember that looser ring gaps won't be noticed, but if the ring gap is too tight, bad

***Most machine shops have a nice electric piston ring filer, which helps greatly in speeding this process up. They do make some very economical manual ring filers for the do-it-yourselfer. As long as you take your time, these work just fine.***

***Once the piston ring is squared up, use feeler gauges to check the ring clearance.***

***Experienced engine builders install piston rings by hand. Beginners should use piston ring installation pliers. The top and second rings are specific to their location. Always install the rings with the dot facing up.***

things can happen.

Always deburr the piston rings after gapping them. Gapping rings takes some specialized equipment. Most hobbyists do not have the correct tools to gap rings. If this is the case, most machine shops will do this for you.

*Piston Ring Installation*

Once the rings are gapped, install them with a ring expander. If you are not experienced at installing piston rings, it is very easy to break a ring, especially if installing them by hand. The instructions also explain which ring is the top ring and which one is the second from top.

Most piston-ring manufacturers mark the tops of the rings with a dot. This dot should always face up. If installed wrong, it is almost guaranteed to lose ring seal and use oil. Oil rings are usually installed first, being careful not to overlap the oil rings or the separator. With all of the piston rings installed, begin installing the piston/rod assemblies.

*Connecting Rod Bearing Installation*

Install all the connecting rod bearings into the cap and rods on the bench. Make sure that all of the bearing tangs sit in the rods correctly. Add assembly lube on all the rod journals on the crankshaft. You are now ready to install the number-1 rod.

The number-1 rod is the driver-side front cylinder. Bearing notches face the pan rails, and stock pistons are marked "front" or have arrows on them pointing to the front of the engine. Performance race pistons are not normally marked with

***Install the connecting rod bearings in the rod cap and connecting rod. Make sure that the bearing notches are always lined up. Put a medium coat of assembly lube on the bearings before installation.***

fronts. However, they will have intake and exhaust pockets on them.

Using break-in oil, lube the cylinder wall generously. Install some assembly lube on the rod journal, making sure to cover the entire journal. Install connecting-rod boots on the bolts, these are available at most machine shops. This prevents you from accidently nicking the crankshaft.

#### *Piston Installation*

Using a piston-ring compressor, install the piston into the cylinder. When installing, move the piston-ring end gaps so that they do not align. Lightly tap the piston into the bore. Once in the bore, guide the connecting rod over the rod journal.

This step is critical so that you do not nick the rod journal. This is why rod boot protectors should always be used. Most seasoned engine builders do not use rod boots, but they have been doing this for years. Nearly all aftermarket connecting rods have cap screws that screw directly into the connecting rod. In these applications, no boots can be used.

If you happen to nick a rod journal, take the necessary steps to fix it. Yes, most of the time, you will have to remove the crank from the block, but this could have catastrophic results if you don't.

#### *Rod Cap Installation*

Install the correct-numbered rod cap onto the connecting rod. Always make sure that the bearing tangs in the rods are aligned. The two most important items to remember here that are *no* rod caps are interchange-

***With the ring compressor held tight, lightly tap in the piston with a rubber hammer. While tapping in the piston, align the connecting rod with the rod journal.***

***Finish tapping the piston until the connecting rod is sitting against the connecting-rod journal.***

***Install the piston into the bore with the bearing notches facing the pan rail. Space the piston rings as such so that the ring end gaps do not align with each other.***

***One of the most important items is to make sure that the correct rod bearing cap always stays with the correct connecting rod. We keep each rod with its correct cap and even have them numbered with the cylinder number. During assembly, all bearing notches face the oil pan rails.***

able and bearing tangs *must* always align.

Install the rod nuts or bolts with engine oil or moly lube and just snug them. Install the lube both on the threads and on the head of the nut or bolt. Follow these steps to install the other seven piston and rod assemblies.

#### Rod End Play

Before you finish torquing the connecting rods, check the rod end play. On each of the rod journals, both connecting rods should move side to side. As long as you have clearance, you will be okay (0.007–0.015 inch is a good number for which to aim).

If using factory rod bolts, always use the factory torque value. If using aftermarket ARP bolts or aftermarket connecting rods, always follow the manufacturer's torque specifications and lube requirements. You will notice that the torque specifications are different for using motor oil than using a moly paste. This is because there is less friction when using moly paste. A torque wrench works off of friction, and when it reaches a certain amount of friction, it clicks.

If you assembled the bolts without any lube, it would build friction and torque prematurely. When it comes to an all-out race engine, most engine builders use a stretch gauge on the rod bolts or a torque angle method.

Set up the torque wrench for 50 percent of the torque value and run through all the rod bolts. Once this step is complete, set the torque wrench to the final value and run through them again. Always do the final torque in one sweeping motion. When completed, run through them one more time and make sure that none were missed.

## Camshaft Timing and Degreeing

Now that the camshaft and crankshaft are installed, install the timing chain and degree in the camshaft if needed. A question that we receive regularly is, "Do I have to degree in my camshaft?" If you are building a high-performance engine, there is no question, we recommend degreeing in the camshaft.

Degreeing in the camshaft means synchronizing the camshaft's position with the crankshaft and valve opening and closing sequences. A few degrees of misalignment can affect the engine's performance and operation dramatically.

There are many items that have to be manufactured properly besides the camshaft for the position of the camshaft to come in line. All manufacturers have tolerances to stay within, but just like bearing clearance, if everything was machined on the low end of the tolerances, you would have what we call a tolerance stacking up. When degreeing in a camshaft, you are relying on the timing chain, sprockets, camshaft, crankshaft, and keyways to all be in the correct location. This is why it is beneficial to degree in the camshaft.

We still degree in every camshaft at the shop. We very rarely to never see a camshaft ground wrong, but with timing chains, we have found that the cheaper the timing chain set, the more we have found them to be off. Usually if they are off, it is only a degree in either direction. If you are new to this but want to give it a try, we'll walk through the degreeing process together.

#### Degreeing the Camshaft

Today, nearly all camshafts are ground with the intake lobe ground 4 degrees advanced. If your camshaft card says it has 110 lobe centers, the intake lobe will usually come in at 106. This is pretty standard. If the engine used a camshaft thrust plate for a roller camshaft, make sure that it is installed at this time. Before we begin, let's go over the camshaft/distributor gear-oil system that we talked about in Chapter 6.

As previously stated, AMC V-8 engines have a one-of-a-kind oil system that requires attention. All V-8 engines supply oil to the distributor gear mounted on the front of the camshaft and to the distributor gear itself through oil holes, grooves, and chamfers to get there. Because of this, these engines need careful and precise preparation to positively provide adequate oil flow.

There are many key areas to watch, and we'll point out the most important of them for you. This discussion applies to all AMC V-8 engines from 1967 and on: 290-, 304-, 343-, 360-, 390-, and 401-ci engines.

#### Camshaft Oil Feed Location

Now that we are at the final engine assembly, the first item to make sure of is to check that the front camshaft bearing was installed properly. Make sure that the oil feed hole is aligned with the oil hole in the camshaft bore to get the best oiling. This oil hole guarantees the proper amount of oil flow to the camshaft's front journal groove. When the oil holes are aligned properly, this allows the proper amount of oil to get there while the camshaft is making its full rotation.

We have seen engines come in with anywhere between 30 percent to 50 percent of this oil hole being blocked. This is enough to cause inadequate oil supply and for gears to be destroyed.

Let's discuss how the oil flows from the camshaft through the timing gear. The camshaft bearing feeds the hole in the camshaft journal. The camshaft has an oil feed hole that goes through the front main journal and exits the front of the camshaft. This oil feed hole has to align with a chamfer on the back side of the camshaft gear.

If this oil hole does not align with the chamfer, grind a small groove to allow the oil to feed the chamfer. This chamfer then feeds the ID groove in the timing gear. This is one of the most important items to check because without oil properly feeding the distributor gear, it will not last minutes.

Once the oil is feeding the camshaft gear correctly, follow it the rest of the way to the distributor gear. The timing gear has a groove that runs the entire length of the ID of the gear. The oil will follow the chamfer

On the front of the camshaft, there is an oil hole bored in the camshaft bearing journal. This hole will come out the face of the journal. The camshaft timing sprocket has a large chamfer on the rear of the gear. The oil will feed from the front camshaft bearing through the front hole to the chamfer and groove on the ID of the timing gear.

Looking at the back side of the camshaft timing sprocket, make sure that this groove lines up with the hole in the front of the camshaft. If the groove is not lined up, the oil will not transfer through, so you may have to grind a small groove to act as a path for the oil. This groove must align with the hole in the camshaft. We had to hand grind this gear to align the oil hole.

The grooves on the front of the camshaft sprocket are designed to feed a small amount of oil to the timing chain and the fuel pump eccentric. This is something to look for because not all timing manufacturers were putting these grooves into their timing gears.

From the timing sprocket, the oil continues on through the passage in the fuel pump eccentric adjacent to the keyway and then to the distributor drive gear.

*Flipping the fuel pump eccentric around, align the keyway and install the eccentric.*

*EngineQuest manufactures a gear kit. However, it is not always in stock.*

*When installing the timing cover during final assembly, do not overlook the installation of the dowel pins in the block. These ensure proper cover alignment.*

that you already made sure is correct, and now it will follow the ID groove. This groove is on the opposite side of the camshaft keyway.

Most aftermarket timing gears also have oil grooves that oil the timing chain and the fuel pump eccentric. Not all gears have this option, so always check the gear. The oil follows through the fuel pump eccentric all the way to the distributor drive gear. The critical oil spot is the distributor drive gear, and if this does not get proper oil feed, all of the teeth will wear off the gear. The drive gear will have a series of very small oil feed holes drilled between the teeth.

It is very important that these oil holes are not obstructed in any way. I have seen aftermarket gears with the oil holes drilled in the wrong location and not delivering enough oil.

#### *Camshaft Bolt and Washer*

The camshaft bolt and washer are unique, and we do not recommend just grabbing any old bolt and washer. The washer serves a purpose of sealing the oil flow off the front. If the incorrect washer is used, it will not seal the oil flow. Using the wrong washer could also prevent the distributor drive gear from oiling properly. If you do not have oil pressure at the gear, it will not oil properly.

We use a camshaft thrust plate when using a roller camshaft, but back in the day, we saw people using a longer bolt with some spacers or washers built up so that the head of the bolts acted as a camshaft bottom. This bolt would be polished smooth and would rub ever so slightly on the front cover. If done correctly, this worked fine, but we evolved to a camshaft thrust plate.

I mentioned that the AMC oil system is unlike any other. I guarantee that many engine builders do not understand the whole idea of how the front oil feed system works.

### Distributor

With the distributor completely seated without the gasket in the oil pump shaft and the pump gear fully seated in its housing, check to see if the distributor flange is seated against the top of the cover or if there is a gap. The distributor should bottom out in the front cover with no gasket when the oil pump is installed.

If the distributor does not bottom on the cover, there could be a timing cover problem or an oil pump shaft groove depth issue. It could be that the radius on the bottom of the oil pump groove is too large, which can be cleaned with a file to achieve the proper fitment.

Those who have assembled a Chevrolet engine have it easy. MSD makes distributors with adjustable collars for situations where they have incorrect gear mesh. For AMC, we have to do things the old-fashioned way.

### Front Cover

There are some aftermarket front covers being reproduced that also contribute to distributor gear failure. Before final assembly of the engine, test fit the distributor, oil pump gear, and cover.

*Dowel Pins for Front Cover*

The dowel pins on the front of the engine block are used to locate the position of the front cover, which houses the oil pump and distributor. Inspect these dowel pins and make sure that they are there and in good shape.

*Test Fit the Cover*

To test fit the front cover, install it with just a couple bolts and a gasket. Using the distributor, make sure that it slides in and locates the oil pump shaft without any misalignment.

## Crankshaft Gear

First, install the crankshaft gear on the crankshaft. A hollow tube that fits nicely on the gear with a large washer welded on the end works well for installing the timing gear. That way, the gear will be installed squarely. I have actually witnessed people splitting the crankshaft gear by installing it crooked on the keyway.

TECH TIP

### Oil System Test

After the engine is final assembled, run a quick test to ensure that the oil system is oiling the distributor gears properly. Using an oil pump primer in a drill (we made our primer out of a junk distributor), install it into the oil pump shaft as you prime the oil system and rotate the engine. You should see a decent about of oil coming out of the distributor gear. Once we have verified this, we are ready to continue. It may seem like a lot of extra work, and it is. This is one of the many reasons that it costs more to build an AMC engine than it does for other manufacturers. We cover dropping in the distributor later in this chapter, but we will also install some camshaft break-in lube on the gears. ■

***The first step is to install the crankshaft gear on the crankshaft. To install the timing gear, a hollow tube that fits nicely on the gear with a large washer welded on the end works well. That way, the gear will be installed squarely.***

Make sure that the gear is seated all the way against the chamfer. On most timing sets, there are three options for installing the gear: straight up, 4 degrees advanced, and 4 degrees retarded. I recommend for it to be installed straight up on a stock engine.

***Mount the degree wheel on the end of the crankshaft and rotate the engine to approximate TDC. Mount the pointer and line it up at zero on the degree wheel.***

Once again, follow the instructions, but the "O" marked keyway is the one on which you install it. Turn the crankshaft so that the "O" on the tooth is at 12 o'clock. The number-one mistake is to align the keyway at 12 o'clock. Do not align the keyway; instead, use the "O" dot on the tooth.

Install the chain and the camshaft gear on the engine while aligning the camshaft dot at 6 o'clock. Once complete, install the camshaft bolt, fuel pump eccentric, and distributor camshaft gear.

If you are running an electric fuel pump, you may ask, "Can I remove the fuel pump eccentric?" Yes, you could, but in its place, you need to machine a spacer so that the distributor gear bolts on the front in the exact correct location. We find it is easier to just install the eccentric, but it does not matter that you don't use it.

*Degreeing in the Camshaft*

The first step to degreeing in the camshaft is to mount the degree wheel to the front of the crankshaft. This time, do this with the cylinder heads off.

***Most likely, you will be degreeing in the camshaft before the cylinder heads are installed, so a dial indicator to find TDC will work well. If you find you are degreeing in your camshaft after the heads are on, you will be using a spark plug TDC tool.***

With the number-1 piston at top dead center (TDC), mark it. Use a dial indicator on a fixture to determine TDC. Rotate the engine over in one direction by hand, bring the piston up until it is at its highest point on the dial indicator. Write the number of degrees on the pointer on a piece of paper.

Turn the engine in the opposite direction until the piston starts to return to the TDC location again. Bring the piston up to its highest point on the dial indicator. Write down the degrees noted on the degree wheel. You can now add these to numbers together and divide by two.

Next, without turning the crankshaft, loosen the degree wheel and move it to the correct degree. After doing this, go through these steps one more time to verify results. The zero on the degree wheel is TDC now.

### *At 50 Method*

There is a lot more to degreeing in your camshaft than it seems. One of the most common ways to degree in the camshaft is what many call the "duration at 50" method.

One of the biggest items to remember is that when turning the engine over, there is slack in the timing chain that is being taken up. If you rotate backward, the slack in the chain will throw your numbers off. If you rotate the wheel too far and you're past the stopping point, do not rotate the engine backward.

So, if you over-rotate, continue rotating the engine over until it comes back around. Because we are doing this without the cylinder head on at this time, we work off the edge of the valve lifter.

Now that we have the indicator in position, zero out the dial indicator. Slowly rotate the engine over in the normal direction while watching for the dial indicator to start moving. As the dial indicator starts to move, continue rotating the engine until it reaches 0.050 inch of camshaft lift. Document the reading on the degree wheel.

Continue to rotate to maximum valve lift. If you check your camshaft card, it will show you the maximum lobe lift. Continue to turn the engine over in the same direction that the lifter will fall down on to the heel of the camshaft. This is considered the closing side of the camshaft lobe.

As the indicator continues down the opposite direction, rotate the engine until you are back at the 0.050-inch reading on the indicator. Document the reading with the first reading at 0.050 inch.

As you rotate the engine back to the base circle or the heel of the camshaft, verify that the indicator again reads zero. This is a great way to double-check yourself. As easy as it is to do this twice, we always check ourselves twice.

The two readings written down are both at 0.050 inch. The first reading is as the valve is opening, and the second reading at 0.050 inch is as it is closing. Now that you have these readings, compare them to the readings on your camshaft card. As long as it is within a degree, it is good. Remember that the key to this is always doing each step twice. After doing the intake lobe, the exhaust lobe can be done the same way.

For what you are doing, we believe that the intake side of things is good enough. As we have mentioned before, this is a great way to double-check your TDC marks on your harmonic balancer. If using an aftermarket new balancer, you're going to be in good shape. However, if using the original balancer, it is very possible for the outer ring to turn on the balancer.

A good way to double-check yourself is to make sure that you come up with the same number twice. On the internet, there is an abundant number of companies that sell degreeing tools, piston stops, and dial indicators for degreeing in camshafts. Even though you might only do this a few times in your life, this is one of those things that every car buff should have on their bucket list.

## Internal Oil Line Installation

The internal oil line can be made of many different materials. We have seen hydraulic hoses, copper with swedged fittings, AN fittings

*The two AN fittings used to build the oil line are Earl's part numbers 820106ERL and 829006ERL.*

with steel-braided line, and the new black line offered by all of the AN companies.

For years, we used the copper line. This is a more difficult line to form to keep the kinks out of the tube. With the copper tube, notch the webbing in the valley of the block and tuck the oil line down tight to still use the factory valley pan. On a mild application, this is okay, but we just did not feel right notching the webbing on a performance application.

Recently, we have moved to the AN line with the black covered stainless steel wrap. All of these will work well. It comes down to personal preference. We do not use liquid Teflon on the pipe threads when turning them into the block. The risk of getting Teflon in the oil-gallery system is not worth the risk.

The internal oil line needs to be kept as low as possible to clear a valley pan if running one. Even when you keep the oil line as low as possible, the valley pan needs to be modified. With the braided line, individual intake gaskets work the best, but if a valley pan is desired, you have to cut a horseshoe loop to clear the front of the oil line. This is common and can be done successfully. The valley pan is more successful for keeping engine oil off the bottom of the intake manifold and out of the PCV valve.

*Don't not use any Teflon sealer on the pipe threads when installing the internal oil line. It is not worth the risk of Teflon getting into the oil galleries.*

## Cylinder Head Installation

Let's start with installing stock cast-iron cylinder heads. Then we will discuss installing aluminum cylinder heads. Before starting, take one last look at the piston tops to make sure that they are all installed in the right cylinders. Stock and some performance pistons will have the fronts marked. This will be the last time you see the piston tops.

*Install the cylinder head with a used head gasket and a few bolts to help secure the head to the block. Install two of the rocker-arm studs with a guide plate if used. We have one intake and one exhaust valve installed with checking springs to hold them up. Now, install your one single lifter in cylinder number-1. The last step before checking is to use a dry-erase marker and mark the valve tips black. This allows you to see the travel.*

*Aftermarket aluminum Edelbrock cylinder heads come with adjustable rocker-arm studs and with the correct valve spring. One of the big advantages to the aluminum cylinder head is the weight savings.*

***Wipe the Deck***

Make sure that the cylinder deck is wiped off with a lint-free white shop towel. Usually, after installing the pistons, there is leftover oil on the deck from oiling the cylinder walls. It is easier if the deck is facing straight up, so rotate the engine on the stand now.

***Head Bolt Holes***

Take one last look into the head bolt holes to make sure that they are clean and no fluids are left in them. Ninety-nine percent of all head bolt holes on an AMC are blind, but there is the rare occurrence that we see where one bolt hole breaks into water from the machining process at the factory. So, check all the bolt holes with a small pick and a flashlight to make sure that they are blind.

Another quick way to check is to put an air nozzle tip into the hole and spray a little air into the hole. If the bolt hole goes into the water, you will hear the air run into the block. What is the big deal if it does? Well, if the holes are blind, motor oil can be used to lubricate the threads. If one goes into the water, liquid Teflon should be used on that one.

The head bolt hole known to break into water is the driver-side number-7. This is the second-from-front bolt from the front of the head on the outside row. If this bolt does not seal, the water will find its way past the threads and leak water between the head gasket or out of the top of the head bolt.

***The factory AMC head gasket is very unique because the cylinder block side is steel and the head side is composite. The aftermarket industry copied that aspect of the factory head gasket. Although these head gaskets were thought to be not as good compared with a composite gasket, they hold up well even is most mild performance applications.***

## Head Gasket

If you are using the stock replacement head gasket made by Fel-Pro, you will notice the engine block side is steel shim and the cylinder head side is composite. This is how the head gaskets came from the factory, and for stock to mild performance, they will work well. The steel side of the head gasket needs to be coated with a brush tack or copper coat spray.

## Cylinder Head Dowel Pins

Before doing this, if the block was resurfaced, make sure that the machine shop put the cylinder head dowel pins back in. These dowel pins are becoming a little more difficult to find, so we have started to machine our own in the lathe. Give the dowel pins a little tap with a brass hammer just to make sure that they are seated all the way down.

We do not want the dowel pins to keep the cylinder head from being torqued down. At this time, take a look at the finished cylinder head and make sure that the deck surface is completely wiped clean and dry. Blow the cylinder head out one last time, making sure that the water jackets are blown clean.

***The steel shim side of the gasket needs to be sprayed with a Permatex spray tack or another form of copper coat. A few other various products can provide the same result. After applying on the spray tack, let it dry just enough to be slightly tacky.***

### *Permatex Spray and Silicone*

Now is the time to spray some copper coat or Permatex spray tack on the steel shim side of the head gasket only. Allow it to dry a little bit. Once it becomes tacky to the touch, install the gasket with the steel side toward the engine block.

Apply some black Right Stuff silicone on both sides of the head gasket just up by the valley. The valley is a common place for an oil leak. We put a very thin amount of silicone one the block side and the cylinder head side.

***When installing the cylinder head bolts, we put just a small amount of oil on the threads of each head bolt. Also put a small amount of oil underneath the head of the bolt, which will prevent the head bolt from torquing prematurely due to friction.***

### *Install the Head*

Once this is complete, install the cylinder head. Don't be afraid to ask a friend for help. It is not that the cylinder head is heavy, its just that it needs to be set down as square as possible.

### *Head Bolts*

AMC cylinder heads can be bolted on either side of the engine; there are no lefts or rights. Once the cylinder head is sitting flat on the head gasket, install the cylinder head bolts. Make sure that the head bolts are completely clean; if any head bolts are eroded or have damaged threads, do not use them. In the worst-case scenario, ARP does make new head bolts.

When installing the stock head bolts, put a little oil on the threads and some on the head of the bolt. It does not take much, just a little to keep the friction down to achieve the correct torque. Once the bolts are installed, run them down snug always from center out.

Stock AMC head bolt torque is different for the 7/16-inch bolts (100 ft-lbs) and the 1/2-inch bolts (110 ft-lbs). Everyone has a different opinion of torque on an AMC engine to keep the cylinder heads from cracking.

***The 1968–1969 cylinder head bolts are 7/16-inch bolts, and the factory torque setting is 100 ft-lbs. The 1970-and-newer engines had 1/2-inch cylinder head bolts, and the factory torque is 110 ft-lbs. Due to how the outside corners of the factory steel cylinder heads crack, torque the four outside-corner head bolts to only 75 ft-lbs.***

### *Aftermarket Heads*

There is not much difference when installing aluminum heads, but here are the items that will be different. When using aluminum heads, we use the Cometic MLS head gaskets instead of the stock Fel-Pro style. The MLS gaskets require no spray sealer

## Head Bolt Torque

We torque the 7/16-inch bolts to 95 ft-lbs and the 1/2-inch bolts to 105 ft-lbs. The major change we make is the four short outside corner head bolts, where the cylinder heads tend to crack. Torque these head bolts to only 75 ft-lbs. Sometimes we will have a cylinder head crack in the corners after installation.

Set the torque wrench for 50 ft-lbs for the first go around. Always torque from center out. For the second step, go to the final torque value and make sure to move smoothly and do it in one sweep. Just to make sure, go over each bolt one last time to make sure that none were missed. Repeat this for the other side and always take your time during assembly. ■

*These are stock factory cast-iron cylinder heads. One of the major differences in AMC cylinder heads is the rectangular port compared to the newer dogleg exhaust port.*

on either side. Since aftermarket heads are being bolted up anyway, install new ARP head bolts. With ARP bolts, use the supplied ARP moly lube and follow the torquing instructions.

On the aftermarket heads, do not worry about the heads cracking, so torque all of the bolts to the same value. If assembling Edelbrock cylinder heads on a pre-1970 engine that originally had 7/16-inch head bolts, remember to use the Edelbrock cylinder head bushing kit. All Edelbrock heads are manufactured for the 1/2-inch head bolt engines but can be installed on the 7/16-inch head bolt blocks with no problem.

When bolting Edelbrock heads on the pre-1970 engine blocks with 7/16-inch head bolts, there are two things needed (as mentioned above): the cylinder head bolt bushing kit (part number EDL 9680) and stepped cylinder head dowel pins (part number EDL 9652). The cylinder head alignment dowel pins are different sizes for the 7/16-inch and 1/2-inch head bolts.

Years ago, there were no head bolt bushing adapters and stepped dowel pins. We used to machine them out of bar stock in our engine lathe. These are all extra items that will need to be purchased when rebuilding an AMC.

## Valvetrain with Pushrod Geometry

Now that the basic long-block is assembled, install the valvetrain. To assemble the valvetrain, turn the engine straight up and down on the assembly stand. Most camshaft manufacturers supply special assembly lube to use on the hydraulic flat-tappet lifters. For roller lifters, dip the lifter in engine oil and install.

*These items are needed to check valvetrain geometry (determining the pushrod length): a rocker arm and poly lock and one lifter (in this situation it is a solid roller). Using the pushrod that was in the motor, pick a checking pushrod that will get us the correct range of length. Now, we are ready to get started.*

*Some builders set the engine up on one bank to install the valvetrain. We prefer the straight-up position to do both sides at once. Using the supplied assembly lube or equivalent brand, coat the bottom of the flat-tappet lifter before installation. When using roller lifters, we lubricate the roller with engine oil.*

Driven (Joe Gibbs) produces a really good flat-tappet assembly lube that is designed just for that purpose.

#### *Install All 16 Lifters*

Lube the bottom of the lifter and install all 16 valve lifters. When installing the lifters, be sure that they are loose in the bore. They should move up and down very easily. This is very important because the lifter needs to spin in the bore very easily.

To lube the sides of the lifter, dip the lifter into a tub with break-in oil. The days of soaking or priming the lifter are in the past and not needed today.

If a lifter feels snug in the bore, it needs to be taken care of before going any further. I recommend asking your machine shop at that point.

Hydraulic- and solid-roller lifters have a needle bearing roller that rides on the camshaft lobe so the normal camshaft break-in lube is not needed. The only form of oiling will be to dip the lifter into the tub of oil so they are not installed dry. It is still important to make sure that this style of lifter moves freely up and down the lifter bore. Though it is not nearly as critical as a flat-tappet lifter that is required to spin.

## Pushrods

When using the flat-tappet lifters, the stock pushrods can be reused if they are in good shape. Clean the pushrods, making sure the oil hole is perfectly clear.

The next step is to inspect the ball ends. These should show no signs of wear on either end. Once the tip starts to wear through the hardness, there is no stopping it, and eventually it will fail. Keep in mind that pushrods are a very inexpensive item when comparing what you have invested in the engine.

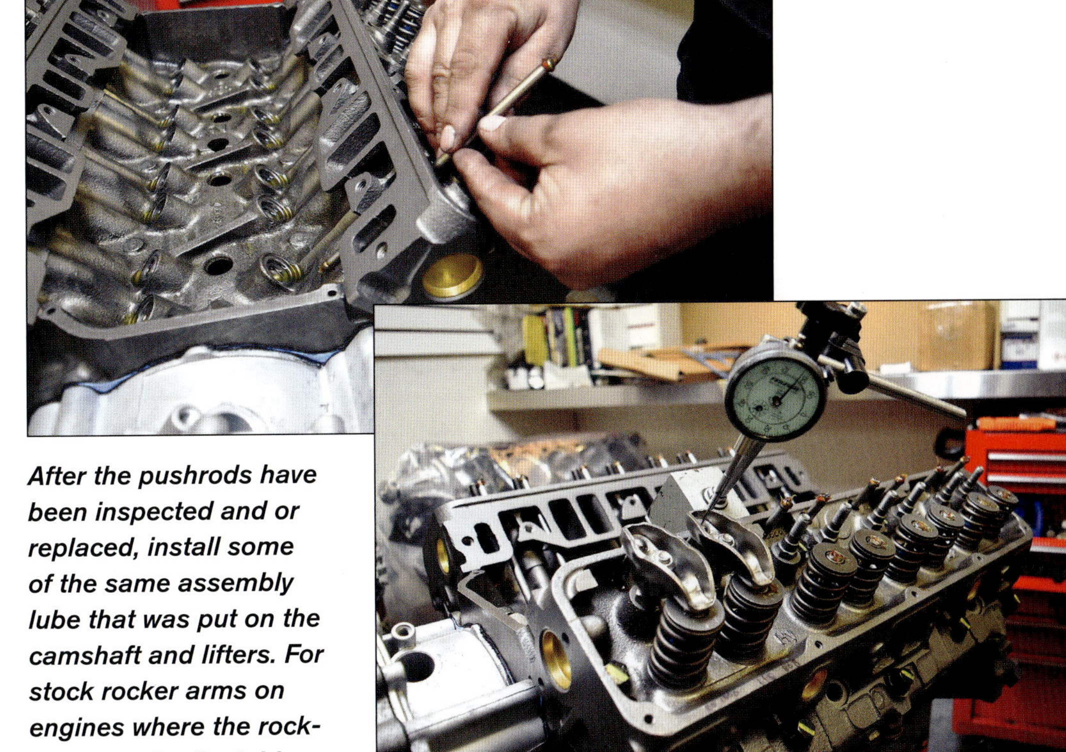

***After the pushrods have been inspected and or replaced, install some of the same assembly lube that was put on the camshaft and lifters. For stock rocker arms on engines where the rockers are not adjustable, make sure that there is the correct amount of lifter preload.***

***By installing a dial indicator, we can check how much lifter preload we have. This is only necessary if we are using the original nonadjustable valvetrain.***

#### *Lifter Preload*

When installing pushrods, apply some of the same assembly lube that was put on the camshaft and lifters. For stock rocker arms on engines where the rockers are not adjustable, make sure that there is the correct amount of lifter preload. If you are building a completely stock engine, most of the time the stock pushrod length will be correct.

## Rocker-Arm Assembly

When installing the rocker-arm assembly, snug the rocker up to a zero preload. This means tightening down the rocker-arm nut to the point where the pushrod seats in the lifter and rocker arm without pushing down the lifter. There are a few ways to check this, and the machine shop would install a dial indicator to check it.

Understanding that you may not have all the tools of a machine shop, tighten down the nut to the correct torque value while keeping track of the turns that it takes for this to happen. The correct amount of preload should ideally be somewhere between a half to one turn. Various engine builders as well as various lifter companies have different preload specifications. Too little preload will cause a lifter tick and too much preload could hold a valve open.

#### *Hydraulic-Roller Lifter*

If switching to a hydraulic-roller lifter, it will need to be checked with an adjustable pushrod and dial indicator. If this is something that you need help with, reach out to the machine shop. For a small charge, the machine shop will come out and measure the pushrod length for you. If you are determined to check your

*Install the adjustable pushrod and the rocker arm that will be running on the engine. Various rockers will align differently, as will different rocker ratios. Set the rocker arm to a zero lash for this test. To play around a little bit, set the pushrod length way too long and then way too short. This will make it obvious to the eye that the rocker tip is riding too far on the edge of the valve. This will wear out valve guides too quickly.*

*After you start to grasp the correct length, remove the rocker arm and check the travel. At no time should the roller tip start to roll off the edge of the valve. The roller tip should start out on one side of the valve and be about centered at full valve lift; then, it should start to return. There are other things to check while doing this, including making sure that the angle is correct to check if the valve-spring retainer is rubbing on the inside of the rocker arm. Don't get too alarmed because this is common. You will frequently see rocker arms that are at clearance.*

own pushrod geometry, there are several quality YouTube videos by reputable companies that are available.

Before we get into establishing pushrod length, let's address how the rocker tip travels across the tip of the valve.

### Rocker Tip/Tip of Valve

Sometimes it's hard to picture how the rocker arm will travel in an arc across the valve tip as the lift increases. The more you study it and try different lengths on the test pushrod, the more you will understand. If you take your test pushrod and try a bunch of different lengths, you will notice that the closer you get to a perfect length, the less the rocker will travel across the valve. At this point, the least amount of travel will also provide the least amount of side loading. In turn, this will have the best valve-guide life.

As the valve opens, the rocker travels across the tip of the valve. After it reaches full valve lift, it starts to retract back across the valve tip until the valve closes. As you are trying different lengths, try making big changes that will give you an obvious idea of what happens with the incorrect length pushrod.

As you try a really long pushrod, you will notice that the rocker arm is already starting over center of the valve. As it rotates through, the rocker will end up on the outer edge of the valve, which creates an extreme side loading of the valve. We have seen brand-new cylinder heads come in with only 100 miles on them and the guides are completely shot. If you are off, it does not take long for the damage to occur.

### Keeping Track of the Travel

I bet you never thought there was this much to a pushrod length. There are some tricks to keep track of the travel. One of them is to use Dykem Steel Blue to mark the valve tip. Run the engine through the valve-lift sequence a few times, then remove the rocker and check for its wear pattern. The pattern should travel from the inside edge of the valve to just over center and then return. Just keep in mind that the straighter the valve is pushed down in the guide, the less side load there will be.

Many companies sell pushrod-length checkers for very reasonable prices. I believe every toolbox should have a set of various length checkers. How many should be checked? Sure, there are race engines with four different-length pushrods, but for the most part, checking one intake and one exhaust is fine. If everything is in line, the intake and exhaust pushrods are the same length.

### Measure the Pushrod Length

Remove the pushrod-checking tool and remember to lock the lock nut so that it does not move. Measure the length of the pushrod with a dial caliper. Pushrods are available in 0.050-inch increments, so average the measurement out to get the length. There are a few other ways to measure, but for your first time, I thought this was one of the clearest to understand.

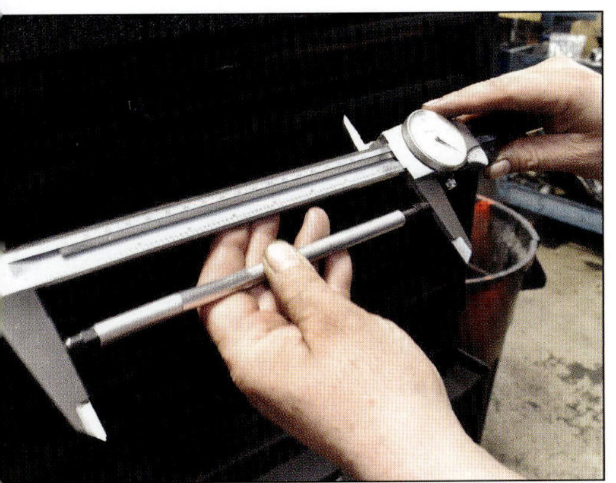

*Once the adjustable pushrod is locked into the correct length, measure the pushrod. We make it a habit to check the intake and exhaust pushrod length just in case there is a difference. If done correctly, both pushrods should be the same length on an AMC.*

*The stock intake gasket was a steel valley pan. It is probably one of the hardest intake gaskets to seal. Pre-bend and fit the intake gasket before installation.*

#### *Rocker-Arm Nut*

If the heads have been converted to an adjustable valvetrain, then determine the correct pushrod length and tighten down the rocker arm nut to a zero preload. Tighten the nut an additional half to one turn. It seems that newly manufactured lifters are set to be on the light side of a half turn.

#### *Rocker-Arm Clearance*

For a solid camshaft application, set the rocker-arm clearance with a feeler gauge. These specifications can be found on the camshaft card. All rocker arms need to be installed and adjusted when the lifter is on the heel of the camshaft. There are a few different ways to make sure of this, but for new assemblers, we like the simple way of bringing the piston to TDC on the compression stroke. When this is achieved, you can set both the intake and exhaust valve on this cylinder. Once both are set, move on to the next cylinder.

### Setting Valves

Setting valves is one of the harder items during the assembly, especially if you have never done it before. Don't be afraid to reach out for help if needed. This is why it is good to buy parts and get machine work done locally, as building a good relationship with your engine builder can be very helpful.

### Intake Manifold Installation

There are two different kinds of intake manifold assemblies: the steel original valley pan and the two-piece intake gasket. A good two-piece intake gasket for AMC V-8 engines is from Mr. Gasket (part number 5844). Fel-Pro (part number MS96011) is the good valley pan that is available.

#### *Fitment*

The first step to installing the intake manifold is to check the fitment. If the cylinder heads and engine block have not been decked very much, the stock intake should bolt right up without any machining.

To check the fitment, take the two-piece intake gasket and tape it on the cylinder heads to keep it in place. Gently set the intake on the engine and start two intake bolts, one on each side. If both bolts thread in very easily, the ports should be close.

Oftentimes when using an aftermarket intake, one bolt will go in but the other will be very hard to get started. Often, the intake ports do not align properly as well. Most aftermarket intake manufacturers will leave the intake manifolds high. This is because material can be removed but can't be added.

If the intake manifold is sitting high, bring it to the machine shop to have them mill it. The hard part is determining how much to remove. Ask the machine shop how to best determine how much to remove from the intake. You might have to do it twice, but that is better than taking too much off and having it sit too low when you get it back.

#### *Valley Pan Gasket*

Now the intake manifold is ready to install. If using the stock valley pan, these are a little challenging for a beginner to install. You will need to pre-fit the gasket to the block, kind of forming it to fit in the valley. Sometimes it helps to run a few bolts into one side of the gasket and then gently form it to the valley.

We do not use the rubber end rails. Use a bead of Permatex Right Stuff on both sides of the tray instead. When dry fitting the intake manifold, make note of the measurement of the gap on the front and rear of the intake. The silicone bead needs to be slightly larger than gap measurement.

#### *Prep the Tray*

Following the water ports, apply Right Stuff completely around all the water ports. The rest of the intake tray will need a good coat of Permatex brush tack on both sides. Once the silicone beads are installed on both ends and around the water ports, use some 3M weatherstrip glue to keep

*When test fitting the intake manifold, it is common for manufacturers to leave the material on the manifolds so they can be milled to the desired location. After dry fitting the intake, determine how much material to remove from each side. Reaching out to the machine shop is usually a great idea, as it can usually direct you on how it would like you to measure the removal amount. We always say that you can remove material, but if you mill too much off, it cannot be put back on. For this reason, doing this in two steps is sometimes the best way.*

*After the intake is installed, if you are using a PCV system, the PCV grommet can be installed.*

the tray in place on the engine. Let the gasket harden just enough to keep it in place.

Put two more beads of silicone on the front and rear of the intake. Also, put another bead around all of the water ports on the other side of the gasket. Make sure that the front and rear beads of silicone are tall enough to take up the gap between the intake and the block.

#### *Installing the Manifold*

Carefully install the intake on the engine. Install the bolts on both sides of the engine and proceed to tighten them evenly from side to side of the engine. Do not try to wipe off excess silicone; let it dry overnight first. The next day, come back and trim excess silicone with a razor blade. One of the mistakes made is trying to remove excess silicone by pulling it off the block. Doing this risks upsetting the silicone bead that needs to seal the engine.

If that sounded simple, keep in mind that when running the internal oil line, you need to notch the intake gasket to clear the line. This makes the valley tray that much harder to keep in place.

*This 390 engine is using a completely stock intake manifold with an aftermarket Edelbrock carburetor. We will not use the exhaust heat crossover, so we will install a plate with a gasket. This plate is used on all of the engines we run. Our final plate will be a nice thick aluminum piece machined out of billet.*

#### *Rubber Grommet for the PCV Valve*

Whenever possible, use the two-piece aftermarket intake gasket. Once the intake is installed, if you are running a PCV valve, install the rubber grommet at this time.

On this 390 AMC engine, we are using a stock factory intake manifold with an Edelbrock carburetor. This particular engine will not be using the exhaust crossover or a mechanical choke. The exhaust crossover can be covered with a plate. We usually machine a nice cover from a 1/4-inch thick piece of aluminum for this purpose. We have not seen very many aftermarket companies making these covers for purchase, so making your own is probably the route to go.

### Oil Pump, Front Cover, and Water Pump

In Chapter 7, we rebuilt the complete front cover and oil pump assembly. Now, we can install it on the engine. It is a lot easier to have the oil pump bench assembled before installing the cover on the engine. You can also bench install the front crankshaft seal in the front cover before installing it on the engine.

Find a socket or a bushing driver that fits your front seal perfectly. Under the front cover, support it with a small block of wood while pressing or tapping in the front seal. Tap the front seal in with a rubber mallet, but be exceptionally careful to install this seal square with the cover.

Normally, this seal is installed flush with the chamfer on the outside of the front cover. Make sure that the seal spring located on the ID lip of the seal stayed in place during the installation.

Before installing the front cover on the block, go through all the bolts and make sure that you have all of them. Some of these bolts are special lengths, some will go all the way through the water pump, and some have special threads on both ends. Hopefully, you took pictures before disassembly because some of the engine accessories hinge on mounting up to these bolts.

Have the water pump ready to install at this time as well. Some of the bolts go all the way through the water pump and front cover into the engine block.

There is a gasket between the front cover and the engine block. Coat this gasket with either a spray tack or a light bead of silicone. You are now ready to install the front cover. Assemble all of the bolts that you can, snug them up, and then install the water pump and put the through bolts in.

GNB offers an aluminum high-flowing water pump. This is the long version designed for the four-bolt harmonic balancers. The water-pump gasket should also be coated with a light coat of RTV or spray tack. Make sure that the bolt location is correct because various models have different locations for accessories. Some of the aftermarket water pumps have a clearance issue with the harmonic balancer.

To check if the bottom bolt boss is going to clear the harmonic balancer, install the water pump just hand tight and begin to install the harmonic balancer. Before installing the harmonic balancer all the way onto the crankshaft, you should be able to tell if it is going to clear. We find that most aftermarket pumps will not clear.

Remove the water pump from the engine and use a carbide cutter on a dye grinder to machine the water pump boss just enough to clear the harmonic balancer. Reinstall and check for clearance. Then, you are ready to final install everything.

After the water pump is installed, the water bypass hose can be installed from the water neck to the water pump. Our hose is just a bit too long. It is on there just for the purpose of running the engine for camshaft break-in.

It is common that the original thermostat housings erode with time. If you are set on using the stock housing and you cannot locate one in better condition, we have used JB-Weld to fill in some of the pitting and then belt sanded the surface for a good sealing area. For a replacement, we use an Oldsmobile water neck (RPC part number R9403).

There are several companies making that water neck. The only modification needed is slotting the mounting holes ever so slightly. Use a gasket to mark the holes to be slotted. To install the water neck (if the aftermarket one has an O-ring to seal it), remove the O-ring, fill the groove with silicone, and use the old-fashioned gasket. Seal both sides of the gasket with Right Stuff silicone and install. For a clean installation, wipe off any excess sealant with a rag.

Surprisingly, there are quite a few companies making aftermarket pulley kits for the AMC engine. You will have your selection of both original-style V-belt and new serpentine systems. These kits are available by pieces and by complete kits that include alternators and power steering pumps. This kit is manufactured by March Pulleys.

Some of these kits can be a nightmare to install. The March Pulleys kit went on with us only having to

*The front-cover bolts and water-pump bolts come in many different lengths. Before installing the front cover, make sure that you have all of the bolts and that they are cleaned and usable. Since we rebuild so many of these, we stock these bolts. Otherwise, you will need to run to the hardware store to get replacements. Once you begin installing the front cover, it is best to have all of the bolts on hand to ensure that the gaskets seal.*

*GNB makes an aftermarket aluminum water pump that is correct for the 1971-and-later engines with four-bolt pulleys. This pump is considered to be the long pump for use with four-bolt harmonic balancers.*

*It is common to have to clearance the aftermarket water pump where it makes contact with the harmonic balancer.*

make three new spacers to align the pulleys. The early AMC cars came with rather small-output alternators. When adding electric fans, ignition boxes, and better radios, a little more output is needed.

PowerMaster produces a GM CS130 alternator (part number 578021) that mounts with just a little bracket modification, and rotating the case bolts in with not too much trouble. This unit puts out 140A while running and 95A at an idle.

Replacing the old original alternator with an updated Delco version provides a modern alternator with 140A while the engine is over 1,200 rpm and at least 95A at an idle. This PowerMaster alternator's is 57802.

## Tinwork, Oil Pan, and Valve Covers

Now that the base long-block assembly is done, begin the final steps of installing the tinwork. The first item to install is the oil pan.

Whether you are installing a stock oil pan or an aftermarket one, most of this procedure is the same. For a stock oil pan, start by installing the pickup tube assembly. On a stock application, this will screw directly into the engine block. Once the pickup tube begins to get tight, final position the pickup in the center of the pan. The hardest part about this is knowing whether it will make it one more turn around or not.

There have been times where some aftermarket pickup tubes thread into the block too far and start to block the main oil gallery. We have shortened the leading edge of the tube before. With the aftermarket Milodon tubes, we have not had a problem with them blocking the oil feed hole. We do not install any thread sealer on the threads; no need to risk thread sealant getting into the oil system.

If you are running the Milodon external oil pump pickup line, remember to install a pipe plug in the

*Once the water pump is installed, install the water bypass hose from the water neck to the water pump. Our hose is a bit long and is installed only for camshaft break-in at this time.*

*The original water necks have a tendency to erode over the years. A lot of them are so bad that we have to fill in the low spots with JB-Weld and then belt sand them to give us a good sealing surface.*

*Several brands of water necks come with O-rings. However, we remove them and fill the groove with silicone. After doing this, we use the original water outlet gasket to seal the housing. Let the silicone harden and trim as needed for a neat appearance.*

*For a replacement water neck, we use an aftermarket Oldsmobile water neck (RPC part number R9403). There are quite a few different companies that make water necks. The only modification needed is the mounting holes need to be slotted ever so slightly.*

*For an alternator upgrade from the stock unit or just something that looks as cool, there is this PowerMaster blacked-out alternator. This alternator is built around the common GM CS130 model. Rebuilding this GM-style alternator is very easy, and the parts are readily available. As far as mounting it up, a few minor bracket modifications give you a modern-day alternator on a classic car.*

*This is a March complete pulley system installed on an AMC engine. Sometimes getting all the pulleys to align can be a disaster. However, this kit is very well made. With just a few bushing modifications, we had everything aligned. If you are looking for a clean, polished look on the front of your AMC engine, this kit does the job. It is also available in black.*

*To prevent an oil leak, install RTV silicone in the crankshaft keyway groove. This keeps the engine oil from following the keyway groove and leaking.*

original pickup-tube location. Failure to do this will result in zero oil pressure. Make sure that the oil pan is free of any dirt one last time. Even if it is a new oil pan, always wash the oil pan before installing.

The Fel-Pro oil pan gasket (part number OS30187C) contains four pieces. If this is your first time installing an oil pan, set the gasket in place so that you can see how it fits. The most important places to put silicone are the four corners of the rubber end seals where they meet up with the cork end rails.

Once familiar with the oil pan gasket, remove it, apply silicone, and install it. We find Permatex Right Stuff works well. Remember that we are installing the oil pan to not have any leaks in anticipation that it will stay on there forever. To do this, put a little bit of silicone at the four

*To install the harmonic balancer, use a harmonic balancer installation tool. Once the balancer is started, thread the installation tool in the snout of the crankshaft.*

*The early 1968–1969 engines used a three-bolt harmonic balancer and pulleys instead of the later four-bolt versions that came out in the 1970s.*

*We used to purchase new dipstick tubes right from the Chrysler dealership. These tubes fit correctly and needed no modifications to fit them into the block. They have since been discontinued, so we have reached out to the aftermarket companies. We now purchase them from Bulltear AMC, and they fit properly.*

*If you are running an electric fuel pump, you need to install a block-off plate. The big-block Chevy block-off plates bolt right up. There are a variety of plates from which to choose.*

corners then install the rubber end pieces. Next, silicone the oil-pan rails on the engine block and install the gasket gently by pressing the gasket down and aligning the oil-pan bolt holes.

This next step is just a precaution, but we actually install the oil pan and tighten a few bolts to allow the Right Stuff to harden. After giving it a few hours to harden, we remove the pan, place Right Stuff on the top of the gasket, and reinstall the pan. We find that doing this prevents the gasket from pushing out the ends.

Next, install silicone in all four corners again, as well as on top of the gasket. You are now ready to lay a small bead of Right Stuff on top of the gasket. After the gasket is covered, reinstall the oil pan.

When tightening down the bolts, make sure that it is an even process all the way around. This ensures that the oil pan is brought down squarely on the engine block. Let this harden up for a day. Then, cut any excess RTV off with a razor blade. Remember to never pull the silicone off the block.

### Harmonic Balancer

Next, install the harmonic balancer. Whether using a stock or aftermarket harmonic balancer, the installation is the same. The balancer can only be installed with the correct installation tool. I have seen bad things happen when you try to install it with a hammer.

A harmonic installation kit actually is pretty cheap, and it is worth the investment. A brand-new harmonic these days is made small. Most all-new balancers come with instructions for how to measure the crankshaft snout to determine the correct press fit. Once you have an accurate dimension of the crankshaft, take the measurement and the balancer to the machine shop to be checked and honed.

Make sure that the keyways are installed in the crankshaft correctly. Apply some RTV in the keyway and install the balancer squarely on the snout of the crankshaft. Put a little bit of oil on the OD of the balancer so it slides in the front seal easily.

Install the harmonic balancer installation tool at this time. With the proper press-fit measurement and the proper tool, press the balancer all the way on. You will notice once it is seated all the way on.

At this time, the harmonic balancer bolts and front pulleys can be installed if they are ready. Our engine is a pre-1971 with a three-bolt harmonic balancer and pulleys. If running an electric fuel pump, you need to block off the fuel pump mount. The Chevy big-block fuel pump block-off is a direct match. The nice part about this is that there are a many varieties of block-off plates for a big-block Chevy. You have a choice of steel or billet and color.

Not many aftermarket companies manufacture dipstick tubes. However, some of the mail-order companies are selling one now. We tried one of these, and the tube that presses into the block is way oversized. We practically destroyed it trying to install it. We have found that the one sold by Bulltear AMC and the original part supplied by Chrysler are good.

The dealer part number is sometimes hard to find. They only seem to run them once in a while. They all come with a yellow dipstick that we paint with the engine. The factory dipsticks have a small bracket that holds the dipstick in place and bolts it to the valve cover. Most of the time, this bracket only works with the stock valve covers.

***The application will determine if the valve-cover gaskets are glued down on both sides or just one. This engine is a completely stock rebuild, so we first glue them to the cover and then glue them to the cylinder head with Right Stuff silicone. If we had a solid camshaft that might need the valves reset a few times, we might only glue them to the head or the cover. On the other side, we might use some grease so that they do not stick.***

***Now that the valve covers are installed but not bolted on, rotate the engine and listen to hear if a rocker arm is hitting the valve cover. Do this before bolting the cover down for good, especially if you are running an aftermarket rocker arm or a full roller rocker arm.***

### Valve Covers

One of the last items to install are the valve covers. We usually silicone the gaskets to the valve covers. If the engine is completely stock, we will use Right Stuff on both sides of the gasket. The valve covers will not have to be removed on a stock engine. This can be done a variety of ways.

On race car applications where you have to set valves each weekend, we'd glue the gasket to either the head or the cover, and on the other side, we'd grease the gasket to make it easier for the covers to be removed.

One of the biggest reasons that valve covers leak is due to the covers not being flat. If using stock covers, taking a little extra time to ensure that the covers are perfectly straight goes a long way.

Before installing the covers for the final time, set them on the engine for checking. We do find a lot of interference with the valve covers and aftermarket rocker arms. The easiest way to check this before you get it into the car is to rotate the engine by hand and listen really well. Usually, if a rocker arm is hitting the cover you can hear it.

With hydraulic lifters, this might not be found until it is running. If you find you are struggling to locate where it is hitting, put some dye on the inside of the cover. Many aftermarket covers will need a little clearancing.

*The oil filler tube presses into the front of the intake manifold. Use a block of wood and a small hammer to tap it in.*

*This is the stock oil filler tube that was removed to clean the intake manifold. Sometimes, to re-press it in, you have to wedge the opening up just a little bit.*

***Oil Fill/Breather Tube***

Another item to mention is that there are no breather holes or oil fill spot on AMC engines. If the stock or aftermarket intake does not have the oil fill/breather tube installed in the intake, now is the time to install it.

These do not come with the new intakes, so remove it from the old intake. For installation, they simply tap into place. To help seal the tube in the intake manifold, use some silicone sealer when you press the tube in. Right Stuff again works well here. Install a breather on top, and it is complete.

As was stated in prior chapters, this is probably not enough of a breather for a high-performance engine. For high-performance engines that will build more crankcase pressure, additional valve-cover breathers are needed. On a full race engine, a puke tank has become popular.

## Painting the Engine

The last item for assembly is painting the engine. Seymour and Eastwood are two of the last paint suppliers for the AMC engine.

Pre-1967 engines were painted Rampert Red. We have seen quite a few engines in 1967 use a gold engine color. All International Harvester V-8 engines were red, and we have seen a few AMC California cars have red engines. This is unconfirmed, but car owners who had true California-ordered cars have said that they had red engines.

*For final painting, mask off all of the parts that you do not want to paint. This engine is first sprayed with a high-temperature engine self-etching primer. Then, the engine is given two coats of Seymour En-66 AMC engine paint.*

The part number for the AMC Blue engine aerosol paint is EN-66. We use a thin coat of primer when painting the engine. Pictures of the engine before disassembly show that a factory stock engine is painted AMC Blue. Some call it AMC Green. Either way, 1968-and-newer engines were painted the same color.

*Seymour's Caravelle Blue (part number EN-66) is the correct paint for 1968-and-up engines. Take your time taping off the engine and spray on a light coat of engine primer on before painting.*

When using aftermarket heads and intake manifolds, most builders leave these items in their natural raw color.

## Flexplate, Shim Plate, and Reinforcement Plate

To prepare the engine to run, install the flexplate and shim plates. All AMC V-8 engines were produced with a shim plate that goes on the engine before the flexplate.

The three components to install are the flexplate or flywheel, the shim plate, and the flexplate reinforcement plate. These items must be installed in this order: shim plate located on the bellhousing dowel pins, flexplate or flywheel, and the reinforcement plate (only used with a flexplate). Do not use the outer ring on a flywheel or aftermarket flexplate, only use it on a stock flexplate.

We are asked regularly why this ring should be used on the outside of the flexplate. We have heard many different opinions, but our belief is that the flexplates were cracking, so this outer shim plate reinforces it.

The first item installed is the shim plate. Make sure that the plate is not deformed. If it is, have it straightened before installation and make sure that it is on the bellhousing dowel pins.

The flexplate and the flywheel can only bolt on one way. This will locate the counterweight, ensuring that it is in the correct position. When installing the flexplate, install the reinforcement plate and then the bolts.

Flexplate bolts should be replaced during the rebuild process. ARP offers a couple 1/2-20 bolts for the Pontiac engine that work well. Always use red Loctite when installing the bolts. These are probably one of the most common bolts to come loose, and of course, they are the hardest to get to.

*Next, install the flexplate or flywheel, shim plate, and the flexplate reinforcement plate. These items must be installed in this order. First is the shim plate, which is located using the bellhousing dowel pins. Then, install the flexplate or flywheel. Then, install the reinforcement plate (only used with a flexplate).*

*Different than most OEM engines out there, AMC engines use a thin plate between the engine block and the transmission. Over the years, this plate has a tendency to bend or become distorted. After a little bit of straightening, the plate is ready to be installed.*

*Inspect the flexplate or flywheel bolts before installation. Remember that these bolts are pretty old, so a little insurance is to install some new bolts. The AMC bolts are 1/2-20, and there are not many aftermarket options for new bolts. We usually use the ARP bolts for a Pontiac engine. Pontiac also used a 1/2-20 flexplate bolt. The flexplate bolts are something you do not want unthreading on their own. When flexplate bolts come loose, it can cause many different noises and destruction. Using red Loctite on the bolts during installation will provide a little peace of mind.*

*The AMC flexplate or flywheel can only be bolted on one way. This is a safety feature that is designed to align the balance weights on the flexplate. If the bolt holes do not line up, rotate the flexplate until all the holes align.*

# Carburetor and Fuel-Injection Units

*The Carter carburetor tags featured four or five characters. The first character was the number 0 through 8, and it designated the specific year. For example, 0 = 1970, 1 = 1971, etc. The second character was the engine size (R, T, W, and D). The third character was either a letter A for automatic or an M for manual transmission. The fourth character was always a number 4, which stood for 4-barrel.*

Spanning all the years of production, AMC hung in there with the same carburetors: the AMC-designed 2-barrel and the Carter 4-barrel. The only other popular carburetor was the Autolite 4300 that was released in 1966.

## Autolite Carburetor 4300

The Autolite carburetor started out with Ford and Mercury and was found on production vehicles until 1974. It was the only carburetor that was used on all V-8 engines from 1970 to 1974.

## Autolite Carburetor 4350

The next version of this carburetor was the 4350, which Jeep vehicles continued to use until 1978. From the factory, AMC used tags on each carburetor. These tags often were not put back on after the carburetor was serviced. So, when we see one of these tags in like-new condition, we take good care of it. The tags were both four and five digits long.

## 4300 Carburetor Decode

The first character was a number that ranged 0 through 8. It always corresponded to the specific year of the engine. If a tag had a number 1, the car had a 1971 engine, (as long as the tag is the original).

The second character corresponded to the engine's displacement (in cubic inches). The main letters that are found are R, T, W, and D. There are a few listings that state the engines with which these codes correspond, but we have seen multiple different listings. The common ones we have seen are: R = 360, T = 401,

W = 390. We have seen examples of these ourselves, and we believe that they were never switched around.

The third character was a letter that corresponded to the type of transmission, and only two choices were available: *A* for automatic and *M* for manual.

The fourth character was a number that was easy to remember. If it was a number 4, it was a 4-barrel carburetor engine.

Not many tags had a fifth character, but we have seen it. We have never been able to confirm this, but we were told that this meant the engine had a revised carburetor.

In much smaller stampings on the tags, there was a date stamping as well. The first character corresponded to a source code, the second character was a single number for the production year, the third character was a letter for the month, and last character was a number for the day of the production month.

### Jeep Carburetor Decode

On the Jeeps, the third character was always an *H*. Jeep's numbering system was very close to the AMC tags.

### Motorcraft 2150

In the later years (1973 through early 1980s), AMC used a Motorcraft 2150 carburetor.

### Hurst S/S Cross-Ram

In the late 1960s and early 1970s, Hurst played a role of some kind in all the American muscle cars. AMC and Hurst worked together starting in 1969, and together, they designed and built an AMX NHRA Super Stock race car.

***AMC and Hurst designed the 1969 AMX together to compete in NHRA Super Stock class. One of the main engine swaps was the specially designed Edelbrock cross-ram intake outfitted with two dual-quad Holley carburetors.***

To produce an NHRA-legal Super Stock race car, 50 cars were required to be produced for purchase by the public. There were 53 of the 390 engine 4-speed cars sent to Hurst for modifications. The engine modifications consisted of removing the cylinder heads and installing smaller-chamber heads to bring the compression up to 12.3:1. The single 4-barrel intake was swapped for the newly designed Edelbrock cross-ram intake with Holley dual-quad carburetors. For exhaust, the stock cast-iron manifolds were changed out with headers.

### Edelbrock Carburetors

An Edelbrock carburetor is the easiest aftermarket carburetor to install on an AMC engine. It is one of the most reliable, easy-to-install carburetors ever produced. For performance, the Edelbrock may not be the best pick, as the difficulty of changing main jets and metering rods holds it back.

### Holley Carburetors

The staple of all carburetors is the Holley carburetor. Its years in existence and parts availability is incredible. The popular hot rod thing to do was to remove the stock intake and install an aftermarket intake with a Holley 4-barrel double-pumper carburetor.

Over the years of building many different makes of engines, the thing that stands out is that the AMC usually wants a larger-CFM carburetor than other manufacturers. If we have an AMC and a Chevrolet engine built at the same time, the AMC seems to want a larger-CFM carburetor—even if they make about the same horsepower.

### Fuel Injection

With the surge in the aftermarket world of self-tuning, fuel injection has become popular. The early models in the past were not very

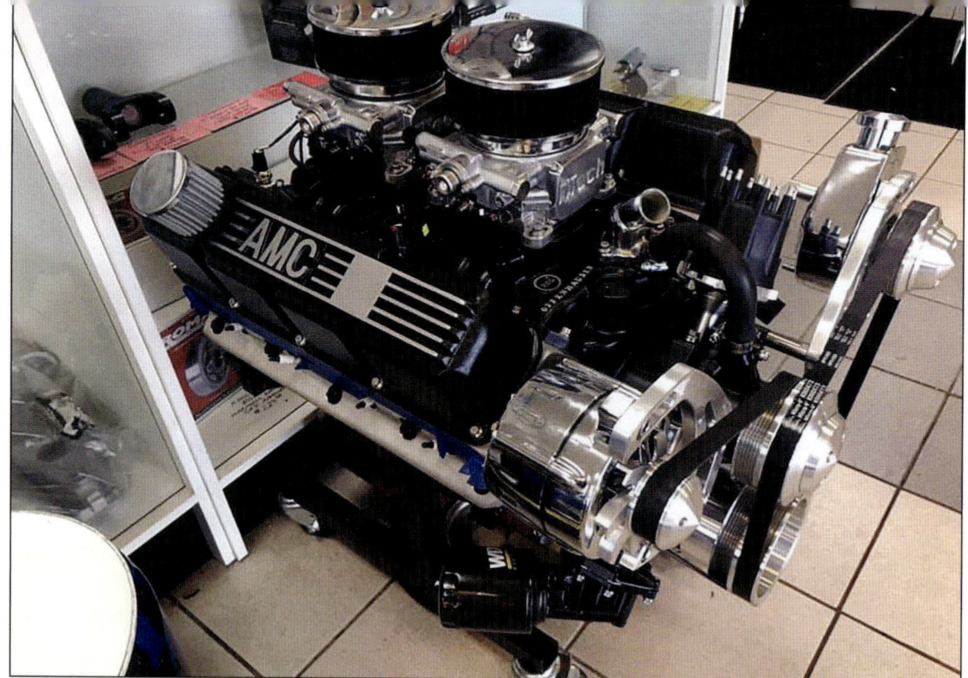

*Almost any imaginable setup can be done with fuel injection, as is the case with carburetors. As the younger generation gets more involved with muscle cars, we expect to see more of these old-school engines swapping to fuel injection, such as this twin FiTech installed on a dual-quad intake manifold.*

consumer friendly. However, since the very early 1990s, most new cars had fuel injection. Most of us have become used to jumping into our new cars and just turning the key. No more pumping the gas pedal, and no more flooding the carburetor.

One of the most common requests is: "I would like for my wife to be able to jump in my classic car and have it start up just like a new vehicle." The newest models made by FiTech and Holley seem to be the most popular. FiTech has a lineup of various models, but we will narrow the topic to throttle-body electronic fuel injection (EFI) units. These units are as close as possible to having a carburetor. Most AMC enthusiasts do not want to voyage far from the original look of the engine compartment.

### FiTech Fuel Injection

FiTech systems are available for various horsepower applications and with different coatings, including black, classic gold finish, and polished versions. They offer an inline frame-mount fuel delivery kit for quick installation. Our preferred method is purchasing a new fuel tank with an electric fuel pump mounted internally.

A company called Tanks Inc. has a huge inventory of new tanks ready to go. The only problem with this is that Tanks Inc. is very slow to add the AMC line to its inventory. When installing a unit on an AMC, we send the tank out to get dipped and modify it to install an electric fuel pump.

### Holley Sniper EFI 4150 4-Barrel

The other popular fuel-injection unit is the Holley Sniper. Holley offers different models as well, but we will narrow the topic to the Sniper EFI 4150 4-barrel. These units are very easy to install for a home mechanic, although the first one will take between 10 and 20 hours. It depends how detailed you get with running fuel lines and wiring.

### FI Wiring

The part that scares the the do-it-yourselfer is the wiring. Back in the day, converting a carbureted vehicle to EFI was thought to be difficult. From complicated wiring and tuning issues to concerns about parts compatibility and flow rates, it was a daunting prospect for shade-tree mechanics and veteran gearheads alike. A lot has changed in recent years, though.

The new Holley systems are a plug-and-play fuel-injection unit. The other item that scared the average mechanic away was worrying about the EFI tuning. Today, there are only six wires with a Sniper system. For those who want to get into the more-advanced tuning stuff, there are plenty of possibilities.

### Which Setup?

It does not matter how extreme the engine is, there are fuel-injections

*Once the Holley Sniper is unboxed, you will see that there actually are not many pieces in the kit. Once the throttle body is mounted, there is only a handful of wires coming off of it. The kit includes the O2 clamp-on fixtures, but you will be hours ahead if you weld them in.*

kits that will cover everything from a completely stock application to an all-out race engine. The hard part is picking the correct kit for the application. This is where it is important to be realistic about how much horsepower the engine will have and how much street driving it will be doing. The more horsepower, the more important your fuel delivery system will be.

## Installing a Holley Sniper

Basic Holley Sniper systems only have four wires to hook up: the battery positive, battery negative, switched on/off ignition, and a wire for engine RPM. We also like to ground the throttle body right to a positive engine ground. Not having a good ground has haunted us for hours on the Holley. One of the Sniper kits comes with an inline electric fuel pump. This kit comes with most of the needed fuel line and connections.

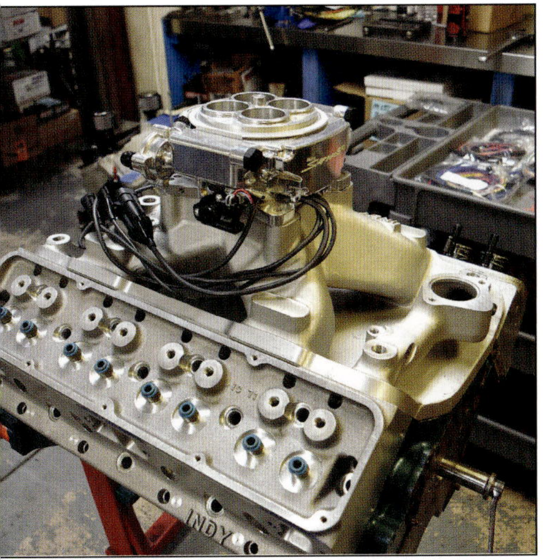

*Another item that we like to pre-assemble is the carburetor or the fuel-injection unit. It is a lot easier to design and fabricate brackets or wire looms ahead of time if needed. Also, fabricating before your engine is final cleaned for assembly will save you from cleaning things twice. Preassembling items also gives time to determine which items will be painted and where the lines of the paint will be.*

## Electric Fuel Pumps and New Gas Tanks

This system works fine for most combinations, but we prefer to install a new fuel tank with an electric fuel pump in the tank. The systems can be run as a returnless system, but we run a return line back to the fuel tank. Quite often, we will see an install where they used the factory fuel lines and just spliced into them. On some applications this is okay, but for a higher-horsepower build, some of the factory fuel lines are pretty small coming from the tank to the front.

Most of the cars that we install them on are 40, 50, or 60 years old (or more) now. And the same goes for the factory fuel tank if it hasn't already been replaced. In some cases that's fine, but in others, you might discover that there's a bunch of rust and other junk in it, and that stuff is going to make its way into the fuel system if it's not addressed. This would cause problems with any system. This is why we prefer to install a new fuel tank with a submerged fuel pump.

There are a few manufacturers offering new tanks for a lot of muscle cars nowadays. Let's hope they show AMC some love and start producing some AMC tanks soon. At the time of this book's publication, there are no AMC tanks with electric pumps available, but there are some aftermarket companies that reproduce some of the AMC fuel tanks. It's worth it to purchase one of these and modify it to fit an electric pump in the tank.

With a new tank, you can weld and cut on the tank without any worry of a fire. The other option is to send your original fuel tank out and have it dipped. After dipping, you can modify the fuel tank as well.

### *Aftermarket Tank*

Everything is already figured out for you if the kit comes complete with the pump, level sensor, tank, and everything else ready to install in your car. There are many companies offering tanks, and we have been told that AMC tanks will soon be available with the pump kits installed.

As with the drop-in modules, Holley states these packages are rated for up to 550 hp naturally aspirated as standard, but builders with forced-induction applications and/or those making more than 550 hp have some options here as well. Most of these packages are available with a 400 liter/hr pump module, rather than the standard 255 liter/hr pump. They also sell that 400-liter pump separately. This one will support 750 hp, and that will cover most of the naturally aspirated AMC builds.

### *Non-Drop-in Module*

If your project isn't going to have a new tank, some options are below. Of course, you are going to still need to dip the tank.

There are units designed to be installed on a tank that don't have an application-specific drop-in module. If this is your project, install the module by cutting a hole in the top of the existing tank and installing the module inside. The system has swing-out clamps that lock the module securely to the inside of tank. Returnless versions are also available (the same kind of system as the drop-in units) as well as return-style systems for those who want to run an external regulator.

While inline external pumps are an option here as well, there are benefits to installing the module inside the tank that are particularly notable for those doing EFI conversions on street cars. The OEMs have been installing pumps in the tanks for years now. The main benefit is that the fuel keeps the pump running cooler. This is true for new vehicles, so if you want a long fuel-pump life, don't run your tank on empty. The other major benefit is silence. Most of you have heard a fuel pump whining and know exactly how loud that old-school Holley blue pump is.

#### *External Inline Pump*

If you have a dedicated race car, an external inline pump offers important advantages over the in-tank style. Many drag racers and road racers use these because it is easy to service and change out the pump when it is not in the tank. Imagine being at the dragstrip and having to drop the fuel tank to change the fuel pump.

One thing that everyone agrees with is that electric motors will fail, and it will usually not give you any warning signs. This setup does not provide the same cooling benefits as the in-tank pumps. However, these pumps are built with cooling designs that are built in for longevity.

#### *High-End Fuel Pumps*

If you have a dedicated race car (drag or road race) or even a heavy-hitting street car, there are high-end fuel pumps available for in-tank mounting. Many companies offer a race version of EFI pumps, including dual-pump units. These fuel pumps are usually used in conjunction with a fuel cell.

As EFI units become more popular with the racing world, we are seeing a large increase in systems, fuel pumps, and accessories being manufactured. The result is a race car easy starting, good drivability, and average fuel mileage.

The Holley fuel-injection kit offers different models, three different finishes, and versions with or without the fuel system. The units that are sold without the inline fuel-pump option are the kits for using an in-tank electric fuel pump. These units bolt to any 4150 intake manifold or a spread-bore manifold.

When installing these units on a spread-bore intake, use a spread-bore sealing plate (part number 9006). The FiTech units also have a few different sizes and configurations available. These kits can be purchased with the inline fuel-pump option or the basic kit can be used with the tank fuel pump.

## Oxygen Sensor

For both FiTech and Holley, an oxygen sensor will need to be installed into the exhaust. They both offer a way to install this sensor without welding, but from our experience, it is better to find a welder to weld in the oxygen-sensor bung. We have seen the clamp style leak air into the exhaust and change the oxygen-sensor readings enough to make the unit run erratically.

Holley's handheld programmer has a touchscreen for simple setup, minor tuning, and gauge displays.

On the calibration wizard, when you answer a few questions about the engine, and it will create a base map to start, and then it will take over self-tuning from there. You have the option of the Sniper to control the ignition timing. For a more detailed install, the timing should be wired into the Sniper. This requires the distributor to be locked out.

When using all the features available, we put the vehicle on our chassis dyno and hook up the laptop with the Holley Sniper software installed. That way, we can write a custom program for the engine. Don't let this scare you away; the Holley unit is designed for the average mechanic to install, start up, and let it self-tune. Even Holley advertises that no laptop is needed.

On Holley's website and YouTube channel, there are some really good installation videos. Take some time and watch a few. If anything, it will save you from making some of the easy mistakes. As millennials grow up, they will only know fuel injection. It is the future, whether we approve or not.

*The handheld programmer for the Holley Sniper is small and easy to use. After a program is written for your Sniper using a laptop, all minor changes can be done with the handheld programmer. The programmer is small enough that it can be tucked away neatly when it is not being used.*

# Distributor and Ignition

As with most manufacturers, the AMC distributors were points distributors. Actually, the point distributors were somewhat reliable, even though the points needed to be reset and even changed more often than any parts in an electronic distributor.

To this day, we have customers who prefer to keep their points distributors. The kits to convert the points to an electronic ignition became very popular, especially because in the past there were not many aftermarket distributor choices.

## PerTronix Distributor

Even today with the availability of quite a few different distributors, the PerTronix kits remain very popular among the car restoration groups. The idea was to keep the distributor looking as original as possible.

*For distributor upgrades that give you the electronic upgrade but keep that stock-looking distributor, the PerTronix brand is the best choice. PerTronix has been making points conversion kits for years. With these kits, there will be no more changing out points and condensers or the ever-popular failures that come with running the old breaker points.*

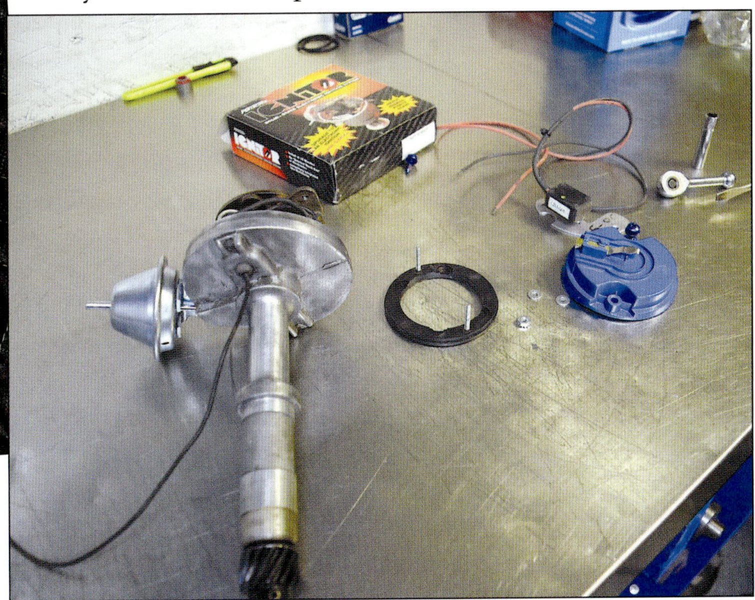

*The first step to installing the PerTronix kit is to remove all pieces from the package and familiarize yourself with the kit. Read through the instructions. One of the most important items to making your PerTronix last is using the proper wiring.*

***Remove the old distributor cap and rotor from the distributor. Next, remove the old points and condenser from the housing.***

***After many years of producing points conversion kits, PerTronix came out with its line of electronic distributors. The AMC distributors (part number D160700) will fit all the V-8 engines from 290 ci through the 401.***

There were a few more vendors that make points conversion kits, but I believe PerTronix is one of the only ones left. PerTronix advertises that its electronic ignition modules help the engine RPM without the engine breaking up. Most AMC V-8 engines use PerTronix (part number 1181).

To install the ignition kit, begin by removing the distributor and setting it up on a clean workbench. We have installed many of these kits in different vehicles, and it seems that each vehicle has a little different setup. Disassemble the distributor cap and rotor (as long as you are removing these items, install new ones if you haven't already).

The next items to be removed are the points and the condenser. These can be thrown out. At this time, clean the distributor out either with a light coat of parts cleaner and a brush or some brake cleaner.

***PerTronix Flame-Thrower II distributors feature the patented Ignitor II (electronic ignition module) with adaptive dwell control and an integrated Hall Effect circuit. The Flame-Thrower II fits applications from 290 ci through 401 ci. The stand-alone design makes them plug-in units that require no additional ignition, but they are compatible with multi-spark CD ignition boxes for outstanding versatility. An MSD box can be hooked up to the PerTronix distributor (part number D160700).***

***Now, install the new rotor in place. You are now ready to install the distributor in the engine.***

## Flame-Thrower Distributor

Once the distributor is clean, begin to reassemble it. Follow the instructions very closely when installing the electronic module. The same company that manufactures the ignition kits also offers a complete replacement distributor. The Flame-Thrower distributors come completely ready to install with an electronic ignition module. This distributor will not need any additional ignition boxes to run; it is what is called stand-alone, or ready to run.

The part number for the ready-to-run distributor is PerTronix D160700. This distributor comes with a gear already installed, but the gear material needs to be compatible with the gear on the front of the camshaft. We remove this gear and install either a factory gear or run any of the matched gears that are manufactured.

## Other Aftermarket Distributors

A handful of aftermarket manufacturers produce AMC V-8 distributors. You will find everything from a high-energy ignition (HEI) distributor to a more common electronic distributor. We have used many different models with great success.

The HEI distributor is a much larger distributor. Sometimes, this style of distributor will create some clearance problems when mounted in the front of the engine. Also, the HEI-style distributors are the furthest from a stock-appearing distributor that is available. We have had these distributors interfere with some accessory brackets mounted in the front of the engine. It is common for us to slightly clearance the distributor or the brackets to run an HEI-style distributor.

Similar to other distributors, the HEI unit uses a control module in place of the breaker points. The HEI distributor was widely used in the later 1970s in many different makes of vehicles. It was known for delivering more spark to the spark plugs.

This distributor was adequate for all street applications but has its limitations in higher-RPM builds. The ignition coil requires more dwell time to charge before it can release. This is why it has limitations at a higher RPM. When an engine operates at a high RPM, there is less dwell time to operate. What this means is that at a high RPM value, such as 7,500 and up, it is possible to have high-end misses.

### TECH TIP: Distributor Gear

When installing an aftermarket distributor, one of the most important items is the distributor gear. When an aftermarket distributor comes with a gear installed, we recommend not using it. At the very least, remove it and install a factory gear. Not all gears are interchangeable due to the diameter of the shafts not being the same. ■

### *MSD*

The most widely used aftermarket distributor is MSD, which offers matched gears for both the distributor and the mating gear mounted on the camshaft. We cannot stress enough how important it is to keep matched gears on your engine.

The two MSD distributors available are the ready-to-run and the Pro-Billet distributor. Ready-to-run is the perfect choice for a street cruiser. For street driving, it comes complete with a mechanical advance. Included in the box is a spring and a bushing kit. For a street hot rod, it is important to bring the timing in gradually and have it all in at 3,000 rpm.

The springs control the rate in which it comes, and the bushing controls the spread of the initial to the total timing. They all come with a vacuum advance. Some applications benefit from the advance, but we choose to not use the advance for most hot rod builds.

*One of the most popular aftermarket distributors is the MSD ready-to-run model (part number 8523). It has a very clean installation with only three wires to connect.*

*The MSD 8519 billet distributor fits all AMC V-8 engines (290, 304, 343, 360, 390, and 401). It must be used with an MSD 6-, 7-, or 8-series ignition. Popular setups are using the MSD Blaster 2 coil (part number 8202) with the Digital 6 box (part number 6201).*

## Distributor Maintenance

This distributor is pretty much maintenance free. The only thing we see is that the climate changes over the winter months create some rust inside the distributor. It is common

*This is what your distributor can look like after a couple years of storage in weather that causes the internals to sweat. A little maintenance goes a long way.*

to have to clean the inside of the distributor well.

One of the great features is the ability to lock out the advance. This application usually will only be locked out on a racing application, in which case the Pro-Billet distributor with an MSD ignition box is a better option. The other application is to lock it out when running a Holley Sniper. As we mentioned, the biggest bonus to this distributor in a street cruiser is how no ignition box is needed. The part number for the AMC ready-to-run is 8523.

Economically, using any ready-to-run distributor will keep the cost down. The Pro-Billet distributor with an aftermarket ignition box provides a reassurance of higher voltage, different rev limiters, and in some applications, a start retard for when the mechanical advance is locked out.

## OEM Look

For years, these distributors were only available with a red cap. We have painted these red caps for years for customers who just wanted a low-key look to their aftermarket distributor. Finally, about a year ago, the black cap was released to fit both these distributors. Unfortunately, you cannot order the distributor with the black cap at this time, so you have to buy it separately and then change it.

As usual, the AMC is the stepchild. The black cap options have been available for other makes but not the AMC engine. At least there is one available now: the Pro-Billet distributor (part number 8519).

## Selecting a Distributor

The time has come to make a choice on which distributor to run: a ready to run or a Pro-Billet with an ignition box. Remember that there are manufacturers other than MSD, and you can mix and match distributors with ignitions boxes from other manufacturers as well. The way we choose is to weigh the benefits of the ignition box and whether or not it is really needed.

### *Engine Rev Limiter*

The first question to consider is: "Do you need an engine rev limiter?" Maybe the car has a manual transmission and you enjoy doing burnouts, and maybe you miss a gear. In this scenario, there is logic to support using an ignition box with a rev limiter. Would you ever lock out your mechanical advance where it would be beneficial for you to have a start retard?

Here is another question: "Will you ever take the car to the drag strip, even just a few times a year for fun?" If so, an ignition box may be needed. The ready-to-run distributors are extremely easy to wire no matter which brand is used. They have an ignition wire, a negative coil wire, and a ground wire. When using an ignition box, there are a few more wires, and you will also need to find a place to mount your ignition box that is away from direct engine heat.

The two distributors do not look any different from each other. When it comes to selecting an ignition box, the sky is the limit. If you are computer savvy and want to really get involved with your engine, there are units that allow you to program timing curves and programs for performance adders, such as nitrous retard options. Even the basic ignition boxes have gone digital. This is just going to continue to get more involved, especially with the addition of the fuel-injection systems out there.

Let's go over one last review to help you decide if you need an ignition box or not. Some of these thoughts are from helping customers throughout the years. For a purely street vehicle that will never use boost or nitrous oxide and if you want something easy to install with very few wires to hook up, then I recommend a ready-to-run distributor.

If you are going one step further and want it to look more original, I recommend the black-cap option. Now, if your build uses nitrous oxide, a blower, a supercharger, a turbocharger, or any form of boost and you need/want a rev limiter and timing controls, I recommend an ignition box.

Now, you are going to have many ignition box options that range from $300 to $1,200. Research the options (and chat with your engine builder) to decide what you want.

Remember that the ready-to-run will have limitations. The Pro-Billet with an ignition box will work fine on the street and will cover you for all your future add ons. Your budget may be a factor in what you decide as well.

## Distributor Installation

You are getting close to seeing all of your hard work pay off! With a few more items, you will be ready to install the engine into the car and hear it run for the first time.

Installing the distributor sounds pretty easy, and really it is, but if done incorrectly, major damage can be done during startup. First, make sure that the number-1 cylinder is at TDC on compression stroke. This can be done by rotating the engine until the TDC line on the harmonic balancer is aligned.

During assembly, this line should have been double-checked that it did align correctly. As you turn the engine over and start to come up to TDC, it is important to hold your thumb over the spark plug hole on cylinder number-1.

When compression starts to push your thumb off the plug hole, you now are coming up on the compression stroke. Continue rotating the engine over until the TDC marks align. You are now ready to install the distributor.

If you are installing a PerTronix kit, follow the instructions at the beginning of this chapter. If using the original points and condenser setup, have your new points installed at this time.

For a new MSD distributor, you might want to pre-curve it before installation. For most street applications, we run the black bushing with the light silver-and-blue spring. The idea here is to have the spread of initial and total be as small as possible and have your total timing be anywhere between 2,000 and 3,000 rpm. This is a personal preference and is different for each engine.

### *Timing Locked Out*

If the engine is mainly a race application, you want the timing locked out. If running an engine that has vacuum advance, install that distributor so that the vacuum-advance canister does not limit the travel while moving the distributor to time the engine.

Most factory distributor installations had the vacuum advance canisters pointed toward the driver's side. Although, it does not really matter where you position the number-1 plug wire, we stay with the tradition that the number-1 spark plug wire aims toward the number-1 cylinder.

Once the distributor is installed and positioned close to the correct position, align the number-1 plug up with rotor. Install the distributor hold-down clamp and just snug it. Further timing adjustment is needed upon startup.

## Alignment

Install some Driven camshaft assembly lube on the gear before it is installed. As the distributor is dropped in, turn the rotor toward the number-1

*The first step is to make sure that the number-1 cylinder is on TDC on compression stroke. This is done by rotating the engine over until the TDC line on the harmonic balancer is aligned. During assembly, this line should have been double-checked to make sure that it did align correctly. As you turn over the engine and start to come up to TDC, hold your thumb over the spark plug hole on cylinder number-1 until it starts to come up on the compression stroke.*

*The PerTronix kit distributor is ready to install if you followed the instructions in the beginning of this chapter. If using the original points-and-condenser setup, have the new points installed at this time. For a new MSD distributor, pre-curve it before installation. For most street applications, we run the black bushing with the light silver and blue spring. The idea here is to have the spread of initial and total timing be as small as possible and have your total timing come in anywhere between 2,000 and 3,000 rpm. This sometimes is a personal preference and is different for each engine. If your engine is mainly a racing application, you will want your timing locked out.*

*Most factory distributors were installed with the vacuum-advance canisters pointed toward the driver's side. This position provides ample room to adjust the timing.*

*The AMC distributor clamp is held down by just one bolt. Once the engine is timed, it is important to make sure that the hold-down is tight. If the distributor were to move during driving, major engine damage could occur.*

*Before installing the distributor, put a coat of camshaft break-in lube on the gear. Most aftermarket distributor companies are suppling this break-in lube with the purchase of a new distributor.*

cylinder. As the gears mesh, the rotor will turn. You might have to turn the rotor back one position before installing it. Even if it takes a few tries to install it with the rotor in the correct position, it is okay.

Some engine builders turn the oil pump shaft to the correct spot so that when the distributor is dropped all the way in, it will drop into the oil pump shaft. We find that it is easier to drop it in when the distributor gets to the oil pump shaft. Slowly turn the engine over while holding light pressure down on the distributor. Once the distributor is aligned with the oil pump shaft, it will drop in. Repeat the procedure of bringing the engine up to TDC on compression stroke.

Once you are there, inspect the rotor alignment. If correct, set the cap on and put a small mark on the cap where the number-1 spark plug wire will go. You can now install the distributor hold-down and just snug it down. Next, install the distributor cap and secure it.

The last items to install are the distributor wires. MSD has a quality wire that you can route, cut to length, and install. The firing order on an AMC is the same as a Chevy: 1, 3, 5, 7 is the driver's side and 2, 4, 6, 8 on the passenger's side. So, the firing order is 1-8-4-3-6-5-7-2. Here is a little trick to remember the firing order: 18 x 2 = 36; 36 x 2 = 72; now, put 4 and 5 in the middle.

The distributor rotates clockwise, so the spark plug wire is installed in the same manner. You can now complete the installation of the spark plug wires.

## Performance Ignition Systems

MSD has performance ignition boxes that must be installed if you are using a Pro-Billet distributor. We narrow this discussion to a few of the most popular ignition boxes available.

### Digital 6

The first entry-level ignition box is the 6A, which is the Digital 6 box. This is the most popular ignition box available, and it also has the most reasonable retail price. The Digital 6 boxes will provide high-end rev control by using the dials under the small plastic cover on the box. If you upgrade to the 6AL2, you will have the option of a two-step starting-line RPM control.

Under this plastic cover, there are four dials: two for high RPM and two for starting-line RPM. One of the best new features is that they have done away with the RPM chips from years past. These RPM chips could get expensive, and you usually needed an organizer for them.

### Digital 7

The next step up are the Digital 7 boxes. There are a few different boxes available and there are still some non-digital boxes offered in the 7s as well. This ignition box covers street/strip and some minor stock-car-racing applications.

As mentioned earlier in this chapter, the addition of the MSD grid has taken everything to a new level with unlimited timing curves available. This just scratches the surface of the availability of ignition boxes. I don't mean to only talk about MSD here, but there is no doubt that the company has most of the market share for ignition boxes.

PerTronix offers a few good reliable ignition boxes. A great entry-level combination at a very friendly price is the PerTronix AMC distributor and ignition box. Its ignition boxes start at about $230 and go up from there for more-advanced digital boxes.

Mallory still has its hand in the ignition boxes also. Although we have not used its distributors for a few years now, it is still active in the ignition-box market.

# Engine Priming and Test Running

It seems that every hot rod magazine and automotive internet site has published some an article about engine oil and the zinc content. Despite this fact, very few car owners actually understand what has changed in the content of motor oils during the last decade.

***Driven racing oil was designed specifically to fix the flat-tappet camshaft problems. Changing to the BR break-in oil from off-the-shelf products nearly eliminated break-in failures.***

## Engine Break-in Oil

Engine builders have learned the hard way how to break in an engine, which can result in a camshaft failure. Some of the terms that are used to describe the compounds in engine oil are hard to understand. A common term that you may see in articles regarding zinc being removed from motor oils is zinc dialkyldithiophosphate (ZDDP).

### *Zinc*

There are different types of zinc, which can get complicated. Zinc by itself is not a lubricant. Only when heat and some kind of load/friction is enforced will it create a glass film. This film protects metal surfaces, such as a camshaft lobe and lifter. After zinc sees heat, or is "activated," it can then be considered a lubricant. This is what we have learned from years from attending oil seminars.

According to our instructors, there are different types of zinc. Some of zinc additives activate quicker with less heat and load. The faster the zinc can protect a surface, the better chance that metal parts have to last.

During the initial break-in period, a glass-like layer of protection is made. If the layer of protection is not made quickly enough, the lifter can stop turning. This will create a large amount of heat, which will wear the lifter lobe right off the camshaft.

The best form of zinc has been called the secondary zinc (Zn), which is a green zinc. This has been known to be the fastest acting form of zinc. The reason that zinc has been removed from motor oil is because secondary zinc was determined to destroy catalytic convertors from the inside out faster than any other type of zinc. So, that is the problem.

The American Petroleum Institute (API) and GM Dexos 1 engine oil has a very low active rate. This engine oil has been determined to be the friendliest but also have the least amount of protection for the older engines that have many metal-on-metal engine parts.

The change in motor oil came unannounced and was required by the U.S. Department of Transportation (DOT). Consumers and engine builders were not notified of these changes (not that we would have known or understood the long-term effects at the time). It seemed that we all learned by failures. For that matter, it seems that we are still learning about dealing with the low zinc levels.

What does this really mean for a classic car owner? Well, if you are still purchasing engine oil from the normal parts stores, you more than likely are not getting a quality zinc engine oil. If you are wondering what year the engine oil was changed, a low-zinc-level oil was introduced in all newer cars being manufactured in 2010. You ask yourself, "How much zinc do I need?" Well, this depends on the engine and the style of the engine valvetrain. If your engine still has the typical flat-tappet camshaft, pushrods, and stock-style rocker arms, you need the best fast-acting highest-level of zinc possible.

Customers often ask, "If I install a roller camshaft in my engine, I don't have to worry about zinc, correct?" Well, it's not quite that easy. The engine will still have some metal-on-metal interaction, such as on pushrods and some rocker arms, but the major change that helps is the roller camshaft. The odds of having a failure dropped by probably 80 percent.

When installing larger camshafts and running greater valve-spring pressures, the need for quality engine oil increases greatly. The more valve-spring pressure that is put on the lifters, the harder it is for the lifter to spin. No lifter spin equals a rapid failure.

The ZDDP level has also been reduced in normal API oil. We were part of the great camshaft failure back in the day. I remember our shop losing 20 to 30 camshafts in a year's time. The failures happened so quickly that within 10 minutes of break-in, it was over.

The ZDDP was first dropped from 1,000 parts per million (PPM) to 800 ppm. This drop was enough to really hurt engine builders. Shops across the United States began to see failures at a very fast pace. There was a point in time that engine builders blamed certain camshaft companies when it had nothing to do with their manufacturing procedures.

## Recommendations

Engine oil can be extremely complicated now. Always listen to your engine builders' recommendations for oil and always start a rebuilt engine on break-in oil. Your engine builder will have his favorite engine oil that he trusts, and he will always know the weight of engine oil that is needed for your specific bearing clearances.

Larger-lift camshafts with longer valve duration require much higher valve-spring pressures to keep the valvetrain stability in line. Especially on flat-tappet camshaft engines, a quality break-in oil is needed to create the anti-wear film on your engine parts. Once the engine is broken in, you still have to use a quality zinc engine oil. This will ensure that you will have many years of protection.

### *Valvoline VR1*

Even if the engine has been upgraded to a roller camshaft, most engine builders still recommend using a high-quality zinc engine oil. One of the most common engine oils is Valvoline VR1. A reason that this oil is so popular is because it has all the qualities to protect your engine. It also seems to be available in many different speed shops and automotive parts houses.

*There are many companies that now manufacture high ZDDP engine oil. Once everyone learned what the camshaft failure was all about, all the major engine oil companies jumped on board and designed high-zinc engine oils.*

The Valvoline engine oil is available as a non-synthetic oil and a partially synthetic oil. It is also available in many different weights for different temperatures. Some other oil companies creating break-in oil with high zinc offerings are Amsoil, Driven BR40, and Lucas.

When the ZDDP information hit the classic car industry, it did not take long for all of the major engine oil companies to jump on board with great choices of high-zinc engine oil.

## Priming the Engine

Now that the engine oil has been selected, one of the most important steps is to properly prime the oiling system. We use a high-pressure oil tank to prime our engines. Many suppliers make them today, and our preferred tank is made by Melling.

The Melling pressure tank is filled with 3 quarts of Driven break-in oil. The engine is rotated over while power priming the engine. The idea is that rotating the engine will feed the

*Priming an engine has come a long way since I learned years ago. Never did I imagine that we would be priming all engines with a power lube tank, such as this one supplied by Melling (part number MPL-201).*

*We have seen many different forms of homemade and store-bought oil priming tanks. We use the Melling pressure tank. Most engines only need 3 to 4 quarts to prime the engine. One of the most important steps is to rotate the engine while power priming. This ensures that oil travels through both sides of the engine and through all of the pushrods and rocker arms.*

engine oil through all of the oil holes and up through the pushrods. The easiest place to hook up the Melling pressure primer is off of the hexagon oil adapter on the front passenger's side of the engine with an adapter threaded into the oil port and a quick disconnect to keep things simple.

Before opening the pressurized valve on the Melling oil tank, make sure that the oil filter has been filled with oil and installed and that all oil ports have been properly plugged. I have seen builders forget to plug an oil gallery and make a mess all over the floor. Keep track of how many quarts you are installing into the pan. For example, if you put 3 quarts in the primer tank and 1 quart in the filter, you already have 4 quarts in the engine. So, you will only need the remaining quarts added.

*The power primer should be screwed into an oil galley located on the engine block. The AMC engine has a main oil-feed gallery located on the passenger-side front. The primer hose should be installed into this oil gallery for priming.*

### *Custom Shaft to Turn the Oil Pump*

For a singular engine build, you do not need a pressure tank. There are many ways to make your own shaft to turn the oil pump. Before installing the distributor, install a shaft that locks into the oil pump gear through the distributor hole.

To make one, take an old distributor and cut off the end. Using the shaft, weld on a hex or even a round shaft that will fit easily into a cordless drill. Make sure that all of the oil ports are covered and an oil-pressure gauge is installed. Spin the oil pump shaft until you have oil pressure. If you are spinning it the wrong way, you will not have any oil pressure.

Once you obtain oil pressure, have someone turn over the engine while spinning the drill. This will enable the oil to get to the whole engine. We try to do this relatively close to startup. In other words, if you are not going to start the engine for six months, wait to prime it until just before start-up. There are engine builders who believe in priming an engine even after it has been stored over the winter. We don't go that far but can understand their precaution.

## Running the Engine for the First Time

There are a few more items to cover before you are ready to fire your engine for the first time.

*For this engine run, the customer's stock carburetor was out being restored. To run this engine and do a camshaft break-in procedure, we installed a house Edelbrock carburetor.*

*Our stock 390 flat-tappet engine is installed on an engine run stand for camshaft break-in. The customer did not want to dyno the engine, but we run all flat-tappet camshaft engines before we let them go out the door so we can ensure that we do not have premature camshaft lobe failure. That way, we can control the break-in procedure.*

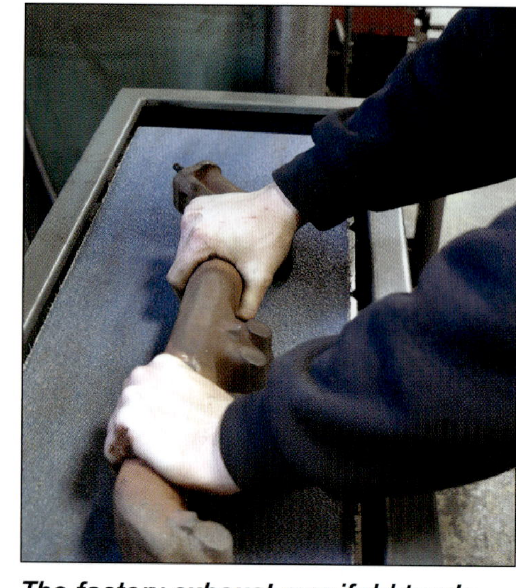

*The factory exhaust manifold tends to warp or even develop a low spot due to an exhaust leak. Have the local machine shop true these up on a belt sander or a surfacer before installation.*

### *Header Bolt Clearance*

While using an aftermarket ARP head bolt kit, the head bolts stick up too high to clear most all header flanges and exhaust manifold flanges. To install the headers, the head bolts that align with the exhaust ports are shortened and installed without the washer. Sometimes even this is not enough to clear the head bolt. Any further clearancing needed will be removed from the header flange or the manifold.

When using the factory exhaust manifolds, we like to clean them up on a large belt sander before installation. This provides the best possible chance of having no exhaust leaks. Always use an exhaust gasket when installing the manifolds on the engine.

*It is very common for the headers on an AMC engine to interfere with the ARP head bolt kit. This is something that is often overlooked until the engine is installed in the car. It is very difficult to deal with this situation with the engine in the car. As you can see, only the head bolts that align with the exhaust port have an issue. Remember to check this before installation.*

*Instead of hooking up all the pulleys on the engine run stand, we prefer to use a small electric motor to run our pump. The engine will only run for two 20-minute break-in sessions, so any quick method you can use to run the water pump will work.*

### Ignition Timing

Preset the ignition timing to start the engine at a fast idle. It is important that the static ignition timing is set as close as possible. If the engine has a carburetor, it should be filled with fuel.

The engine needs to start quickly without excessive cranking to ensure immediate lubrication to the camshaft lobes.

### Water Pump

To operate the water pump on the run stand, we use an aftermarket electric water pump from Moroso.

### Initial Start

Start the engine and immediately bring it to 2,200 rpm. Many engine builders have a different RPM that they like to see. For the most part, getting it off of an idle is the main focus.

### Adjust Timing and Vary Engine Speed

Timing should be adjusted as quickly as possible to reduce excessive heat or load during break-in. Get the engine running fairly smooth and vary the engine speed from 1,500 to 2,200 rpm in a slow-to-moderate acceleration/deceleration cycle.

### Check for Leaks

During this time, check for any leaks and check out any unusual noises. If something doesn't sound right, shut off the engine and check the source of the noise. Upon restart, resume the high-idle-speed cycling.

## 20- to 30-Minute Break-In

Continue varying the break-in speed for 20 to 30 minutes. If the engine starts to get warm, it is perfectly okay to shut it down at 10 minutes and continue after it cools down. This is necessary to provide proper lifter rotation to properly mate each lifter to its lobe. Of course, lifter rotation is only for flat-tappet cams. Roller lifters do not turn. That is why roller lifters are a safer bet.

If the engine needs to be shut down for any reason, bring it to 2,200 rpm upon restart and continue the break-in for a total run time of 20 to 30 minutes. At this point, the initial break-in is complete. The engine can be run normally.

## 500 Miles

It is recommended that you change the oil and filter after 500 miles. You may want to put another 5,000 miles on the camshaft before switching to a synthetic oil if that is your preference.

### Camshaft Life

For extended camshaft life, flat-tappet camshafts should not be run with more than the recommended open valve-spring pressure. Racing applications often need to run more spring pressure at the expense of reduced camshaft life. To break in a camshaft with high open pressures, the inner springs should be removed to reduce break-in load. The inner springs can then be reinstalled after initial break-in is complete.

Flat-tappet cams (both hydraulic and mechanical) have the lobes ground on a slight taper, and the lifters appear to sit offset from the lobe centerline. This induces a rotation of the lifter on the lobe. This rotation draws oil to the mating surface between the lifter and the lobe. If it is possible to view the pushrods during break-in, they should be spinning as an indication that the lifter is spinning. If you don't see a pushrod spinning, immediately stop the engine and find the cause.

# Source Guide

Alfano Performance (Nick Alfano)
262-308-1302
alfanoperformance.com

American Parts Depot
409 North Main St.
West Manchester, OH 45382
937-678-7249
sales@americanpartsdepot.com

ARP
1863 Eastman Ave.
Ventura, CA 93003
805-339-2200
arp-bolts.com

Bullet Cams
8785 Old Craft Rd.
Olive Branch, MS 38654
662-893-5670
techinfo@bulletcams.com

Bulltear
24543 Olinda Trail
Scandia, MN 55073
1-651-433-3689
Toll free: 1-855-433-3689

Campbell Enterprises
6520 Boundary Run Dr.
Mechanicsville, VA 23111

Canton Products
232 Branford Rd.
North Branford, CT 06471
203-481-9460
Cantonracingproducts.com

Clevite Mahle Engine Parts
1-888-255-1942
usmahle.com

Clifford Performance
2330 Pomona-Rincon Rd.
Corona, CA 91720
cliffordperformance.com

Cloyes Engine Parts
7800 Ball Rd.
Ft. Smith, AR 72908
Cloyes.com

COMP Cams
3406 Democrat Rd.
Memphis, TN 38118
CAM HELP® 1-800-999-0853

Diamond Pistons
35075 Automation Dr.
Clinton Twp, MI 48035
877-552-2112
sales@diamondracing.net

Don's Auto Parts & Machine Shop
6814 39th Ave.
Kenosha, WI 53142
Donsautoparts@tds.net

Dura-Bond Bearing Company
3200 Arrowhead Dr.
Carson City, NV 89706
775-883-8998
dura-bondbearing.com

Driven Racing Oil
3416 Democrat Rd.
Memphis, TN 38118
Toll Free 1-866-611-1820
drivenracingoil.com

Edelbrock Inc.
2700 California St.
Torrance, CA 90503
edelbrock.com

Federal-Mogul/Sealed Power/
Fel-Pro
1-800-325-8886
Monday–Thursday: 7:30 a.m.–
4:30 p.m. (CST)
Friday: 7:30 a.m.–4:00 p.m. (CST)

FiTech
12370 Doherty St., Ste. A
Riverside, CA 92503
951-340-2624

Holley Performance
1801 Russellville Rd.
Bowling Green, KY 42101

Galvin's AMC Rambler Parts
522 South 5th St.
Klamath Falls, OR 97601
209-365-6315
ramblerparts.com

Indy Cylinder Heads
8621 Southeastern Ave.
Indianapolis, IN 46239
indyheads.com

K1 Technologies
7201 Industrial Park Blvd.
Mentor, OH 44060-5396
440-497-3100

Keith Black Pistons
1040 Corbett St.
Carson City, NV 89706
1-800-648-7970
775-882-7790
tech@uempistons.com

Kennedy American, Inc.
7100 State Rte. 142 SE
West Jefferson, OH 43162
614-879-SAVE (7283)
kennedyamerican.com

Kenosha Automotive Museum
kenoautomuseum.webs.com

Manley Performance Products,
Inc.
1960 Swarthmore Ave.
Lakewood, NJ 08701
1-800-526-1362
732-905-3366
sales@manleyperformance.com

Melling Oil Pumps
2620 Saradan Dr.
Jackson, MI 49202
517-787-8172

Milodon Inc.
2250 Agate Court
Simi Valley, CA 93065
805-577-5950
milodon.com

Molnar Rods
Motorsports Parts Corporation
6520 Boundary Run Dr.
Mechanicsville, VA 23111
804-779-0888

MSD
915-855-7123
holleybrands.com

PerTronix
440 E. Arrow Hwy.
San Dimas, CA 91773
pertronixbrands.com

Planet Houston AMX
1902 Wycliffe
Houston, TX 77043
planethoustonamx.com

Quick Fuel Carbs
915-855-7123
holleybrands.com

Rare Parts Inc.
621 Wilshire Ave.
Stockton, CA 95203
rareparts.com

RaceTec Pistons
15681 Computer Lane
Huntington Beach, CA 92649
714-903-4362
racetecpistons.com

Romac/RollMaster
rollmasterromac@aol.com

Seymour Paints
917 Crosby Ave.
Sycamore, IL 60178
seymourpaints.com

Smith Bros. Pushrods
2895 SW 13th St.
Redmond, OR 97756
1-800-367-1533
pushrods.net

Trend Performance
23444 Schoecherr
Warren, MI 48089
800-326-8368
trendperform.com

Wiseco Pistons
804-779-0888